WEAR YOUR DREAMS

WEAR YOUR DREAMS

My Life in Tattoos

Ed Hardy

WITH
JOEL SELVIN

THOMAS DUNNE BOOKS
ST. MARTIN'S PRESS
NEW YORK

THOMAS DUNNE BOOKS.
An imprint of St. Martin's Press.

www.thomasdunnebooks.com
www.stmartins.com

Book design by Jonathan Bennett

ISBN 978-1-250-00882-4 (hardcover)
ISBN 978-1-250-02107-6 (e-book)

Thomas Dunne books may be purchased for educational, business, or promotional use. For information on bulk purchases, please contact Macmillan Corporate and Premium Sales Department at 1-800-221-7945 extension 5442 or write specialmarkets@macmillan.com.

First Edition: June 2013

10 9 8 7 6 5 4 3 2 1

To Francesca, for everything, forever

CONTENTS

CONTENTS

WEAR YOUR DREAMS

1.

My Life in Tattoos

Today there have been nearly one billion Ed Hardy retail items unleashed on an unsuspecting but highly receptive public. That staggering sum makes no more sense to me than it does to you. It's more than T-shirts, hats, and running shoes. They've got everything. For a while, there were seventy sublicenses. A licensee sent us a bitchin' iPad cover with a leaping koi. There is red wine, white wine, champagne. My designs appeared on everything you can dress yourself with, on cigarette lighters, or air fresheners, you name it. I asked one of our guys just what the fuck does that have to do with air fresheners? "Nothing," he said. "People like the designs."

The big snarling tiger with the crazy green eyes I first painted in 1968, when I was just starting out doing tattoos in Vancouver. I took it from an old-time tattoo design, which I'm sure was taken from a circus poster. The "Love Kills Slowly" heart and skull design, something I first drew in 1971 at my shop in San Diego, is the most popular. It's like the Ford insignia of the Ed Hardy line.

I'm not a public figure. People don't know what I look like and I don't get out and around a lot. I was riding the subway in New York last year and there was a lady with this totally bling Ed Hardy bag. We were jammed up together. When I got off at my stop, I handed her a card and told her, "I'm Ed Hardy and I really appreciate you supporting the brand." I was in North Carolina for a tattoo convention and the maid came into my room, a young, hip gal with a couple of tattoos. She asked what I was doing in town and I said, "tattoo convention." She took a look at me in my plaid shirt and cardigan sweater. "Really?" she said.

"I'm a tattooer," I told her. "My name's Ed Hardy."

She whipped out her cell phone. "Wait a minute, wait a minute," she told me, then shouted into her phone, "Do you know who I'm standing here with? Ed Hardy! I love Ed Hardy."

When he signed me up, Christian Audigier told me they were going to make me a star and I would travel around the world in private jets and limousines and sign autographs for a half hour wherever I went. I told them, in only the nicest possible way, that I'd rather they would pay me and leave me alone.

That I became the best-known fashion brand in the world today is beyond laughable. Francesca and I are like the Beverly Hillbillies. All this is so strange to me. I've had to learn to pay attention. We had to mount a lawsuit to gain back control over the brand, but all that was settled. Today we are partnered with the New York brand management firm Iconix, and things are on a more even keel.

All I ever wanted to do was to make art and be an artist. I didn't want to be judged by the medium of my expression. When I started, nobody thought tattoos were art or that people who did tattoos were artists. Of course, I knew the tattoo shops and the people who tattooed lived in an underground world, but I never thought it *wasn't* art. When I took this up as a life calling, the so-called world of high art, needless to say, had no idea what to make of tattoo artists. We didn't exist in the world of galleries and museums. I never took that very seriously anyway, except that I didn't want to be viewed as a lesser human being because I didn't paint on canvas. The art world erects these artificial barriers and then gets to say who is an artist and who isn't. With tattoos, you are always going to get that to a degree because it's got that loaded thing—it's on skin and it's messy—all ink and blood. You have to look at people's bodies, which pushes all sorts of buttons. And they can't resell it, so they don't know what to do with it.

Today there is more tattooing than any time in history. Tattoos go back as far as civilization. The early Egyptian mummies were tattooed. The Pictish people in pre–Anglo-Saxon England, where we get the word "picture," were all tattooed. Tattoos may have predated cave paintings. I have no idea why people get tattoos. You might as well ask why people make art. The tattoo is a marker of life's journey. Tattoos are found in all cultures. The Pacific Islands had great tattoo traditions. Sadly, the Judeo-Christian bunch rejected tattoos as pagan markings, which pretty much assured the underground status of the tattoo in the Western world, where it's done in sketchy parts of town, by people with strange, noisy machines. When I opened Realistic Tattoo in 1974 in San Francisco, the modern tattoo movement was barely beginning to mass on the horizon.

I started corresponding with Sailor Jerry, the greatest tattooer of his generation, when I was first working in San Diego in 1969. We traded several letters a week because we had a lot of dead time in shop. We swapped photos of our work, compared notes, delved into aesthetics, techniques, and all aspects of the art of tattooing. We were both pushing epic tattoos, more breakthrough work with an Asian theme. We wrote each other constantly, but we only talked on the phone a couple of times. The first time I put a big tattoo on a woman, Jerry happened to call and ask, "What are you doing?" I told him I was fixing to put a big Japanese design on a good-looking young lady's back, just to bust his balls, because I knew he would be mad with envy.

She was a hippie chick who had been in my shop before. I remembered her when an old friend from my San Francisco Art Institute days called and said he met a girl in a bar who had some tattoos, which was highly unusual in those days. He was one of my few friends from school who showed any interest in tattoos. He was with me the night I got my second tattoo in Oakland and

3

was wearing a couple of my earliest pieces. He was back in San Francisco after a long time living out of town. At the time, he was a total lush, slamming them back at bars with strangers, and ended up one night taking her home with him. She gave him a dose. "God damn it, watch out if she shows up in your place," he said.

She did come back down and turned up at the shop, looking to get another tattoo. She picked something off the wall, but was vague about what she wanted and pretty much left it up to me. I had this design on the wall, sort of a Japanese grim reaper in a large, fluttering robe, brandishing a big Japanese ax. On the ax is the *kanji* (Japanese symbol) for death. I think maybe it was my idea, a good spot for it. I put it on her inner thigh. I didn't mention what was on the ax. I thought this was appropriate—a little warning to those in the know.

A couple of months later, the day Sailor Jerry called, she came back in with a man, a native Japanese. He barely spoke English. He was an architecture student who picked her up hitchhiking in the Haight-Ashbury and she talked him into driving her down to San Diego so she could get a big tattoo. He was more than slightly baffled by the whole thing. In Japan, tattoos are traditionally associated with the *yakuza,* the criminal underworld, and not something for anyone in polite society. He wore a deer-in-the-headlights expression and who knows what he thought the payoff was. He drove her. He was her patsy.

I pulled the curtain over the front window and locked the door. I had a private area I could close off if I was tattooing, and everything out front was nailed down, so if people were out there looking around, you wouldn't lose anything. But I figured I'd better lock the front door. She stripped down (following Jerry's lead, I would tell females not to worry about taking off their clothes—I'm just like a doctor) and got everything off. I drew the tattoo on her back. When I started outlining, she began squealing, "Whoa, whoa, whoa." She had multiple tattoos. "You know what this feels like," I told her.

Who knows what substance she was on? "If I could just have a drink," she said.

I do not do tattoos on people who have been drinking. I always held to that. You might get a sailor with a couple of beers in him and that would be okay, but I do not work on drunks. I really wanted to do this tattoo, though. After arguing with her a bit and more wiggling, I gave the Japanese guy some money and sent him around the corner for a half-pint. I handed her the bottle and told her to take a swig. She drained it.

Immediately her true inner beauty came out. I was trying to do the tattoo and she was moving around, moving around, and started to get incoherent. I was thinking *Jesus Christ*. The Japanese guy was terrified. You couldn't tell whether she was trying to beat the shit out of me or fuck me. She was very small. She jumped up and was hanging on to me like a monkey, with all this ink and grease on her back. I was thinking it would be better not to get involved in something like this again.

I had some of the lines on her back, but she finally passed out. Many times in this business, you find yourself in a situation with a person where things are going wrong, but this always stood out in my memory as an especially bad choice on my part. I should have steered clear of this dame from the start. When she passed out, the Japanese gentleman looked even more terrified. "Is she dead?" he asked.

"No, she's just blacked out," I told him. "I've got to get her out of here. She can't stay here. You're going to help."

It was early in the afternoon. I opened at noon and ran until midnight or later. They had showed up around opening time. Sailors were going to be coming off the ships. I had business coming in. I had to get her out of the shop and he was hopeless. He didn't know what to do.

I told him we had to take her somewhere and called a Travelodge down by the Pacific Coast Highway. We got her clothes on. She was in full drool, out of it. I got her into his car and we drove her down there. It completely looked like we were transporting a body. I went into the motel office and pointed to the car. "My cousin is really ill," I told the clerk. "I'm getting the room for her. I'll pay for it and take her to her room."

They gave me the keys. We pulled into the back of the parking lot and took her out of the backseat. She was disheveled, reeked of booze. Her vest was riding up and you could see the big bandage on her back. We were shuffling her down the hall when another room door opens and there was a full family—Mom and Pop, Buddy and Sis—out for a clean, wholesome time in San Diego. They did a full freeze as the Japanese guy and the tattooed man dragged this unconscious wretch past their doorway. It was full saucer eyes for all of them.

I did the entire ink drawing for the tattoo on her back and took a photo that I was going to send to Jerry. I got about half the outline down before she started going crazy on me. I took the money out of her vest, left her in the motel room, and advised the guy to be careful about picking up hitchhikers. I guess he drove back to San Francisco. That was my first experience with putting a big tattoo on a woman.

When I started in the business, ladies didn't get tattoos. The tattooed lady was strictly a sideshow attraction. In fact, when I started, most men who got tattooed were in the military.

I must have put more than ten thousand tattoos on servicemen before I even started with the epic stuff. There is probably somebody wearing an Ed Hardy tattoo in every city in the country.

Tattoos were always more than a way to make a living to me. From the beginning, tattoos were a mission and I was an evangelist. I wanted to expand the possibilities of the medium and I wanted to elevate the art form. Having graduated from art school, I brought with me to the field of tattooing—for better or worse—a sense of art history, a fierce dedication to the medium, and something of a chip on my shoulder toward the rest of the world that failed to hold the art of tattoo in the same regard I did.

When I began tattooing, there were no more than five hundred other tattooers in North America. Tattoos were not a part of polite society. My early clients at Realistic came from the peripheries of society—closet cases, Hells Angels, hippie visionaries—and the whole practice of tattoos oozed from there into the mainstream culture over the next twenty years. Nor was this a process I witnessed from the sidelines. My fingerprints can be found on every major wrinkle in the worldwide movement, from introducing Japanese-style tattoos to the West (or American-style tattoos to Japan) to the new tribalism that returned the tattoo tradition to the South Seas islands for the first time in a hundred years. I watched the entire world get tattooed. I tattooed more than a few of them myself.

2.

Kiddie Tattoos

Corona del Mar, where I grew up in the fifties, was just a small beach town about forty miles south of Los Angeles. It was actually part of Newport Beach, which was a millionaires' playground. A lot of movie stars such as John Wayne and those types had yachts moored in the beautiful harbor in Newport. The whole area had great surfing spots. Duke Kahanamoku, the great Hawaiian surfer, introduced surfing to California there. Before the jetty was built on the Corona del Mar side, they used to get big waves in the twenties. The beaches are really beautiful.

It was a conservative, small town. Officially part of Newport, unincorporated Corona del Mar was a distinct community with lots of open land on each side. Laguna Beach, which was always known as an art colony, was six miles down the road.

I was born Donald Edward Talbott Hardy on January 5, 1945, in Des Moines, Iowa. My father was serving in World War II, and my mother went to live with her parents while he was away. After the war, she quickly moved back to California. My father, Wilfred Ivan Samuel ("Sam") Hardy, was from England originally. His passion really was photography, but he would do anything to bring in a buck. He did a lot of aerial photography. My parents met when my mother, Mildred Sandstrom, was hand-tinting photographs in a big lab in Des Moines, my mother's hometown, where he was stationed with the Air Force. But I grew up a few blocks from the beach in this little beach town.

My father Sam was a real soldier-of-fortune, a world traveler. He came over to North America from England, first landing in Canada when he was about twenty, and always wanted to travel. He had been married before he met my mother and eventually took off and worked other places while they were married. He was in Saudi Arabia, working for Aramco, when they were laying the first oil pipelines in the late forties. I have photographs of him wearing a burnoose and standing next to a camel. They both took lots of photographs and my mother saved everything. Sam landed a position as an engineer in Japan during the Occupation. He went there when I was six. He'd never been to Asia. He'd been in Europe a lot, and the Middle East, but he completely went nuts for Japan. My mother figured out shortly that he wasn't going to come back and she filed for divorce. He ended up marrying a Japanese woman, a secretary who worked in the office.

He did stay in touch with us and sent child support. They had a pre-fab house that they'd built with a GI loan in 1947. My father did a lot of the work on the house himself. He kept making payments, and he sent over all this exotic stuff from Japan. There were always these things from where Daddy went, this mysterious land across the sea: tea sets, little framed pictures, a silk jacket with embroidered dragons, tigers, and hawks.

We went back to Des Moines for a year. My grandfather was very sick and I attended first grade in Iowa, before we came back to Corona del Mar. After my grandfather died, my grandmother moved out with us, so I was raised with a strong base of sympathetic female support. "What kind of pie do you want when you get home from school, Donnie?"

"Apple, Grammy." I was a tubby kid.

My best friend, Len Jones, lived a block away. The Second World War still loomed over us. Lenny and I used to play war. Both our dads had been in the war and we had fatigues, dummy M1 carbines used for training, and helmet liners that looked like actual helmets. I always tried to be accurate. If you're going to play cowboys and Indians, you want to wear the right gear. We also lived with a great sense of the Wild West.

Our street ended at the top of my block, the town limits, where there was barbed wire around the Irvine Ranch. In the summer, we could go to the end of the block and watch cowboys on horseback round up horses. The West was totally alive to me. The beach was just down the street and cowboys were only blocks away.

There was an old character named Colonel Blake who ran a Wild West Museum on Highway 101, a block away. It was a funky, old plaster building with a dirt floor and displays behind chicken wire. The colonel was a Buffalo Bill look-alike who dressed the whole part right down to the white goatee. He had this antebellum Southern-style, two-story house with a fish pond in front across the street from Lenny's house, where he'd sit on the porch in a rocking chair. In the fifties, there were still direct connections to that kind of Americana, although it was rapidly disappearing.

Lenny's parents, who were from Chicago, were much younger than mine. His mother was a gorgeous Italian-American and his father was Irish. His dad was a hip guy who drove a '49 fastback Cadillac, wore a Ronald Colman moustache, and listened to jazz. Len Sr. had been in the army and had several tattoos. When we were about ten, we got the idea to take a serious look at his dad's tattoos.

He had a clipper ship on one arm, an anchor on his hand, and a few other things. And he had the word "Stardust," his favorite song, on his forearm. He was a big Artie Shaw fan. I thought that was so cool—to have your favorite song tattooed on you. Len and I locked onto this tattoo thing and, along with playing war, cowboys and Indians, engineers on a train, we started playing tattoo. And we started drawing tattoo designs.

Tattoo designs were hard to find. You would see tattoos in cartoons in the *Saturday Evening Post*. Tattoos, for some reason, commonly cropped up in cartoons in the fifties, maybe because so many men had been in the military during World War II and

Korea. Beyond that, what did we know about tattoos? We drew anchors, eagles, and hearts and ribbons that said "Mom." I began obsessively drawing up flash (the sheets of designs that could be turned into tattoos). When we found Mongol colored pencils you could dip into water and turn into watercolor, we started figuring out ways to draw tattoos on the neighborhood kids.

We collected soda bottles on the beach to raise some change for Maybelline eyeliner, which we used for the black outlines. Len's mom suggested that. We set up a toy tattoo shop in the spare room in my house that we called the den.

The den was plastered with souvenirs from my father's travels. A bow and arrows from the Philippines were on the wall, alongside a German officer's dress dagger and an Arabian knife with a curved blade. Flags hung all over the ceiling—including a big Nazi flag from Nuremberg Stadium from when he was in Germany during the war trials. There was a flag from Saudi Arabia with a big scimitar and Arabian writing. There was a Korean flag with a yin-yang and trigrams. The walls were painted screaming blue with a bright red door that went out to the backyard. Sam did have a penchant for drama.

I taped up this tattoo flash we had been drawing and started trying to get neighborhood kids in. "Hey, I'm going to draw some tattoos." You'd try to charge them for it—"Two cents for that one"—but I put them on anyway, because I just wanted the excuse. There were strict rules: you had to have your parents' permission and you had to be at least nine years old.

There was a crippled guy named Tommy who ran a shoe-repair shop three blocks away on the Coast Highway. He had a typewriter and we had him make us tattoo licenses, complete with our fifth-grade photos for mug shots.

My mother took photos of everything with her Brownie box camera. She took lots of photos of me sitting and drawing tattoos on kids. The town was small enough that people started seeing these kids wandering around with tattoos that looked pretty damn real, and it came to the attention of the proprietor of the local weekly. He caught up with us on our way to Cannon's Market, where we would sit around, drink Cokes, and read comic books. He said he had heard about the tattoo shop we set up and wanted to know if he could come by and take a picture for the paper.

He ran a good-sized shot of us posing the way I knew the tattooers posed. We had a kid in the chair and another one standing behind us with stuff on his chest. We sat on either side and I knew to look at the camera with the tattooing tool poised. And we were holding our typewritten licenses.

Our education began in earnest when we figured out there were tattoo shops twenty-five miles up the coast on the Long Beach Pike, a big, scary, pre-Disneyland, pre-theme-park amusement park built on a pier on the beach. Disneyland wouldn't even open for another year. We would take the Greyhound bus, a seventy-five-cent fare. Our parents let us go. We'd get somebody to buy cigarettes for us. We'd smoke a pack of Marlboros and spend the day hanging out, combing our ducktails, looking at all the crazy shit on the Pike, maybe go on a few rides. Mainly we went for the tattoo shops. There were six shops on the Pike and most of them would kick kids out. You were supposed to be eighteen years old to be in a tattoo shop. But there was one guy who didn't mind: Bert Grimm, the greatest tattooer on the Pike.

He had come over from St. Louis a couple of years before and would let us hang out in his shop as long as we beat it when a cop came around. Bert was the quintessential tattoo flim-flam man—great storyteller, great bullshitter, great self-promoter. But Bert could also really tattoo. He had a strong, bold, power-hitting Americana style. He wore a green eyeshade, suspenders, and always had his long sleeves rolled down because all the work on his arms was old, blown-out, and faded. He never showed his own tattoos. There were photos of him from when he was about fifteen, from when he learned to tattoo in Portland. He had a big portrait of Geronimo on his chest. He'd tell the stories—how he had tattooed Bonnie and Clyde—and you could never distinguish what was true from what wasn't, but he sure knew how to roll them.

When he was in St. Louis, he owned a chain of photo studios, and took fabulous big-format, Speed Graphic black-and-white photographs of his work. It helped make him famous. He got hip to the power of photographing and displaying the tattoos you're doing. His window on the Pike was stacked with photos of impressive tattoos. He did a lot of large chest and back pieces. He worked extremely fast, blasted the work on. He developed his speed tattooing workers on the riverboats running the Mississippi, who only had a short time on shore between stops. He painted beautiful flash, a lot of it only in black and red. It made for faster application, but also was a masterful style challenge, to imply full-color range with limited means.

Bert had a real folk style, not fine-tuned like Sailor Jerry or other guys with more finesse, but you could read it a block away. He was my role model. I pestered him to show me how the machines worked. He told me if I was still interested when I was fifteen, he would teach me how to tattoo. That seemed like a long four years away to me.

His place was everything a tattoo shop should be. I copied designs off the wall. I would do thumbnail sketches, go home, and draw more finished versions. I was obsessed.

There were almost no books on tattooing, but there were ads for tattoo supplies in the back of *Popular Mechanics*, one of the magazines that showed you how to build a helicopter in your backyard, raise chinchillas for big money in your spare time, that kind of stuff. It was all part of the can-do postwar spirit of America.

I wrote away for the information on tattoo supplies. They couldn't know I was a ten-year-old kid. They sent me the order forms and pictures of the tattoo flash, which I copied. The flyer from Milt Zeis said it was a pleasant and profitable profession that could be done at your kitchen table. That sounded good to me. My mother worked in a factory. I knew I didn't want to do that. There were pictures of the tattoo machines that I would stare at and try to will them into life. I knew what it took to do real tattoos with these electric machines from watching at Bert Grimm's on the Pike and I never screwed up any kids trying to do any actual tattoos by hand. I did a few little pieces with sewing needles and India ink. I put a few dots on my hand and my initials on my arm and a set of initials on Lenny. But I never did anything grandiose. My drive for authenticity did lead me to put spools of thread electrical-taped to the end of the colored pencils when I "tattooed" to simulate the coils of the tattoo machine.

For a paper about professions in the fifth grade, I wrote about the prospects of drawing greeting cards for a living and a couple of other jobs involving artwork, but I quickly worked my way to tattooing. I included the flyer from the correspondence course and presented it like it was as normal as wanting to be a banker or a lawyer, but I'm sure the teacher must have been thinking, "What the fuck?"

When I decided to write a history of tattooing for school, I utilized a family drive we were making to Los Angeles. Mom went to visit a relative after she dropped me at the main library there and I spent the whole day absorbed in *Memoirs of a Tattooist* by the famous British tattooer, George Burchett. It was one of the very few books published about tattoos, all of which were beyond my little local library. I sat in that library and devoured almost the whole book, but I realized I needed a lot more information to really do the job.

I kept drawing the tattoo things for a few years, until that summer of "Yakety Yak" and "Purple People Eater" in 1958, when cars entered the picture. Our great coastal town drew people from all over Southern California. It had a wide beach with an enormous parking lot where people would park these outrageous customs and hot rods. There were booths that sold sno-cones and rented mats to ride in the surf. There were fire rings for hot dog and marshmallow roasts and all that.

We would go to the beach, check out the cars in the parking lot, and scout tattoos. You could see a lot of tattoos on guys who had been in Korea or World War II. They were still pretty young, out on the sand, in their bathing suits. I would see a good design, then go home and draw it up. (I used to look for designs on the wanted posters at the post office, too, because they had descriptions of tattoos. Some murderer? No, source material.)

Car customizing was starting to happen around Southern California. Len and I took a real shine to it. Len was very mechanical and ended up being a complete car guy—racecar driver, dealer, the whole bit. For me, they were sculptural objects. I was totally disinterested in mechanics and cars as things, especially things to work on. But the way they looked, with those vivid paint jobs and all that gleaming chrome, I understood. They started holding car shows on the beach in Long Beach next to the Pike. I was still going to hang out with Bert Grimm when I went to the first one, where I saw Ed Roth airbrushing shirts, before he was Big Daddy Roth.

We could cruise the Pike, go to the tattoo shops, take a couple of rides, and go to the car shows. There were guys there who painted sweatshirts—it was before T-shirts were commonly decorated. They had stacks of sweatshirts in these distinctly modern, new DayGlo colors—lime green, rancid pink—that they sprayed with black airbrush ink. This was my introduction to what was called Monster Art, also sometimes known as Weirdo Art. These artists would do portraits of cars and bang them out freehand with the airbrush—some guy's '57 Chevy, with a big monster at the wheel, his hand on an ape-hanger gear shift. It was a whole look, largely created by a young painter named Dean Jeffries, who called himself Kid Jeff and his work Krazy Shirts. I read an article about him in a teen hot rod magazine called *Dig!* that had some other cool stuff in it, including a big tattoo article.

Southern California was the birthplace of hot rods and custom cars. For one thing, the land is almost all flat and there is no winter. There is no salt on the roads to screw up paint jobs. The automobile really built Los Angeles. In the early days of Southern California, when they practically gave away lots to get people to move out there, the place filled up with people from the Midwest. My mother was part of the diaspora. We used to go every summer to a big Iowa reunion picnic in Long Beach. Land in Southern California was cheap. Life was good. The city spread out from the mountains to the sea. The Red Car system ran trains all the way out to where I grew up in Newport, although the oil companies took out most of these by the thirties. Broad boulevards were built that went for twenty miles. It was a real car culture, and everybody knew it. Every new building came with a parking lot around back. In the prosperity after the war, almost anybody could afford a car.

Around Los Angeles, the Barris Brothers and a few others were building custom cars. A big part of the look, besides the mechanical alterations, were the paint jobs. At first, it was mainly flames and stripes. Von Dutch was the guy that really kicked it off, when he invented that flying eyeball thing and did the wildest, most unexpected work. He was a legendary crazy bastard, a total loose cannon. Von Dutch did art on things besides vehicles, but not too much. I've seen an incredible hi-fi that Dutch oil-painted with these crazy figures and outer-space fantasy. He was the centerpiece of a group of people painting cars around the area that also included Dean Jeffries, who started out pinstriping, but ended up making custom hot rods for the movies. There were people developing their work in other parts of the country, but for me, it was Southern California–centric.

The Southern California culture was so fluid, ideas and designs flowed freely over boundaries. The "finish fetish" artists who were part of the Los Angeles art scene in the early sixties, doing stuff with poured resins, airbrushing, all that, and clearly were drawing directly from the people who custom made surfboards, while also taking a lot of their cues from the hot rod guys. Many of these artists were surfers and car enthusiasts.

I bought a ratty little compressor and an airbrush. I collected every hot rod and custom car magazine I could find that ran features with photographs of cars with these incredible paint jobs. Len and I would buy Revell plastic models and customize them ourselves using hot knives we heated on the stove to cut slits in the plastic (this was before the company made deals with customizers such as Ed Roth and Dean Jeffries).

Mom wanted me to get a job that summer so I started airbrushing my Monster Art on shirts and would wear these to the beach to drum up interest. One featured a monster guy pulling his eye-ball out with a fork. People would bring me their shirts, which I would paint, sign, and sell for small change. By the end of the summer, I had gone through a lot of shirts and made fifty dollars, serious money. It was beginning to dawn on me that this was the dream—to do my art and get paid for it.

My mother was impressed enough with the summer wages my Monster Art earned that she signed me up for classic watercolor lessons from a woman who lived a few blocks away. Mrs. Klaris, a painter, was one half of a European lesbian couple who seemed so exotic in sleepy Corona del Mar. Her partner was a dancer. She taught me fairly classic still-life watercolor techniques, which was the beginning of my formal training outside of school. But at that stage, all I really wanted to do was draw these monsters—and Mrs. Klaris would say in despair, "You have so much talent." She just didn't go for it. My buddies did. That was cool.

I grew up at the beach. Besides drawing, being in the water was my main obsession, snorkeling, body surfing, and riding the inflatable rubber mats in the waves. I started stand-up surfing for the first time shortly after my fourteenth birthday, and that to-tally took over my life. I bought a used, wood board and spent every spare minute at the beach. Surf culture was only beginning to develop along the south coast. Filmmakers John Severson and Bruce Brown used to rent high-school auditoriums and give live narrations to their sixteen-millimeter surfing movies, backed by some rock-and-roll records. All I wanted to do was make surf art.

Through hanging out with the surfers at the beach, I also be-came connected with the beat scene. Café Frankenstein opened in Laguna. That was where I bought a copy of Gregory Corso's *Bomb,* that came printed on a foldout with the type in the shape of a mushroom cloud. I also bought Allen Ginsberg's *Howl.* A bit later, I read Jack Kerouac's *On the Road* and William S. Burroughs's *Naked Lunch,* which thoroughly blew my mind. Another coffee shop opened in Newport called the Prison of Socrates, which was a totally cool name. They played jazz in the coffee shops and I started listening to cool jazz. I became fascinated with the beatnik thing. And I knew San Francisco was where the beatniks were.

I kept my grades up. I lucked across a great high school art teacher, Shirley Rice. She was a leftist New York Jewish intellectual and her husband Ed Rice taught literature at Long Beach State. They were well read, hip, and socially conscious. She definitely stood out in my Orange County high school. It didn't hurt that she was also a great-looking lady. I paid attention. She would tell me I could do so much more than my surf art and I started to think it over. She turned me on to Picasso. She showed me art with social consciousness, like Ben Shahn, who did a series on Sacco and Vanzetti. She brought this liberal, sophisticated East Coast sensibility that really fired me up. I started studying art history and getting more serious about my own art.

I surfed through senior year and when summer came, put my board away in the garage and began drawing obsessively. I told all my buddies that I was going to only make art. I had taken some crummy jobs, like washing dishes in the pancake houses, but I knew I had to focus on this to get anywhere.

With my bad-boy surfer friends who didn't know or care anything about art, I was alone. And the people in my high-school class who were interested in art were not people I wanted to hang out with. I was kind of a lone wolf in the deal, trying to dig all this stuff, reading art history voraciously.

I connected with Doug Hall, who worked for the city on the beach clean-up crew, was a few years older than me, and was getting ready to go to Long Beach State. He lived probably six blocks from me and had a wicked sense of humor. We were typical bad boys, drinking beer and hanging out, but he was into art. He was already going to junior college and was on a different level than I was. We started investigating the Los Angeles art scene, which in the early sixties offered an exciting, vibrant counterpoint to the established gallery scene in New York.

I was kind of interested in New York painting, the abstract expressionism after World War II in the fifties, Willem de Kooning and Jackson Pollock and all that. But in Los Angeles, there was so little awareness of art and so few serious collectors, younger artists without any expectations of being taken seriously in New York were free to follow paths of their own. They basically didn't care about New York.

Walter Hopps and the artist Ed Kienholz opened the Ferus Gallery in 1957, which became the entry point for a great many important new artists. Walter Hopps was a really complicated guy, an eccentric genius who looked mature for his age and could get into the black jazz clubs along Central Avenue with a fake ID. He saw Billie Holiday and all the greats there. His father was a doctor and Walter was trained as a scientist. He was a pothead from early on, and an avid drinker, and when he found speed, he became Mr. Bennies and Martinis. But he was a prophet who became the greatest art curator of the twentieth century.

Walter had vision. One of the first things he staged was an event on the Santa Monica Pier merry-go-round in 1955, where they mounted all this art on the carousel, backed by some weird soundtrack. They attracted like-minded people working in the film industry. Dennis Hopper, who was getting noticed for *Rebel Without a Cause,* was around and taking a lot of photographs. Doug and I realized that a lot of these guys were not that much older than we were. And they were making really interesting stuff.

We saw the Campbell's Soup Can paintings by Andy Warhol when they were first exhibited in 1962 at the Ferus, Warhol's first solo show. Doug Hall and I burst out laughing; we couldn't believe what we were seeing. Some of the Los Angeles painters really turned me on. There was John Altoon, serious painter, Armenian guy with a walrus moustache and thick dark hair, probably bipolar—he had a lot of serious mental problems and did a lot of pretty crazy things. He worked as an illustrator to pay the bills, but he did these phenomenal abstract paintings. His Ocean Park series, named for a street in Santa Monica, explored bright, sexy, biomorphic shapes. It knocked me out. We'd see these guys around—Altoon at a café, drinking coffee.

I met the swashbuckling ceramic artist Pete Voulkos when Doug and I came across him installing a show in an empty gallery. He was up on a ladder and he came down to introduce himself. I knew who he was. He was really important; he had practically single-handedly taken clay out of the "crafts" category into recognition as a serious medium, on a level with painting and other mediums. It was just amazing to me that I could walk among these gods, these people who were really doing it. You could do your own art and land a spot in one of these galleries—things seemed possible.

We saw a breathtaking Jean Dubuffet show at the Los Angeles County Museum of Art. By then, Ed Kienholz had sold his share in the Ferus Gallery to another partner, Irving Blum, a suave, former businessman from New York. Irving was good with the business end, whereas Blum knew how to connect with collectors. Ed was farther out than most of the artists, and eventually landed a position as curator and then director of the Pasadena Museum of Art.

Doug Hall had a sister about a year older than me, Martha, who was dating another Corona del Mar artist named Richard Shaw, who had gone to a different school and wasn't part of my set. Richard was about four years older and he knew all these artists. His father had worked for Disney as an animator for many years and hung and swung with all these hard-partying, laugh-a-minute cartoonists, which is how Richard met Llyn Foulkes. He was doing super-disturbing, beautiful paintings of people and animals and these big looming rocks in strange colors. Foulkes was married to Kelly Kimball, the daughter of Ward Kimball, one of the prime animators at Disney who had worked on everything from *Fantasia* on down. Llyn and Kelly were making assembly-line, nonconfrontational paintings for furniture stores—lay out twenty canvases and go through them with all of one color, then the next, and so on. This paid the bills while Llyn developed his gorgeous, disturbing personal work. I found out about Foulkes through Richard and Martha. Ed gave Foulkes a big show at the Pasadena Museum.

Bruce Conner was another artist whose work spoke to me. He did scary assemblages covered in wax and painted black—women's stockings, nudie magazines torn up—supercreepy. I was drawn to dark stuff, to art that came from a different place, reflections of angst and deeply troubling things that were not part of California sunshine, the beach, the convertible car, and the nice life that my mother wanted me to have. But she had an artist's soul. She wrote a lot of poetry when she was young. She loved that I could draw and would say, "Donnie-Ed's going to be an artist."

My mother was of Swedish descent, and maybe that is why I found myself attracted to the gloomy Nordic art, especially Edvard Munch—*The Scream* and his *Death in the Sickroom* drawings of the dying of his beloved sister. Munch would piteously etch her over and over, observing this horror in detail. And then there was Francisco Goya, who I discovered when I was still surfing. I did love melodrama as a teenager.

I did a collage, kind of an homage to Bruce Conner, called "The Life of a Tattooer." I ripped up these tattoo catalogs and pictures of flash and pasted them across a background of black oil paint, smeared around. I included pictures of me and Lenny, my old childhood tattoos. At the bottom, there's a picture of an old man in a wife-beater T-shirt, sitting in front of his display in a carnival midway, drawing flash. *Wasn't that funny?* I thought. *I was going to be a tattooer and now I'm going to be a real artist.*

I was making all kinds of work and Shirley Rice encouraged me. She submitted a number of my pieces to something called the Scholastic Art Awards and my work won more awards than anyone ever had before. My mother and Mrs. Rice took me to the awards ceremony in downtown Los Angeles. They gave me gold keys, blue ribbons, and a tiny bit of money. I was in my total cool-guy phase, all Peter Gunn with blazer, skinny tie, topcoat, shined shoes, all that.

I was brought up with an appreciation of art. My mother loved the fact that Laguna Beach, six miles down the road, was an artists' colony. It was home to California Plein-Air Painters in the early twenties. The beaches were perched on spectacular rock formations. There were a lot of people there painting the scenery, as well as more adventuresome artists. The town had a long-running Festival of Arts at Laguna Canyon that featured something called the Pageant of the Masters, *tableau vivant,* where people posed as famous paintings. We went every summer and toured the artists' booths, looking at the work. I realized people could make a living doing this. My mother had a good friend, Mildred Waters, mainly a watercolorist who sometimes did oil paintings. She had her own gallery on the Pacific Coast Highway, a tiny clapboard house built in the twenties where she showed her work and that of others. You had to audition for the Laguna Beach Art Festival and show them your work to see if you would be accepted. When I graduated from high school in 1962, I qualified for a booth, showed my work, and even sold some.

The art festival was an eye-opener for me on many levels. I met a lot of older artists, people who were painters that were doing things, hip guys, already living the life. I sat in my booth, painted black, cool in my Ray Charles wrap-around shades, displaying my tormented drawings. No seascapes here; only serious art. One of the most exciting browsers I met in Laguna was Adele Ipsen, whose mother had modeled for my hero Munch and who, impressed with my "homage to Munch" drawings, invited me to see her collection of Munch prints. She also alerted me to some of my work's similarity to George Grosz, so I looked into that.

I also met the Interlandi twins. Phil was a cartoonist who had things in *Playboy* and his brother Frank had a booth displaying his abstract expressionist paintings. He liked his screwdrivers. We hung out, sitting in the sun, getting buzzed, and I felt like I was part of a wild, wonderful community of artists.

By then, I'd been drinking every weekend since I was thirteen. At the Laguna Art Festival, I smoked pot for the first time and added that to my repertoire. A couple of the artists I met, a few years older than me, helped broaden my perspectives. I started hearing more about San Francisco. Richard, Martha, and some other friends decided they were going to go to art school up north and I found out about the San Francisco Art Institute. That became my destination.

3.

San Francisco Art Institute

I didn't know quite what I was going to do. I figured I might go to Orange Coast Junior College in Costa Mesa, a two-year school where people from my area went to get on track for a full four-year college. But that summer in 1962, I met Ken Conner, a ceramicist who was five years older, and we became friends.

He had surfed a bit, but he was serious about his art. His parents had some money and he was living on an avocado ranch, ten acres of avocado groves in north San Diego County, which he was tending for his folks. His parents were art collectors. They had a John Singer Sargent watercolor; I had never seen anything like that in somebody's home. Ken and I were two cool cats, zonked on "Sketches of Spain" and "Mulligan Meets Monk."

Ken had gone the previous summer to an art school that was attached to the La Jolla Museum of Art, about thirty miles from where he lived. He suggested I could live with him on the ranch and commute to school.

It was a big jump. I was still living at home with Mom, but I was restless. My circumstances were fairly autonomous. When I was fifteen, my mother decided to add a room to the house for me. That way, my grandmother could have her own room. I'd been sleeping in that den where I'd had the tattoo shop, with the knives and flags on the walls. I drafted the plans for the addition (I took mechanical drawing in high school) and chose the color scheme. I selected black and white: black walls, white ceiling, and checkerboard floor. All black furniture, white bathroom, black towels. I had my drawing board set up in the corner. I had my own entrance so when I came stumbling home, puking after a night of drinking, I didn't have to walk by Mom.

I don't think she ever got over Sam taking a hike. His Old Spice shaving brush stayed in the medicine cabinet. She knew he had been married before and she remained close with his children from the first marriage, my half brother and half sister, who would come down and visit us. People didn't get divorced back then; it was a big deal. She got something going with a guy who had lived next door to us. His wife had died. He ran a dry dock in Newport and they were going to get married, but he broke it off.

She never remarried. She had a real close friend, a cereal salesman who traveled all over working for Kellogg's. He drew great cartoons and had a terrific sense of humor. He would visit and sleep on the living room sofa, but I don't think they had any physical relationship. She just liked being around men.

She had other friends, lots of women she could relate to. When she was working in that factory, she was in a bowling league. The factory job made her furious because she made half the money of what men doing the same job were paid. She knew that wasn't right.

I was excited at the possibility of taking classes from John Altoon, who had taught at the La Jolla's museum art school that summer. He was one of the art heroes whose work I had been seeing in Los Angeles galleries. I applied and was accepted. I moved down to San Marcos with Ken and would go home to Corona del Mar on weekends to do my laundry and hang out. My mother gave me her old pink and gray '52 Chevy two-door and I would commute down to La Jolla for my two classes a week. It was a fine art museum and there were great studios in the basement. La Jolla was a beautiful, wealthy seaside town. Raymond Chandler had lived there. There was a fantastic bookstore and coffeehouse next to the museum, so it was a kind of bohemian immersion. Ken introduced me to classical music. We would sit up on the roof, drink red wine, listen to Wagner, and contemplate the glory of the universe and what we were going to do with our lives. He was a serious ceramicist and had a big kiln in his garage.

I ran across a book by a critic named Selden Rodman, *The Insiders,* which was anti–abstract art and anti-elitist, focusing on art that celebrated—big catchphrase in those days—the human condition. This is where I discovered José Luis Cuevas. He was a prodigy from Mexico City, getting his work shown when he was a teen. He did caricatures, but dark. He didn't paint; he mostly did ink drawings of how bad things could be—pictures of whores, cripples, the underbelly of Mexico City—and a lot of self-portraits. He did a great set of illustrations for Franz Kafka's *The Metamorphosis.* I got into Cuevas in a big way. He showed at a La Cienega gallery, the Silvan Simone Gallery. Ken Conner was really into him; his parents had a couple of Cuevas pieces. On one visit, Simone told us Cuevas was in L.A., making lithos at Tamarind Press, and said we should visit him. We went over to the little bungalow where they'd set him up, and awkwardly tried to express how much we admired his work. Only thing, he spoke virtually no English and Ken only knew a smattering of Spanish.

Ken and I were touring the La Cienega galleries and went into the Rex Evans Gallery. He had an elegant space above an ivy-covered jewelry store. Ken's parents bought the Sargent watercolor from him. He carried big-name, blue-chip art, and had a Magritte hanging on the wall. He sold high-priced art to Beverly Hills collectors such as Vincent Price and Edward G. Robinson. Rex was a big, jolly, Santa Claus–type character, with a large twirled mustache, elegant white hair, and a red vest. He spoke with a plummy British accent and had played character parts in the movies. He was the Bavarian inn owner who led the villagers to get the monster in one of the Frankenstein films. His partner and much younger boyfriend, Jim, helped handle the gallery.

Ken introduced us and I told him I was making art. Of course, Rex had sold a lot of art to Ken's parents and even sold some pieces to Ken. He asked to see what I was doing. I took my stuff to show him. "Oh, these are wonderful," he said. "What do you think, Jim? Shall we put Don in a show?" At age seventeen, my work was being exhibited. I might have sold one drawing, but he put my stuff on the walls. I was in some group shows. That happened so quickly, I really didn't know what to think, but it definitely gave me incentive.

Ken and I made a run down to Tijuana while I was still living in San Marcos and stopped in San Diego on the way. We were knocking around downtown when I saw this sign, TATTOOING—OLD DOC WEBB, and a buzzer went off inside. Doc Webb had a mezzanine shop above a magic store run by a Chinese guy on Horton Plaza, off Broadway, the main Sailortown strip. Those were busy days in San Diego. I went inside and looked around. I didn't really dig Doc's style of drawing flash. He'd been a sign painter and show-card letterer for museum lobbies and stuff like that. There was also an early forties cartoon touch to all his tattoo flash. I still decided to get a black widow spider tattooed on my leg and was sitting in his chair, my pant leg rolled up, with him getting ready to shave my leg when he asked to see my identification. I was still seventeen, under the legal age to get a tattoo. I told him I left it in the car. "You'll have to go get it," he said. I tried again at another shop on Broadway, but no luck.

We continued on to Tijuana, where Ken was loudly heckled all over the street for wearing a beard. Guys would yell, "Hey, Castro!"

I finished the semester at La Jolla, but, since I was about to turn eighteen and become eligible for the draft, I needed to enroll in an accredited school for a deferment. I moved back to my mother's house and entered Orange Coast Junior College in January 1963.

At Orange Coast, I met a terrific teacher, Bruce Piner, a younger guy in his thirties, with a great sense of humor, who liked to tip back the wine. I used to spend time hanging out at his house with him, his great-looking wife, and their two young kids.

We knew about the bigger art world. Pop art was the thing. The big names in New York were Robert Motherwell, Jasper Johns, Roy Lichtenstein, and, of course, Warhol. We caught a documentary on television while we were sitting around Piner's house one night that showed Warhol at work. What struck me was that Warhol was playing girl-group oldies while he was working. As much as I had come to appreciate classical music and dug cool jazz, rock-and-roll was still my true love.

I liked Pop Art okay and I understood how important it was. I did a series of three Pop paintings of tattoos, pink arms on flat, colored backgrounds. They all had tattoos about "Mom." There was a famous old-time tattoo of a garland of flowers with the slogan, "The sweetest girl I ever kissed was another man's wife. My mother." It probably originally came from an embroidered pillow, something for sailors. I called it Mom Art.

I was hanging out a lot with Richard Shaw and still saw Doug Hall, who was attending Long Beach State and started etching. He became a printmaking major, the first person I knew to get into etching. I signed up for printmaking at Orange Coast.

Piner was eager to have all of us explore things, but he wasn't making his own art. We all thought we would go through graduate school and get a job teaching art, but we hoped we wouldn't wind up like that, not having made a new piece of art in years. I was reading so much art history, musing over a biography of Toulouse-Lautrec and all the other artists who were in the mix with him, wondering if our crew was going be like that. None of us had any idea what we were doing. We had no agendas. But we were eager to make the work and carve out a place in the world that wasn't what was expected of us.

In Piner's art history class, I sat next to David Mackenzie, a talented young artist from Huntington Beach. He and I were very taken with surrealism and Dada-esque pranks, and fancied ourselves as apple cart upsetters. When Piner showed the darkened auditorium the slide of Meret Oppenheim's fur-lined teacup, a famous surrealist piece, Mackenzie blew a huge *whoop* through a superloud plastic whistle and disrupted the class. Like the Dadas did. Like the Impressionists, Picasso.

Newport was so right wing, birthplace of the John Birch Society and all that, that when Mackenzie pulled a stunt in the school courtyard where he came to school wrapped in an American flag, he came close to getting thrown out of school for desecrating the flag. It was a great pressure cooker, though, because it made us really want to get the fuck out of there. I went through two semesters at Coast. I learned to etch a little bit. I made a bunch of art.

Mackenzie and I took a run to San Francisco. I had not been on an airplane since I was an infant. Our friends who were going to the Art Institute picked us up in their VW bug and drove straight to North Beach, where they were all living near the school. We quickly made our way to Grant Avenue, Dean Moriarty's neighborhood from *On the Road* and ground zero for the beatnik coffee houses and jazz joints on a Friday night. I couldn't believe I was still in California: the Victorian architecture, weird stores, ethnic restaurants. There was a gay club holding a drag queen contest and these limos kept pulling up and the queens would climb out and walk into the club. California? I could have been on Mars. I was smitten.

I applied to the San Francisco Art Institute and was accepted for the fall 1963 semester. My mother helped with the $385-per-semester tuition. I didn't work all the time I went to Orange Coast, just skated, living at home with mom, selling a piece here and there. At the Art Institute, I took a job on the maintenance crew, swabbing out the bathrooms and sweeping up the cafeteria. Dave Getz worked on the same crew, but he hadn't yet started playing drums in Big Brother and the Holding Company. David Mackenzie was also accepted and he and I moved up with another art student we knew from Orange Coast College. We rented a duplex between Columbus Avenue and Taylor Street in the heart of North Beach. It was my first apartment and the rent was seventy-five bucks a month.

The Art Institute was located in an ivy-covered building from the twenties. They had a big Diego Rivera mural, which, in those days, was covered over. Only about four hundred students attended and classes were small. People would come through. Rothko and a lot of great New York painters had taught there. But San Francisco was a long way from New York and, although I loved a lot of the ab-ex painters, de Kooning and Franz Kline and those guys, and, of course, all the great cultural energy that emanated from New York, we were hyperaware that it was a different thing in San Francisco. The Bay Area figurative painting was a big breakthrough from the tyranny of abstract expressionism. Richard Diebenkorn, Joan Brown, Elmer Bischoff, and other Bay Area painters, segued out of the real muscular slash-and-burn abstract expressionist stuff and began going back to recognizable subject matter.

These were important distinctions, almost philosophical concerns or belief systems. Abstract art was supposed to be a search for purity of expression and it was not cool to do recognizable subject matter (although de Kooning and others always floated in and out of that and kept the figurative stuff going). But these Bay Area people were fantastic painters who decided to turn back to landscapes and figures, but with loose paint, very expressive. It wasn't tight, representational work, but beautiful, killer paintings. The Art Institute may have been a long way from the Park Avenue galleries, but it was a hive of intellectual activity and creative expression.

There were people on the faculty such as Richard Miller, who was a total raging, political subversive, and would give firebrand talks to his classes, and Ken Lash, a poet who lived in Bolinas. We read Joseph Campbell's *Hero with a Thousand Faces* in one class. I was getting a glimpse of a wider world.

I took a drawing class from Joan Brown, somebody whose powerful work transfixed me when I'd first seen it in Los Angeles galleries. She was married to Manuel Neri, who led a sculpture class I took. She was another reason I had wanted to come to San

Francisco. Her work was supergutsy: thick paint, great, crazy brushwork, and everyday themes. She grew up in San Francisco, attending Catholic schools, when she saw an advertisement for the Art Institute on the side of a bus and decided to pursue art. She was something of a prodigy and was enrolled in the Art Institute while she was a teenager. Joan studied with Diebenkorn and Bischoff, among others. She was really cute and also full of piss and vinegar. She swore like a trooper, could drink anybody under the table. Joan was like everybody's sweetheart. We were all in love with her.

When I got to the Art Institute, Shaw had been there already for a semester and was very involved in ceramics. He was painting also, but ceramics became his thing, largely through his work with Ron Nagle, the madman of clay, a protégé of Peter Voulkos who scared all of us a little. I came to San Francisco wanting to be a lithographer. I was in love with lithographs, all the dark tones and the washes that you get working on the stones. They had these ancient Bavarian limestones at the Art Institute, the traditional printing medium for lithography since the beginning of the eighteenth century. These came, along with the big old presses, from when the school started in the late 1800s. They were supposedly used for ballast on the sailing ships that brought Gold Rush miners to the city.

I loved artwork that had a specific craft, stringent demands involving tools and techniques that had to be done a certain way. Whether it was ceramics, printmaking, tattooing, or pinstriping, if you couldn't handle the utensils, you couldn't get it right. I dug the history of printmaking and the eccentricity of a lot of printmakers. Even if they were primarily painters, it brought out a certain thing in artists that I really responded to. I liked monochromatic art, stuff in black and white and gray tones. I loved the dark shades you could get with lithos, and I liked the idea that it was a multiple original. I liked the democratic, anti-elitist nature of that. It was a people's art.

I took a lithography class from the head of the print department, Dick Graf, and also signed up for an etching class. The big-city swagger of the other students intimidated me. One character actually wore a beret at a jaunty angle, about the corniest thing in the world, but he did it with such arrogance and authority, I couldn't help but be impressed. I had been worried about how I was going to fit in with these people, how I could compete, feeling threatened and insecure. I knew how green I was. But then I looked around at the art they were making—especially the guy in the beret—and realized they weren't that advanced after all. *These people don't know what they're doing,* I thought. *I can draw rings around them.*

I was inspired to make my move and work hard. I started do-ing the lithography, which can be difficult, just working with the medium, but I wasn't loving it. Graf kept asking what the deeper meanings of my work were, what I was trying to convey. I had no idea, no big intellectual program to articulate, and he didn't think much of that. The etching class met two nights a week and on Saturdays with Gordon Cook, who was unlike anybody I ever met before. He was a tough, blue-collar guy from Chicago who dis-trusted academia and kept his day job in the printing trade, and only taught on the side. He was a big guy, dour and contrary, kind of scary, but he did these incredibly nuanced, delicate etchings of still lifes, nudes, and landscapes, all drawn from life, minimal means, supermasterly. The first time I met Cook was before I was enrolled, when I was up on a visit with Richard and Martha, who were taking printmaking. I sat in with them and they told me to work on a plate. I etched kind of a fantasy thing of my buddy Mackenzie as kind of a heroic figure with the kind of eagle wings that I learned to draw when I was tattooing. Cook came over and looked at what I was doing.

"That's not very straightforward," he said.

"Maybe I'm not a very straightforward guy," I said. It just popped out. I didn't think about what I was saying. We instantly hit it off.

He talked about art in a way I had never heard before—no

bullshit, superintelligent, from his blue-collar perspective—which I could understand, talking about it in a way that combined a complete embrace of colloquial things of the way life is, down to the metaphors he used, with his deep grounding in art history, tying in Rembrandt and Dürer and this great printmaking tradition. He saw my potential. He kept coming up with stuff that was really hard to do, challenging me. ("Why don't you do this?") He showed me the value of looking at nature, very hard, and figuring out a way to translate it into something that would convey one's feelings in the picture. You were creating a picture with very fine lines and matrices of lines, networks of things, stipples, making marks to create an illusion of something, whether it's a can full of dried flowers or a landscape of a San Francisco backyard with a million leaves and bushes. Essentially it was about perceiving the greater network of the world through hallucinatory attention to details, instead of imposing an attitude or agenda with the work. Cook kicked open a door for me that nobody else had. He became my mentor.

Gordon was well versed in Asian aesthetics. He had been very close to the late Kenneth Patchen, the beat poet who had lived on the Peninsula. He was a journeyman union typesetter, and only taught classes at night and on the weekends. He worked setting hand type, and he was proud of the tradition of book-making. One day, he showed me something from a magazine by two American expatriates living in Kyoto, artist Will Petersen and beat poet Cid Corman: an English translation of a text by Zeami, the fourteenth-century Japanese inventor of Noh drama, about how to act. Basically, it was a Taoist way of looking at the universe in a nutshell, instructions on how to behave in life and make it work, specifically related to the medium that you happen to be working in. For them, it was theater. Zeami related everything to nature: like a flower, you open up, and all the parts come together. I was stunned. Cook asked me what I thought it was about.

"It's about acting," I said.

"It's about everything," Cook said. I copied that damn thing down and still keep it.

We all started hanging out together, going for drinks at the San Remo, a couple of blocks down the hill from school. I was on a social footing with my teachers. I was working hard, making prints and drawing, even painting a little bit. I desperately wanted to be a painter, but I did not know what to paint. I loved the physicality of oil paint, but I was always completely lost with what I should do with it. I didn't have an original thought in my head about that. I didn't have an original thought about printmaking, either. I tended to imitate somebody that I admired. I'd done that all the way through. When I got into Goya, I did a self-portrait à la Goya. I wanted to be like these people. I wanted to mind-meld with them by looking at their work and imitating it. I did it with Cuevas.

The answers seemed to be floating in the San Francisco air and all you had to do was breathe them in. One of the first times I smoked pot in the city, Mackenzie and I walked all the way across town to the Primalon for a party. It was an ex-skating rink and ballroom in the Fillmore district with a rich history in rhythm and blues during the fifties (it was where Johnny Otis discovered Etta James). It had been taken over by artists, who jerry-rigged tiny, cramped living spaces and studios in a kind of communal environment. We got high in this den of bohemians—music in the air, artwork everywhere, everything so cosmic—and walked back to North Beach in the sunshine, intoxicated with more than the marijuana.

Once I was in school, I was filled with anticipation. They're going to give us the keys to the kingdom. They're going to draw back the curtain, and give up the secrets of how to do art. They maintained a great tradition, which may have originally come from the abstract expressionists, of not being explicitly verbal, avoiding intellectual flights of claptrap, and not sitting around pontificating about cosmic essences. I still have a terrible aversion to that, although I am often guilty of it myself.

Very quickly during the first semester, I became frustrated and impatient. I had taken a few sessions of my sculpture class with Neri and I went over to Shaw. "Neri won't really say anything," I said.

"That's the way it is," he said. We had to figure it out for ourselves.

I didn't have any money. I'd go to City Lights Books and sit in the basement and read whole books, spending many nights down there. I was drinking it all up. I lived in that apartment for a couple of semesters. I was doing serious etchings. Martha and I were kind of the leading lights of the printmaking students and Gordon was giving us very hard things to do. He told us to do an etching of the city of San Francisco. We went to Twin Peaks and each of us did a 24-by-30-inch copper plate, drawing the exacting details of a vast panorama of houses and trees with a needle through beeswax.

My dad had reentered my life a number of years before. He first came over when I was fourteen. We went on a fishing trip in the Sierras with my half brother Bill and half sister Betty. He moved back to California a few years later, before I went to San Francisco, with his Japanese wife, who he had renamed Bonnie. She seemed surprised to learn that Sam had a son, my half brother Bill, twelve years older, who was almost her age. Sam's looks held up and Bonnie thought he was much younger than he was. He landed a civil service job working for the navy at Port Hueneme, near Ventura. He and Bonnie visited me in San Francisco and he told me he had taken a job in Guam with the navy. He asked me if I would like to come spend the summer there, where he could line up a job for me, and we could go to Tokyo at the end of the summer. I was right on that. At age nineteen, I qualified to fly as a dependent in the military air transport system.

I was seeing a Japanese-American girl from Santa Barbara who went to the Art Institute and lived in a basement apartment on North Point Street, beneath an old Italian couple. I was desperate to be attached, wanted a wife or a mom substitute, really. This gorgeous young lady had hair down to her ass and I was gone on her, but it wasn't going to work out between us.

She was going to leave town, move to New York with some other guy, but we arranged for me to take over her apartment at the end of the summer. So I stashed some of my stuff with somebody else and, at least, I had a pad to come back to in San Francisco.

I was flying to Guam on a space-available basis out of the military air base near Sacramento, Travis Air Base. Three times I made the trip by bus, only to be turned back after waiting five hours or more, before I finally got onboard a flight. When I got to Guam, after flying through the night over the Pacific Ocean in a propeller plane, Sam met me with more bad news. The only job he could find me was as pickup boy on a construction crew. I was the only *haole* (Caucasian) on an all-Filipino crew, working outside in blistering heat, heavy rain, no trade winds. The guys I worked with thought I was a spy for the bosses. They pressured me to buy wholesale groceries for them at the PX. I didn't think I could, but they wanted to use me for whatever.

It was different over there. We drove through one village in the jungle where everyone was out on the lanai, everything in the open air, no windows. They had a giant lizard nailed up to the wall and next to it were stacks of 45 RPM records on pegs. The intense tropical environment was overwhelming. I lasted a little more than a month on the job before I quit. My old man didn't say much about my quitting. It was the first time that we lived together since I was six years old. He and his wife had an apartment in a town house, a navy housing development. Bonnie was an avid bowler and did *ikebana*, or flower arranging. I knew how to bowl, so I spent the rest of my time in Guam bowling in air-conditioning. Bonnie and I had a good time getting to know each other. When I brought up the subject of my dad, if she missed Japan, and all that, she said, "Before is before." With her limited English, I felt it was a valuable *koan* about not being crippled by things from the past.

To my disappointment, the promised trip to Japan never materialized, but it was a long way from sunny California. When I came back to San Francisco, I had been dipped in the exotic.

At Hickam Air Force Base in Hawaii, I got bumped out of my seat on the return flight. It was nighttime, and the next flight wasn't until morning. I took a bus from the base into Waikiki, and rolled right down Hotel Street in Chinatown, where it was jumping with penny arcades and bars and all these neon signs advertising tattoos. I almost got off the bus, but I didn't know how I would ever find the bus again to go back, so I rode back to the base. If I had gotten off, I know I would have gotten a tattoo.

When I came back to San Francisco, the Japanese chick had split—taking some of my art books with her—but I had this excellent apartment. San Francisco was buzzing with music that fall. Change was in the air. In the spring of 1965, I had attended a Rolling Stones concert at the San Francisco Civic, and only a few months later, a number of people who were also in the crowd that night had grown their hair and started their own rock groups with funny names like Jefferson Airplane or Great Society. The first few dance/concerts were held in Longshoreman's Hall, only a few blocks down the hill from school. I was making prints and digging the scene.

Soon after I came back from Guam, I hooked up with a woman I knew in high school. Christine Podolak moved to the Bay Area with her brother and was working as a dental assistant in Berkeley. We started going together and it quickly got intense. Within a couple of months, she was pregnant and we got married over Christmas break 1965 at an Episcopal church in Newport (my mother, a staunch Lutheran, tried to raise me religious, but it never took; Christine's mother was the Episcopalian). Chris wasn't showing much. I was twenty years old. *I guess this is how life works,* I thought, as I waited to say my vows.

I worked my way off the maintenance crew at school and into a job at the school library, but I still couldn't afford a wife and child on the peanuts they paid me. Luckily, I landed a job at the post office, pitching mail on the swing shift at Rincon Annex. This nice government job came with full medical benefits, which would cover the costs of the birth of our son, Douglas, who was born July 9, 1966. The post office was one of the few places in town that would hire people without haircuts, so the place was crawling with pot-smoking, long-haired hippies. There were plenty of people bumping around there every night, tripping on LSD. Of course, all the old-time management types were shit-faced on booze they kept sneaking; they all kept "short dogs," or half pints, in their lockers.

We were living in an apartment on Stockton Street, in a building that didn't allow kids, but we finally found a duplex on the slope above the Castro district, which was still an old-fashioned neighborhood, over the hill from the Haight-Ashbury. I used to roll Doug in his stroller down Haight Street and take in everything that was starting to happen. I went to the dances. I saw Bo Diddley at the Avalon Ballroom, The Who, Howlin' Wolf, and other greats at the Fillmore. I was smoking a lot of weed, but I didn't take anything else. To satisfy the grandmothers, we had Doug baptized, and went for the class joint, Grace Cathedral on Nob Hill. Ken Conner and Joan Brown were his godparents, about the only friends I knew who had enough churchy backgrounds to satisfy the requirements of the place.

It was an incredible scene at Rincon Annex, tossing mail, going to art school, getting high, keeping it together. I was working at being an adult, responsible for a wife and kid. I could only get crazy along the edges. My floor at Rincon was a big, bright, noisy room with fluorescent lights and the constant clatter of hundreds of people hand-sorting mail before they had machines that could do that. There were long stretches at Rincon where there wasn't that much to do. You'd get waves of mail, where you would be busy, but much of the time you were trying to make it last. You would nurture your tray of mail, down to reading every postcard, because if you didn't look like you were doing something, they put you downstairs throwing heavy mail sacks. They only gave you thirty minutes for lunch, but you also got two breaks. I'd meet up with these hipsters, like this jazz buff, Earl, a big Charlie Parker fan. We would go on our break and everybody would break out something to smoke, then head down to one of the wharfside dives around the corner on the Embarcadero for short, twenty-five-cent beers. You would smoke as much shit as you could, slam down three or four drafts, and go back to work. Of course, the bosses were already bombed, so they didn't notice. Or care. It was a great environment.

I had already applied to graduate schools and had little left to do toward my undergraduate degree in printmaking, so I put in for a day job and something opened up down the street at the U.S. Post Office mailroom in the Customs House. It was a full taste of Uncle Sam's sugar. There were three guys working there who would take packages apart to inspect them and tape them back together. They were postal employees, but they worked under Customs. It was cool to be working the day shift and be home with my family at night, but the Customs House post office operation was weird, even by Rincon standards.

There was almost nothing to do. One guy was from the Midwest, a career post office man, probably in his forties: Bob, a total beer lush. He got fucked up every lunch hour, so I started going to lunch with him. We were knocking back as many drafts as we could on the lunch hour, and stumbling back to work. The other postal employee, Everett, was much older. He had worked there a long time. You had to punch a clock, but there were no post office bosses around. I brought books and sat around all day reading. After a while they brought in another young guy, a long-haired ex-Marine with a mustache named Cliff Garcia. His brother played guitar with one of the bands with funny names around town, the Grateful Dead.

My career track after my impending bachelor of arts degree was obvious to me. I would get a master's and then a teaching job. It was a snap. They needed art teachers. All of us were on the same plan, headed to teach in some institute of higher education.

Chris had lived briefly on the East Coast and had a glad eye for the high life and elegance, the money and the action. I didn't mind the idea of getting out of California. I applied to a bunch of eastern universities like Tufts University and Pratt Institute in Brooklyn, places with strong printmaking programs. I looked into the University of Hawaii, thinking I could start surfing again and still make prints, but they didn't have a graduate program in printmaking. I got accepted by Yale, which was not only a famous school all the way around but also a breeding ground for famous artists. But I got more than merely accepted. I had great grades at the Art Institute, a bit of an exhibition history, and they liked the work I was doing, so they made a generous offer: full scholarship and a job as a teaching assistant. I was a made man.

4.

Phil Sparrow

The summer Doug was born and I was finishing up my courses at the Art Institute, I was supposed to give a talk for one of my last remaining academic classes. For some reason, I got the notion to do a talk on tattooing as a forgotten American folk art. I had not really thought that much about tattoos since I was a kid. I don't know what brought it back to mind. Tattoos were a long way from the Summer of Love. Maybe every so often, you would see one on an ex-serviceman's arm, but that was about it. There was no consciousness of it at all.

I went so far as to call Milt Zeis, a tattoo supplier I remembered from ordering his catalog back when I was ten years old. He had been selling tattoo supplies since the forties out of the same address in Rockford, Illinois. My brother-in-law worked for some big company with a WATS line where he could make free long-distance calls. I had never really called anybody long distance, but I got Milt Zeis on the phone. "I used to buy catalogs from you ten years ago," I told him. He sent me his latest catalog and I ordered a few sheets of flash. At a dollar and a half a sheet, they weren't cheap—that was about what I was making per hour at the post office. The design sheets he sold weren't too good, either. They were about 25 percent smaller than they really should have been, probably to fit on standard copy paper. They were classic Americana tattoos in black and white, done by mimeograph, and it was a bitch because he made the designs a little too

43

small. They were originally drawn to fit a certain size, say, a forearm. But his were all shrunk down a little bit. I ordered some that I thought would serve as good examples. I got a religious sheet, with Jesus heads and crosses. I got a sheet of panthers. These were going to be my visual aids to accompany my talk.

I took everything into class and gave the talk. I knew a lot about the topic because of how much I had learned when I was twelve years old, and it went over great. The talk wowed the class. There was a lot of interest. Questions came flying. Somebody asked if I had any tattoos. I told them about Len and me doing the little tests with India ink and sewing needles, and told them about how I drew tattoos on all the neighborhood kids. At the end of my story, I looked at them. "I don't have any professional tattoos," I said.

It was only a few nights later when Kit Clark showed up at the student show at the Art Institute. He was a friend of Richard Shaw—they had gone to private school together at some place for upper-middle-class misfits—but I knew him from Newport. When we were both in eighth grade, I had hand-poked a little tattoo on his arm. I had not seen him since junior high and he had just returned from a West-Pac tour and was dressed in his full navy blues.

"Hey, Don," he said, "you remember those tattoos? I've got a bunch of tattoos now."

He had been to Hong Kong, Manila, Honolulu, all around that end of the Pacific, and he had collected tattoos. It put an electric charge through me.

After the art show, there were a few of us sitting around, drinking, and smoking weed, and the idea of getting tattoos came up. I looked up "Tattoos" in the Yellow Pages. The only places listed were Lyle Tuttle's in San Francisco, and a few across the bridge in Oakland. Then I saw a name I recognized.

Phil Sparrow was featured in the brochure for a tattoo correspondence course that I got all those years ago when I first sent away to Milt Zeis. There had been a picture of him, showing these roses on his chest. He wrote one of the lessons for the correspondence course. He was a famous Chicago tattooer back then, and now here he was across the Bay Bridge in Oakland. A bunch of us headed out to get tattoos from Phil Sparrow.

We didn't think to call; we just piled in a car and drove over there. I assumed tattoo shops were open at night. But he wasn't. Down the street a block and a half, next to the Greyhound bus terminal, despite the fact we were in Oakland, was another tattoo parlor called Frisco Bob's. The tattooist, Ray Steiner, had full sleeves of tattoos up his arms. The only person I had seen like that before was Lyle Tuttle, who worked at Bert Grimm's when I was a little kid on the Pike. Frisco Bob's was a large corner shop with a pool table and pinball machines to help cover the rent. I didn't know it at the time, but it turned out that Lyle owned the shop. I also found out later that Ray Steiner was in college at that time, studying anthropology.

I decided to get a rose tattooed on my shoulder. I was sitting in the chair, sleeve rolled up, the machine buzzing, the surprisingly painful needle starting to outline the tattoo in my flesh and it all suddenly came over me. I was pretty juiced and high, but it was just this sort of "holy shit" moment—*something is really happening here.* I blacked out. Passed out cold. It didn't last more than a few seconds, but long enough that I came to hearing Steiner saying, "Are you all right?"

"Yeah, yeah," I said. "Finish the tattoo."

So I got the tattoo, a little rose on my shoulder. My pal Richard Shaw got the next tattoo and the rest of our bunch followed him. I completely had the bug.

I came back the next night with another friend from school who saw mine and decided he wanted a tattoo, too. We went looking for Phil Sparrow, only to find his shop closed again. This time, I went down the street to another tattoo shop and had a second rose put on my arm—I was starting a collection—by an old wino called Oakland Jake. I soon found out he was popularly known as Shakey Jake, not exactly a nickname to inspire confidence in a tattoo artist.

The next day I went over with another friend during the daytime and Sparrow was open. I could tell right away his place wasn't like the others. The placards in the window were drawings of bare-chested beefcake sailors showing off their tattoos. The interior was done in all red and black. Classical music was playing. The flash was hung more carefully than in the other places. There was no dummy rail—he did his tattoos in an open space. Sparrow was dressed in all black, his hair slicked back, pencil-thin mustache above his lip, a lit cigarette between his fingers. He was obviously a cultured, educated man. When I told him I was an art student, he pulled down a book. "This is real art," he said. "You should see this."

It wasn't a large book, about ten-by-ten inches square, published that year in Tokyo with a small press run of five hundred. All the photos were by a Japanese photographer. The bilingual text was written by Donald Richie, a film critic who had introduced Japanese cinema to the West in the forties. He served in the Merchant Marine as a conscientious objector during the war and worked as a movie reviewer for the *Stars and Stripes* military newspaper in Tokyo during the MacArthur era. Donald was a closeted gay guy from Ohio who found the Japanese culture quietly hospitable to his lifestyle and fell in love with everything Japanese. He wrote this book on Japanese tattooing, *Irezumi,* which was the first to show images of epic Japanese tattoo work in this country. I thumbed through the pages, dumbstruck. I felt the shock wave crash through me. My head was in flames.

I didn't get a tattoo from Sparrow that day, but I started hanging out with him and picking up some souvenir tattoos as I did. I began to hear some of the story. Years later, he filled in a lot more things he kept private. Phil Sparrow was born Samuel Steward. He grew up in a small Ohio town and realized at an early age that he was gay. He read voraciously and was some

46

kind of prodigy. He gravitated toward bohemians and artists, but pursued an academic career at Midwestern universities. He was drummed out of his post at the State College of Washington for all the frank sex talk in his 1936 novel, *Angels On the Bough*, and went to teach at Loyola University in Chicago, before joining the faculty at DePaul.

He came to know Gertrude Stein and Alice B. Toklas and visited them in the French countryside (he corresponded with Toklas for twenty years after Stein's death). He met Thomas Mann, was close with Sherwood Anderson, and had a long love affair with Thornton Wilder. He kept a secret index of all his sexual encounters, a lifelong collection of three-by-five cards he called his "Stud File." In his file, he noted liaisons with silent-screen star Rudolph Valentino, Oscar Wilde's lover Lord Alfred Douglas, and young Roy Fitzgerald before he changed his name to Rock Hudson.

Phil was also part of the inner circle around sex researcher Alfred Kinsey, his unofficial collaborator. He brought Kinsey new subjects and was filmed by Kinsey taking part in an orgy at his apartment. He had his place outfitted as a full rumpus room with all these murals that he painted. The guy could paint. He was a good visual artist who had been trained somewhere along the line as an illustrator. In 1952, he began tattooing in Chicago. He took the name Phil Sparrow, so they wouldn't find out at DePaul.

He paid a thousand dollars to learn how to tattoo from Amund Dietzel, who was one of the great champion tattooers in America, a grand old man of tattoo who worked in a tie, a vest, and sleeve garters. He tattooed in Milwaukee and had been shipwrecked off Nova Scotia as a young Danish cabin boy. He got some tattoos from Dietzel, but Phil didn't have a whole lot of tattoos. He had a couple of things on his upper arms and he had a big garland of roses across his chest based on a Pavel Tchelitchew painting done in the thirties. Tchelitchew, another Gertrude Stein confidante, did a kind of fantastic surrealist art. He was a famous Russian painter in his day, no longer well remembered. Phil took the roses from a painting Tchelitchew did of some hunky young guy in a chair with this rose garland. The Mob controlled all the tattoo places in Chicago in those days, but they left Phil alone probably because he was this small operator who just wanted to hold young men's arms.

Sparrow had some of Dietzel's flash, which included a beautiful, large dragon design, very Japanese, that I wanted him to put on me. He said no, it's too big for your arm, which it wasn't. He wasn't hip to the Japanese style of larger images that would contain an area of the body instead of being placed within it. So I drew up a pretty clumsy dragon that he put on my arm. I'd previously designed a symmetrical butterfly with a woman's face in the middle of it, a real turn-of-the-twentieth-century tattoo design, which he had put on my shoulder. I got a little bird. Everything was under T-shirt level. At the same time, I was bugging Sparrow to teach me to tattoo, just wearing him down on that front.

He really tried to steer me away from it. "It's a dying art form," he kept saying. "There's no future in it. It's a deep, dark, mysterious world. You don't want to get involved in this. You've got a family, a wife and an infant son. You've got an art career. This is not something you want to get into."

Maybe some of these guys had lives beyond the shop, but they kept it pretty well hidden. Most of them simply looked like bums. I naïvely thought everybody who tattooed did it because they loved it and probably did something else to support themselves. Most were very good at hiding the fact that they made out okay doing tattoos. It was an all-cash underground economy, but not especially visible. It wasn't like these guys were driving fancy cars and wearing diamond rings. At least, I hadn't encountered any of those yet.

But with Sparrow, it was obvious that here was a guy who had both a brain and a life outside the street. Sparrow also admitted he made a pretty good living. He never told me how much he made. This was probably half the actual figure and was real money to me. But he also told me he kept a Swiss bank account. It started to dawn on me that you could make a decent living in the tattoo business.

I dug history, book learning and read deeply. I loved arcane art history. At the Art Institute, Gordon Cook taught me how to etch, but he also shared Phil's suspicions about academia. I was growing more and more intrigued with Asian art and culture, but the idea of teaching in schools for nine months a year was sounding less appealing. I knew from the post office what it was like to work in a big organization and be under somebody's thumb, and I didn't like it. And, once I began to realize that I could support my family by putting tattoos on people, there was no question. I had never lost interest since I was a little kid. It was just something I never thought was in the cards for me.

I was hanging out with Sparrow and picking his brain as much as I could. He never let on that he was gay, not that we didn't know or cared. He was still in the closet, a very sophisticated cat. He continued to try to keep me away from tattooing, but I kept pushing him to show me the basics. I told him that I already knew where to get all the gear. I told him my whole story, how I used to paint tattoos on the kids, that I already had catalogs from all the main suppliers. "I'm just going to screw up my friends if you don't give me some help," I said. "I know where to buy the stuff mail-order."

That did it. He relented and I ordered the tattoo machines. I got some gear, and put my first tattoo on over at his shop with him watching—a little test piece on my ankle. It is customary to put your first tattoo on yourself, if only to make sure you know how much the needle hurts. I had handpicked the initial "H" on my ankle when I was a kid, but now I drew up a design based on an early twentieth-century tattoo of a rose with a woman's face in it, went over to Sparrow's shop, and covered the initial. Instant shock: it was a deceptively hard medium. Sparrow insisted I not use my real name, but take a needle name, so I simply went with my middle name, Ed Talbott.

When I first saw those Japanese tattoos in the book at Sparrow's shop, it flipped a switch. In an instant, I knew that tattoos didn't just have to be an eagle and an anchor. It captivated me as an idea. As an art school student, I understood that it was spectacularly transgressive. Nobody was doing it. It wasn't on the menu. Yet, it seemed to me it could be done so that it was a challenge as a visual art form. It was like an undiscovered country. It also offered me a way out. I didn't have any other prospects. I would go to grad school and teach printmaking somewhere. I even considered the post office as a career because it was safe and the insurance was good. I thought I could either do this, and wonder what it would have been like to go into tattooing, which was a total dive into the dark, or I could go into tattooing and if it didn't pan out, I could go back to school and resume my position on the track I left. That did it.

It was a very big deal among the people I knew. Most were shocked. It was such an out-of-left-field decision to them. I was a promising artist with a fellowship in the offing at Yale, already being exhibited in a good gallery in Los Angeles. Tattooing was just not part of the bigger art picture. You couldn't even find paintings of people with tattoos. It was like tattoos didn't exist in the art world.

There were a few of us who were totally dedicated printmakers, and Gordon Cook really was giving us his all. He was pretty dismayed that I was tattooing, although he had long advised me against getting caught in the trap of academia. He earned his living as a typesetter. He taught because he was dedicated to it and he liked being around the students.

One of the last etchings I did at school was called *Future Plans*, a self-portrait where I pictured myself covered in tattoos, including the few that I already did have. It hung in the student art show and was the first time I publically showed myself as tattooed. In it, I covered myself in real American tattoos: a panther, an eagle, a ship—the standard menu.

I was working days at the post office and my nights were free. I started tattooing some friends. The first few tattoos I did were at Phil Sparrow's. Ron Nagle brought his band mate Larry Bennett from their rock group, Mystery Trend. He was a hipster San Francisco artist who found himself embarrassed about his tattoo of the Marine Corps bulldog and wanted to know if I could cover it. I did a campfire coffeepot—the first pop art tattoo I did. Pop art was still new. Far out, man, a coffeepot. It was also the first cover-up tattoo I did (excluding my first attempt on my own ankle).

I knew how to make prints. I knew how to draw. Most of the tattooers I had seen couldn't really draw. What they did was more like tracing. I figured I could step up and take over, but the primitive machines turned out to be extremely difficult to use. They were these heavy, buzzing, goddamned temperamental instruments, with an impenetrable finesse. The pigments were strange. And you're working on skin. There is the whole psychological thing of working on people. It's an insanely complicated medium, especially at that time when it was unexplored and undeveloped. It kicked my ass. The first tattoos immediately humbled me, even with Sparrow watching. It was like, damn, this is really hard. I can do this elegant drawing, but to make it happen that way on skin is a whole different deal.

I sent away for the gear and set up a workspace on the back porch on Douglass Street, up above the Castro, off Seventeenth Street. I didn't do too many tattoos, but I was surprised at the number of my art school friends who were interested in getting one.

5.

Dragon Tattoo

I started wondering what it was like down at the Pike, where I used to hang out. With my wife and infant son, I went back down south to see our families over Easter break 1967. I left Doug with his grandparents the first night and headed off to Bert Grimm's on the Pike. Business was thriving. The place was a brilliant, gaudy success. There were six guys working and a big crowd gathered around the guy in the lead chair, about six or seven years older than me, doing the most fantastic work I had ever seen. His name was Hong Kong Tom Yeomans.

Up to this point, my return to the Pike, the only tattooer I had watched up close was Phil Sparrow. Now Sparrow was an intellectual, a weird and wonderful character, and a big help to me, but he was not a great tattooer. Hong Kong Tom was a great tattooer—strong, clean lines, bold, powerful colors. I learned he had worked with Sailor Jerry. I had heard about Sailor Jerry from Phil Sparrow. When I asked him if there was anybody outside of Japan working on the epic Japanese-style tattoos, he mentioned Sailor Jerry of Honolulu. The tattoo world existed almost entirely on the grapevine. There were no books and magazines, no listings of tattoo shops. People traded photographs around or somebody came through a shop with a tattoo they got somewhere else. It was a small world and tattoo people didn't necessarily trust one another with trade secrets.

I had Hong Kong Tom stick another rose on my arm. He and

I immediately shared a rapport. We had a lot in common. He came from the street and was my kind of guy—a hipster and a pothead. The rose came out so well, I decided to take the plunge. I had him put a tiger on my forearm—below the sleeve, big deal, a tattoo that shows all the time.

Somebody came through Sparrow's shop one day with a tattoo of the basic crawling black panther, which had been a staple of tattooing since the thirties, only this one had been done as a tiger. I thought that was the hippest thing I'd seen. It was a slight change-up on this well-known design that had all kinds of class, great motion, and fit the arm well. So Tom put this tiger on my forearm. As he took his time doing it, we talked. I told him I was trying to learn to tattoo, that I had been tattooing some friends on my back porch in San Francisco.

He knew way more about the tattoo world than Sparrow did. Sparrow was gay, a lone wolf in the tattoo world. He was demonized by the other operators. He didn't really have any use for any of the other tattooers and they didn't have any use for him. Tom was connected. He knew all this stuff. He asked me what kind of machines I was using. He knew other suppliers. He had a client in San Francisco and he used to take his Jaguar XKE and zoom up to San Francisco. It was only a couple of weeks after I met him in Long Beach that he showed up at my Douglass Street apartment.

He came over with the guy he was doing all this beautiful work on. He checked over my setup and hipped me to some better pigments, turned me on to his East Coast suppliers. It wasn't long before I was headed back down to Long Beach to see Hong Kong Tom at the Pike. I took a couple of friends with me. Bill Wissman was a poet from the Art Institute who had gone with me the second night I went looking for Phil Sparrow in Oakland. Kit Clark was my old hometown buddy from Newport who was now out of the navy. I had given Kit another tattoo on my back porch on Douglass Street. I got a peacock from Tom that was a Sailor Jerry design. He talked to me about Sailor Jerry and showed me some photos of Jerry's work.

ABOVE: Colored-pencil tattoos for the neighborhood kids, 1956.

BELOW: Bert Grimm's Tattoo Shop: On the Long Beach Pike, 1956.

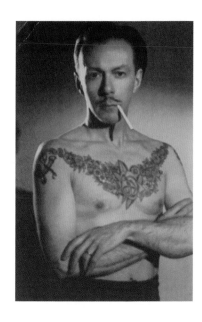

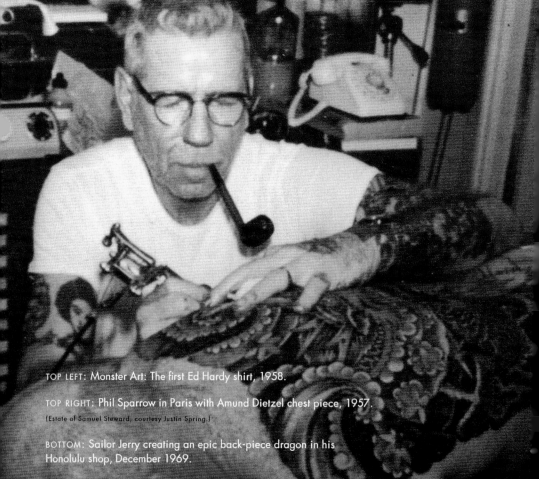

TOP LEFT: Monster Art: The first Ed Hardy shirt, 1958.

TOP RIGHT: Phil Sparrow in Paris with Amund Dietzel chest piece, 1957.
(Estate of Samuel Steward, courtesy Justin Spring.)

BOTTOM: Sailor Jerry creating an epic back-piece dragon in his
Honolulu shop, December 1969.

ABOVE: *Future Plans*, D. E. Hardy, etching, 1967.

AT RIGHT: Ed working at Doc Webb's, 1969.

BELOW: Dragon Tattoo: Ed's first shop, Vancouver, B.C., 1968.

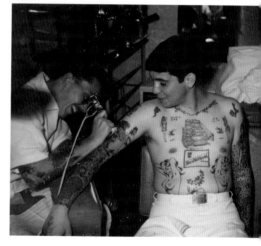

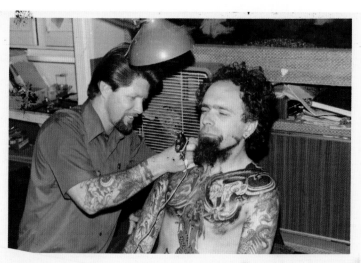

TOP: Ed and Francesa with client in Gifu, Japan, 1973.

ABOVE: Zeke Owen tattooing Thom deVita, San Diego, 1973

AT LEFT: Realistic Tattoo Studio business card, 1975.

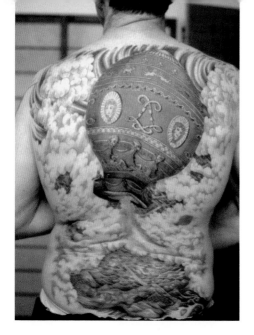

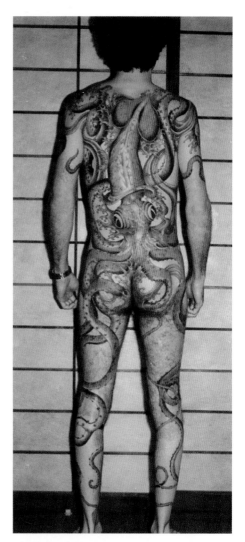

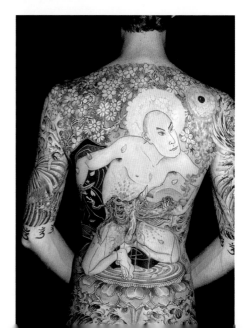

TOP LEFT: *First Manned Ascent, Montgolfier Bros., 21 November 1783* (from an 18th century engraving), 1977.

TOP RIGHT: *Squid Man,* 1974–76.

BOTTOM LEFT: *Witch Spitting Rats* (after Hokusai), 1974.

BOTTOM RIGHT: *Shunga Satori (Coming and Going),* 1986.

TOP LEFT: Goodtime Charlie
Cartwright (left), Jack Rudy, and Danny
Cartwright, smoking in the back room
at Goodtime Charlie's, 1977.

TOP RIGHT: The Last Night at Goodtime
Charlie's: Blood on the sidewalk, 1978.

BOTTOM: Tattooland, East L.A., 1978.

Photo: K. Shimada

TOP: Bob Roberts and customer at the Spotlight Tattoo booth on the *Queen Mary*, 1982.

BOTTOM LEFT: The end of Tattoo City, San Francisco, 1978.

BOTTOM RIGHT: Ed with Horiyoshi II in Tokyo, 1983.

NEW TRIBALISM

ABOVE: Neo-Samoan, quasi-Japanese matching leg tattoos, photographed for the cover of the first edition of *Tattootime*, 1982.

AT RIGHT: Flyer for Ed's first solo exhibition, 1980.

BELOW: Mike "Rollo Banks" Malone at his China Sea Tattoo Company, Honolulu, 1991.

SKINS & SKULLS

SUMMER LONDON 1980
D.E. HARDY
BARBARY COAST GALLERY,
394 BROADWAY S.F.
PREVIEW & SOUNDTRACK SUNDAY 3 AUG 1 P.M.

When I went back to work at the post office, I showed the peacock to Cliff Garcia. He knew I was finishing up art school and planning to go to work as a tattooer. The peacock blew his mind. The colors were neon; they practically vibrated off my pasty white skin. He rolled up his sleeve and timidly showed me his tattoo. It was darkened and his olive-colored skin and thick, hairy arms didn't show the tattoo off, but he had an old Marine Corps classic—an eagle poised on top of a bayonet with the slogan "Death Before Dishonor."

"Do you think you could cover this tattoo?" he asked.

I wasn't sure about that at all and begged off. I had already done Larry Bennett's coffeepot, but that had been a different deal. I didn't feel at all confident about covering Cliff's old tattoo. I was beginning to think about my future. I knew I wanted to settle eventually in San Francisco and live my life in this crazy, beautiful city, but I didn't want a lot of my early work walking around the town where I was going to make my living as a tattooist. I needed some practice potatoes.

In his correspondence course, Milt Zeis recommended tattooing potatoes. After you practiced the tattoo on the potato, you could skin it and see how deep the ink went by slicing it to see if you're at the correct depth. Years later I was told Sailor Jerry, in one of his humorous moods, laid his hands on a good spud and tattooed a Christ head on it—he wasn't much for organized religion—put ointment on it, bandaged it up, and mailed it off to Rockford, Illinois. "Milt, how am I doing?" he asked.

I had a couple of friends at school who were from Canada, including a woman who worked at the library with me. They told me about Vancouver, what a hip town it was. I had been thinking about ways I could open my own tattoo shop, because I was so green and nobody was going to hire me. It would have to be a seaport city. That summer Chris, Doug, and I made a reconnaissance mission to check out the city. The weather was perfect. The city looked sparkling. It was like a little San Francisco in Canada. I snooped around the local tattoo shops. I went to see Doc Forbes, probably the most famous tattooer in all Canada, and pumped him for as much information as I could get without giving up any of my plans. I knew if you walked in and said anything about opening a tattoo shop, they would throw you out. Subterfuge has always been an integral part of the business. Years later, Lyle Tuttle told me about Chris Nelson, who used to tattoo in a penny arcade on Market Street in San Francisco. He always kept a brown paper bag neatly folded beside his tattoo chair. "If they ask any questions," Nelson would explain, "I tell them not to ask any questions. Anything—*How many needles are in that thing?* Anything. If they do it a second time, I put the paper bag over their head so they can't see what I'm doing. They have to sit there with a bag over their head until their tattoo is finished." That's how tattooing was. A secret world.

I got another rose on my shoulder from Doc Forbes. He was a little eccentric, but he kept a clean shop. Circus Leo Leopold worked in the back of a barbershop on Robson Street, on a block where there were a bunch of German restaurants. He was glad to see anyone. That was how it used to be on the Bowery in old New York—the guy doing haircutting, shaving, bloodletting in the front, and, in the back, a tattooer. The setup looked antique even to me. He insisted on putting a free tattoo on me, although I didn't particularly like the idea. I could see he was not much of a tattooer, but I relented, playing for time to see if he'd give me any useful info. He drilled a bird into my arm. The guy was no Rembrandt. He buried the outliner in my shoulder. Now there is a black cloud covering the tattoo, but I've still got a little lump from the scar in the bird's beak.

My father-in-law Jim Pena was a Los Angeles homicide detective and when I asked him over Christmas that year if he would front me the several hundred dollars I figured I would need to start a tattoo shop in Vancouver, he surprised me by telling me that he knew Captain Jim, the man who controlled all the tattooing in downtown Los Angeles. Jim kept his shop on Main Street in the heart of honky-tonk downtown L.A., skid row, burly-Q houses, dive bars, penny arcades, and tattoo shops. He had a couple other shops around town, and my father-in-law knew him from fishing trips when Captain Jim used to take the police on his boat. He asked if it was a good business and I told him I thought it could be. He agreed to loan me the four hundred dollars.

Ever since Sparrow told me about his Swiss bank account, I knew people could make a decent living from tattoos. It might not have been obvious unless you happened across a shop at a particularly busy time, but it was a completely cash business that operated, for the most part, out of sight. If you said something about tattooing, people would say, "Do people still do that?" People said that to me when I told them I was going to open a tattoo shop. The last time they saw tattoos was when men wearing them came back from World War II.

I couldn't think of anything but finishing my undergraduate degree and opening the tattoo shop. I applied to Canada as a landed immigrant. I thought we might stay in Canada five years. I was painting flash—the designs for tattoos that would hang on the wall—cutting stencils and getting ready to open a shop. I took a week off from the post office and made a solo trip to Vancouver in February. I was disappointed to learn that meant missing Jimi Hendrix at Winterland, but I figured I could always catch him the next time. It poured rain in Vancouver all week. I slogged around the city and found a shop location for fifty dollars a month down near the water on Carrall Street. There were a lot of Canadian sailors and merchant marines around. I didn't realize the place was in the middle of skid row because the rain had driven all the rummies indoors. I went home, ready to return and open the shop.

All I wanted to do was tattoo and develop what I saw as potential in the medium, based on the Japanese thing. I wanted to do mythological-style epic Japanese tattoos. I had already done the pop art coffeepot on Larry Bennett's arm, so I knew you could do tattoos of anything, but the Japanese thing was what really fired me up. I painted up some big Japanese pieces for the windows, like I could do tattoos like that.

The building turned out to be a shack that had been jerry-rigged to fit in an alley between two actual buildings, corrugated tin front, maybe twenty-five feet deep, heated solely by a small, wood-burning stove. We hitched up the VW to a U-Haul trailer and drove off to Vancouver to start my life in tattoos. I knew enough carpentry to measure and cut things. I nailed up some four-by-eights, built a dummy rail, split the back section. I made a small front room, and painted it like what I thought a big-time tattoo parlor should look like, the full carny atmosphere with bright primary colors—blue wall, yellow door, red trim. I modeled it after Bert Grimm's place on the Pike.

There was an enterprising fellow named Bernard Lyle Kobel in Florida, who used to do wholesale trade in photo enlargements of tattoos. His catalog contained about fifteen hundred different examples, some with full descriptions. You could order these photos and display them in your tattoo parlor, as if you had done that tattoo. I bought a photo of his of some guy from the 1890's with a handlebar mustache and big tattooed chest. I wrote "Dad" underneath it and put it up in the shop as a joke. I hung out my shingle and Ed Talbott's Dragon Tattoo Shop opened for business in March 1968.

My first customer came in with his girlfriend. He studied the flash on the walls and selected a Bugs Bunny design. He wanted it on his stomach. I had built a dummy rail behind which I would do my tattoos, carefully calculating the space I would need to tattoo in, which is not much. I kept a file cabinet with my stencils and a working sink. There was space for a chair for the tattooer and a chair for the customer. There was no place for anybody to lay down. I had never done a tattoo anywhere but someone's arm. When I built the place, I was only thinking arm.

So I had him stand, hand balancing on the rail, and started trying to put this Bugs Bunny on him. He started to weave and it

dawned on me he was on heroin and going into a nod. It also oc-
curred to me that I was in over my head with this tattoo shop.

I was young, twenty-three years old, and, with my wire-
rimmed glasses and bushy hair and mustache, obviously a hipster
from Frisco. I was acting a role, trying to be cool, but people
would come in, take a look at me and ask "Are you the tattooer?"
Tom Yeomans put these really beautiful tattoos on my forearms.
His stuff on me was exquisitely executed with screaming, super-
bright colors. It was as good as tattooing got. People I would be
tattooing would look at my arm and look back at what I was putting on them and wonder out loud. "It will look different when
the colors set in," I would tell them.

I was getting business and the tattooing wasn't terrible, but I
quickly realized this was something you need to learn working
next to somebody. I would call Hong Kong Tom and ask questions, but that wasn't the same. Phil Sparrow always said you
can't learn to tattoo from a correspondence course. It's like learning to swim in your living room. You have to do it to learn it. You
have to put on the tattoos. The best way is to work with somebody who will show you what you're doing wrong.

Vancouver was cool. I saw the Velvet Underground in some
tiny club called the Retinal Circus, where the stage was so small,
you could look the band members in the face. They were hanging
out at the bar between sets. I went over to Lou Reed and told him
how much I liked the music.

I did become friendly with one old tattooer in Vancouver,
Curly Allen, who was crippled in a car accident on his way to
Callao, Peru, an old Latin America port city, where he was going
to open a shop with Tattoo Jack from Copenhagen. He had already painted the signs and had been studying Spanish in prepara-
tion for the trip long enough that he was close to bilingual. Some
of the more enterprising Danish tattooers would have shops in
port cities in other parts of the world, and fly south for the winter.
Curly never made it out of Vancouver. For the rest of his life, he

limped and lost the use of his left arm. He was a one-armed tattooer. His customers had to pull their own skin tight when he
would tattoo. Curly used stencils, but he could freehand. He loved
to talk and knew the whole Canadian tattoo history. His bedroom
was a cot in the back of the shop. Curly was also a mathematical
genius.

He tried to teach me his system of mathematics, but I'm totally helpless at math. He gave me a mimeographed guide to his
system. He claimed it was a new way to do math and sounded
completely logical. I don't know how important it was, but it was
interesting that this guy in this shit-hole shop out at the end of
this big boulevard on the edge of the Western world, was sitting
there doing math equations. It was a world I wouldn't have seen
if I had gone to Yale.

6.

Seattle Winter

Hong Kong Tom told me about Zeke Owen, who used to have the lead chair at Bert Grimm's before taking off for Honolulu, which is when Tom joined Bert's crew. Now Zeke was the only tattooer working in Seattle. "If you're going to Vancouver, you have to go to Seattle and see Zeke," Tom said. "He's a trip." I took the bus down to meet him, but he wasn't there.

The shop was every young man's dream. It ran along one side of a building with a porno bookstore on the other side and a pool table in the back room. Next door was a bar. The shop had a street entrance, painted bright colors, and a Dutch door from the bookstore. John, the bookstore owner, was a hard-bitten, former fight promoter. He grumbled about Zeke. People kept coming in wanting tattoos and Zeke wasn't there. "He takes off riding a motorcycle with a bunch of friends," he said disgustedly. At the moment, he was on a run to New Orleans.

I stared at the window. His flash was spectacular. There were not only photos of great tattoos by Zeke, but there were photos of tattoos by Sailor Jerry. Phil Sparrow was the first person to tell me about Sailor Jerry. Hong Kong Tom, who worked with Jerry briefly in Honolulu, showed me some photos of Jerry's tattoos. He had some designs he had gotten from rub-offs of Jerry's stencils. Zeke knew Jerry from when he worked at a penny arcade down the street from Sailor Jerry's shop in Chinatown (from Hawaii,

Zeke went off to Guam). As I looked at the work I saw in the photographs in Zeke's Seattle shop window, I realized Sailor Jerry was the mother lode of tattoo.

His landlord John told me when Zeke was expected to return and I took the bus down again. Still no Zeke. "I don't know where the fuck he is," said the landlord.

Finally, I called down a week or so later, and Zeke was there. I rode down again. We got along instantly. Zeke was a smartass Southern California hipster and bad boy—definitely wilder than I was. He was well known in tattoo circles and was only five years older than me. Raised as a street guy, Zeke was a biker, a gambler, a fighter, a regular Marlboro man. But he also had a Japanese stepfather and a passionate connection to Japanese culture. He had practiced *kendo* and other martial arts and understood the soul of the Japanese thing. Most important to me, he had large Japanese designs hanging on the wall of his shop and he was tight with Sailor Jerry. Zeke was clearly the key to my vision of learning the real Japanese ways.

On my first visit, he told me he was planning to move to Callao in Peru, the same port city where Curly Allen dreamed of living. "It's a gold mine," he said. "We should go to South America." He was trying to talk me into going with him and I just hoped to get some advice from him about tattooing, and wanted to get a tattoo from him.

The next week I came back and he was going on about something else. I asked him about South America. "What?" he said. He was on to something else—he didn't even remember that plan. With Zeke, there always had to be a scheme, a game, something going on.

He had a Japanese demon head on his sheet of flash that I liked and asked him to tattoo on my chest. "You went to art school," he said. "You draw your own."

It was the face of a female demon from a Noh theater mask, a complicated, powerful symbol in Japan based on old myths from hundreds of years ago. It is also a popular tattoo design from

deep in the traditional culture. I knew the mask from the first
Japanese movie I ever saw, *Onibaba,* which scared the shit out of
me when I was an art school student in San Francisco. This demon mask really riveted me and I rode home from the theater on
the bus, still totally petrified by the spooky movie.

The next trip down, I brought my version of the image and
Zeke put the *hannya* mask on my chest, over my left pectoral. We
got along well: we shared an interest in Japan, we had both grown
up in Southern California, drank beer, the usual stuff. He came
up to Vancouver and saw my shop. I started to work on him, just
like I had worked on Sparrow. I had plenty of business and I liked
Vancouver, but I was simply too green and I knew it. I realized I
needed to work with somebody. It was hopeless otherwise. I didn't
understand the machines—I'm not a mechanical guy. All I knew
was how to draw and are were only about a million things that
come up about trying to put on a tattoo beyond being able to
draw.

I told Zeke that I would give him my shop. "If you move up
here, I'll give you this place and I'll go to work for you," I said.
"There's a lot of business here." And there was.

I kept pestering him. I told him I would move down to Seattle
and work in his shop. He put me off. Finally he grudgingly agreed.
"You can come down here and work, but I don't know what I'm
going to be able to teach you," he said. He respected my drawing
ability and he said some really smart things immediately about
how I could tailor it more to tattoo-style drawings. He pointed
out I used too many layers. Because I wasn't trained as a commercial artist, I didn't know how to use tracing paper. He showed
me how to do overlay tracings to tune up a design.

After six months, we left Vancouver in October. I took my
flash off the walls, packed up my equipment, and turned the shop
over to a guy who was supposed to pay me. He was a shady character who used to tattoo on State Street in Chicago, where the
Mob controlled all the tattooing, except for Phil Sparrow's place
(everybody left him alone). All the tattoo shops were in penny

arcades. There was always a cashier in a tall booth that looked over the whole arcade and could keep watch on what was going on. If somebody wanted a tattoo, they would pick out the design in the tattoo shop, pay at the cashier's cage, and take a slip back to the tattooer. At the end of the day, the tattooer would turn in the slips, and get 50 percent. But some of the customers would get the heart or the anchor or whatever, and say "How much extra to put a girl's name under there?" The tattooer could pocket the extra money. If the Mob guys watching found out, they would beat him, even for a dollar. Tough town to tattoo in.

Anyway, I made a deal with this guy from Chicago for my shop in Vancouver. Of course, he never paid me. I was too young, dumb, and desperate to really get a handle on the business.

Once again, we packed everything up, hired a trailer, and moved the family. I rented a house right on West Alki facing the ocean, which was cool. Seattle's a beautiful city when it's not raining. My wife loved the greenery, but the weather was still good.

As soon as I showed up and Zeke had someone to watch the shop, he instantly took off for Alaska. He was an inveterate gambler. He was bankrolling a left-handed pool player called Mexican Joe, a slick, slender, dark-looking guy who dressed in black, and they hit the road to the north, where the pipeline workers had plenty of cash. Zeke could shoot a mean game of nine-ball himself, but Mexican Joe was really an ace. I was left in the shop by myself. I still didn't know how to tattoo any better, and nobody was there to tell me what to do.

Things stumbled along with Zeke and he did show me a lot of stuff. We got to be good friends. We both really liked to drink beer. We shared that. But when winter came, business dried up. There were layoffs at Lockheed, where we got a lot of our business. The military contingent, largely the Seabees based across the straits in Bellingham, thinned out. The coldest winter anyone could remember slipped over Seattle.

I was also starting to realize that Zeke was something of a loose cannon. There were some business things that came up as we went along, but Zeke also could be a mean drunk. He would get drunk and start bad fights with people. He would do seriously irrational things like break a store window. There were petty criminals drifting in and out of the shop. I watched as these guys who had knocked over a drugstore or something dismantled a shotgun and hung it up over a beam in an empty part of the ceiling where nobody could find it. Zeke treated the whole thing completely casually.

A year before I had been in art school, thinking about going to graduate school, and having romantic notions about the street life and the tattoo world. I felt like I had fallen into a lost chapter of William S. Burroughs. The guy John who owned the building and ran the bookstore used to warn me about people like Zeke. "That guy's a sucker for his own game," he would say, and I began to understand the wisdom in not falling for your own bullshit.

As snow started falling on Seattle, I started to worry about paying the rent and feeding my wife and two-year-old son. I had gotten used to the post-office paycheck, where you could count on the money coming in. In tattooing, you can't depend on the money coming in. It started getting really thin. It made me nervous.

Then Zeke moved in with us. He got in a big fight with his stripper wife and had to get out of their place. He'd been married before and lost a lot of money. He was sleeping on our glassed-in front porch. He also introduced me to bennies, cross-tops, street Benzedrine. Zeke was fond of those.

He came home New Year's Eve totally wiped out from some bender, probably hadn't slept in three days, and crashed on the porch. My wife, Chris, and I decided we would finally try acid. We had some really clean LSD that her brother obtained from somebody in Berkeley. I started getting worried about Zeke. He was supposed to be somewhere. He was sleeping like a dead man. We put on the new *White Album* by The Beatles and turned it up loud, but he couldn't be budged. We finally got him out of bed and he shook himself off.

It was snowing and he got all dressed up. He was a totally natty guy, who liked golf sweaters and button-down shirts and used hair spray. He had that Mexican-American *cholo* thing down. I think Zeke was of Hungarian descent, but he had me using hair spray, too. Zeke told me the samurai put stuff in their hair. We looked like young wolfmen.

He was getting dressed just as we were starting to come on to the acid. He got his overcoat, and put his pool cue under his arm. We watched from the window as he walked out, hair perfect, into the snow, gesturing with his pool cue like it was his sword and he was marching off on some big adventure.

We had a good trip, real pleasant. The ocean was literally right across the street and, across the bay, were the snow-capped Cascades. The sun was shining. The snow was falling and, as I watched the waves come into shore, I realized with sudden certainty I had to get back to Southern California. I had no business living in this cold weather. I had a wife and son. Who knew when business was going to get better? Chris and I decided that afternoon we were going to move again.

At first, I wanted to go to Hawaii. I tried to get Zeke to introduce me to Sailor Jerry, who he was close with. My dream was to get next to Jerry because I knew he was the *sine qua non* of great tattooing. I had written him a letter and sent some pictures of my work, but never heard back. When I told Zeke that I used Hong Kong Tom's name as a reference in my letter to Jerry, he straightened me out. "Jerry hates him," Zeke said. "He'll shoot him if Tom ever walks back in his shop. He's really pissed off at him."

Zeke told me he didn't think Jerry would hire me, but he did write to Muzzy Marcelino, a Filipino who owned a penny arcade on Hotel Street, downtown by Chinatown in Honolulu, where the sailors came through. It was near Sailor Jerry's and I thought that would at least bring me closer to Jerry, but Muzzy wouldn't hire me, said business had dried up in the area.

I went down to Southern California to the Pike, where there were still four shops going, a dozen years after I first went there.

Zeke warned me about the Pike. "Stay away from Long Beach," he said. "Those guys are like a bunch of old washerwomen. It's always some backstabbing shit."

But, of course, I did try to get a job there with one of the other shops on the Pike, down the street from Bert Grimm's. Nobody was hiring and I was almost broke. We camped out with my mother in my old room. I needed to land a job and Hong Kong Tom was my main contact. "Don't worry," he told me, "I'll take you to San Diego and get you a job with Doc Webb. He'll hire you in a minute. There's plenty of business in San Diego."

7.

Sailortown

Hong Kong Tom drove me down in his Jaguar XKE to meet Doc Webb in January 1969. We went out for lunch with him and Doc agreed he could use me.

San Diego had a hell of a lot of business. It was the height of the Vietnam War. Thousands of soldiers and sailors went through that port every week. There were only three tattoo shops. Tahiti Felix Lynch had a place opposite the Greyhound bus depot on Broadway, which was a honky-tonk street with sailor bars, jewelry stores, and all kinds of businesses geared to separating the American serviceman from his money.

Felix had traveled around the Pacific rim with a Tahitian dance revue—his wife was one of the Tahitian dancers. He had been tattooing for a good while and had two sons who also tattooed. His shop was strictly business: no frills, no decoration, no nothing—get them in and get them out.

I knew about his operation from Zeke, who had broken into the business at Captain Jim's in Los Angeles in the late fifties. For several years, Jim and Felix had been partners, running shops in L.A., San Diego, Oceanside, and even one barely on the American side of the border at Tijuana—which I'd looked into on a family trip in about 1957 with my mother and her friends. Jim and Felix were sort of the Axis of tattooing for servicemen in Southern California. Zeke had spent a summer working at Felix's in San Diego. When he asked Jim if he'd make money down there, Jim assured him he would be able to buy a Cadillac at the end of the summer.

One of the guys who worked for Felix was Al Miller, who was actually from Hawaii. Part Filipino, part Portagee, he started tattooing in the thirties when he was a teenager, until Pearl Harbor, when he joined the army. Al came from a family of tattooers. And he'd actually worked in the same shop with Sailor Jerry when Jerry first came to Hawaii in the thirties. They both worked Chinatown (tattooing was not allowed in Waikiki). Al would not talk to you at all. I remembered him from the day I tried to get a black widow spider on my leg on that Tijuana trip with my art school friend, Ken. Before I tried Doc Webb, Al was another one who wouldn't put the black widow on my leg until I showed him my ID. So I'd met him before.

The other shop in town was Painless Nell's, in the back of "Funland," a noisy, neon-lit penny arcade on Broadway. There was an attraction called Outdraw the Marshal, which featured a wooden dummy with a recorded voice that said things like "Think you're fast enough?" and other taunts, over and over. If you accidentally pulled the trigger while the six-shooter was still holstered, it switched to a Gabby Hayes–type voice saying "Hey, Marshal, they call this guy Old No Toes." This rusty repartee went on all day long, and drove you nuts on a slow day in the tattoo shop. Nell's shop was in the back corner. Her husband, Huey Bowen, had been a carny. Nell and her sister tattooed in this little slot about fifteen feet wide and ten feet deep. She tattooed at the Golden Gate International Exposition in San Francisco in 1940 and then moved down to San Diego in time to catch the wartime prosperity. Old timers used to say the streets were a sea of white hats.

Huey Bowen owned a string of shops during World War II and Korea and hired a lot of women to tattoo. He thought having a woman doing the work would appeal to young sailors. The way Huey operated was that he owned all the equipment and would go around at the end of the day and collect all the tattoo machines in a wheelbarrow and clean up everything—they were strictly sponge-and-bucket shops, no sterilizers. The next morning, he would come around with his wheelbarrow full of tattoo machines and drop them off at all the locations.

Hong Kong Tom told me, "You've got to go see Painless Nell's—it's like stepping back in time." It was like visiting a tattoo parlor of the twenties. Those old dames were in there, with the sponge and bucket, tattooing the guy: ink, blood, wipe it off, squeeze it out, throw it in the bucket. They ran their machines with these rigs that would convert AC to DC. It was primitive. Sponge and bucket had been the standard decades before, and that was the way it was. I heard a story about Chicago's Tatts Thomas being asked by a customer if the needles were clean. Tatts took the ever-present cigarette out of his mouth and dunked it in the bucket. "See," he said, "that sterilizes it."

They had strict health inspectors in San Diego, although nobody was sterilizing. Doc, at least, hung his machines in cold sterile solution and he had an autoclave, a glorified pressure cooker used to sterilize medical equipment. Phil Sparrow had showed me cold sterilization, where you put your gear in Zephiran chloride. Sparrow also had an autoclave, but he was afraid the thing would blow up and never used it. Everybody owned an autoclave, but they were for show. They'd just keep them dusted off for the Health Department. The Health Department didn't care. The inspectors would come in and run their fingers along the windowsill looking for dust. Those were the kinds of things that were paramount in their minds.

They also made everybody wear white coats over their clothing to tattoo. Nell and her sister used to wear hairnets. It was like working in a restaurant. I bought a number of coats because you would get a lot of ink and crap on you and every day you had to send them down to the Chinese laundry. They were big, clunky, starched white coats with a tie around the middle.

73

I went from being a fledgling hipster in Vancouver with my hair kind of long to someone with short hair wearing a butcher coat while he worked. Right away, Doc, in a courteous enough way, let me know I needed to trim my mustache and get a haircut. I didn't argue. I needed the job.

Doc Webb's place was off Broadway, just up from the docks where the launches would deposit the guys from the ships. His shop was part of the same building that housed the movie theater on the corner, a couple of doors up the street. It had wide display windows full of carnival stuff: a wooden Indian, a wavy funhouse mirror, and other trappings from allegedly exotic places. Doc was a big circus buff and had friends who were elephant trainers and such. On his off hours, he liked to wear a pith helmet. He rigged his truck like an expedition vehicle, water canteens on the outside, and would make occasional forays into the desert.

He was anything but the typical hustler or smartass, although he had a little carny in him. He was a supernice guy and a great storyteller. He was a little overweight and always wore one of those yachting caps with the crossed anchors. He had been a sign painter, an art closely allied with tattooing. He also painted show cards for movie entryways and the like for a little extra money and had been tattooing quite a while in Alaska, then in Vallejo for a number of years. He had an odd, cartoony style that I completely despised. I had no respect at all for his work. In later years, I came to appreciate that Doc was trying to do something that wasn't cookie-cutter tattooing and was a very intelligent guy. Most American tattoos pretty much came off the same stencils. He altered the style, but in a way that I thought was incredibly dopey. I was on a mission to bring art to tattooing and was not comfortable tattooing these things verbatim.

His wife, Carol Webb, who looked like a little-old-lady schoolteacher, ran the front room. It was her job to collect the money. There was a sign that said NO CUSSIN', NO FEELTHY TALK. As much as this was not what I thought a tattoo shop should be, a lot of the young sailors, away from home for the first time, probably responded to Doc and his wife like they were surrogate grandparents.

It was a small, narrow space, but he had two stations: his work setup, and another one with a left-hand sink in the same room with a bodywork table in between them. Doc worked from four in the afternoon to eight at night. "Doc Webb will give you a job," Tom had told me. "He only works four hours a day."

I couldn't understand that. "Why would he do that?" I said

"Because he makes enough money," said Tom.

I still couldn't understand why he wouldn't want to tattoo as much as he could. I was on fire to tattoo.

But Doc knew what he was doing. They got off ship or came out of the Marine Corps recruiting depot in the mid-afternoon, and that was the sweet spot of the day, before they started getting drunk. When I showed up, he figured he could keep the shop open longer. He hired me to work a split shift, noon to four and then eight to midnight.

As soon as I raised enough scratch, I moved Chris and Doug down, and rented a bungalow built in the thirties in Ocean Beach, a hell-raising, surfing beachfront neighborhood on the edge of downtown San Diego. I immediately started surfing again. I had been out of the water since finishing high school and getting serious about art. OB has good waves. That whole area is a great surf area. I called up an old friend, and got a board built. The surfing community had changed substantially in the seven years since I stopped surfing. It was about a twenty-minute drive from the shop. I'd drive back to OB and go surfing before dinner, eat dinner at home, go back and work the evening shift.

San Diego was a huge military town and most of its economy revolved around that. In those days, a lot of the old tattooers had died off. With only three tattoo shops in the city, when the military payday came, it was like turning on the tap. You had business, insane business for a couple of days, solid business for a week. Then it would taper down. Then the next payday would come and the whole deal would start all over. That happened twice a month. It was a guaranteed deal.

We were doing a lot of work. Twice a month, when payday came, you just were swamped, turning away people. You wouldn't be doing larger tattoos on the chest or back, mainly punching out small tattoos on the arm. They'd come in. You didn't waste any time, just process as many as you could or they'd go down the block to another shop. I was stamping out tattoos. A lot didn't even take ten minutes to do. Plus, Mrs. Webb would presell. They came into the shop together at four o'clock and she took over. When it was busy, she would take money from guys in line and give the sailor a receipt. "Ed will see you at nine," she would say.

I would come to work and guys would be lined up, the money already in the till. She would have receipts written for guys coming back at nine thirty or ten or later. I had to process these guys. Sometimes my whole shift was booked.

She could watch her pennies, too. She would write on the ticket, "No blue! No purple!" Extra colors took extra time. Time was money. In other words, this was a shop working with a limited color range and that's the way we wanted to keep it. Don't let them get butter on their pancakes. Who knew what they would ask for next?

I was fast and efficient from the beginning. The first time they came in after a payday for their four o'clock check-in, Doc Webb came in the back. "How's it been?" he asked.

"It's been busy," I said, not looking up from the tattoo I was putting on somebody.

He looked in the till. "Oh, my God," he gasped and grabbed his wife. He was thrilled because I was making them money. I had processed a lot of arms.

I got my chops up. It was instantly busy and it was endless repetition—putting on predictable designs over and over again until you had no concern about aesthetics. It was get the eagle on, the anchor, the whatever, and get it on straight. The fact that

Doc's designs were drawn in this dorky style, which I totally disliked turned out to be helpful getting me up to speed with my facility. I wasn't going to tattoo things that looked like that. I would cherry them out. Even freehand, I could go over his stencil prints, and make the tattoo look better.

Stencils are crucial to how a tattoo is going to look. To make a stencil, you draw a line image of the design reversed out on a piece of tracing paper, and inscribe it with a sharp tool into twenty-thousandths-inch acetate. After you shave the skin and apply a coat of Vaseline, you take a salt-and-pepper shaker full of powdered charcoal and rub it into the stencil so it's like inking an etching plate, then print it on the skin. Working up from one corner, you trace the charcoal rubbing with the outline tattoo machine. There's no automatic feed; the machine has to be dipped like a pen or brush. It takes a fine calculation to know how much line or shading you can lay in on one pass.

To make things easier, Doc Webb cut his stencils with some kind of electric engraving tool, which, instead of making a clean, sharp line that printed well on the skin, made lines that were kind of mushy. Sometimes they had a dot pattern. His stencils weren't very good. I would print these things and the target was kind of amorphous. It forced me to tune up the designs by myself and put the tattoos on right.

It was all classic American flash—cartoons, sailor designs, pin-ups, some ships. I was a novelty because, at age twenty-four, I wasn't that much older than some of these young sailors. I talked to them about the tattoos. Some of them were more avid people who dug the idea that they could ask for a specific design. I talked up the Japanese designs and very quickly began doing some custom stuff, which I would photograph and then show to other guys.

I put myself in a delicate position. I didn't want to make Doc look bad. He was the established tattooist. It was his shop. He was my boss. When he realized my capability, he did ask me to paint up some flash and put it in the window. He had a turnstile thing that went around and I painted these four sheets of flash with designs kind of based on stuff I got from Zeke. I made them more modern, tightened, and tuned them up. This flash immediately began selling; it was noticeably more "modern" than everything else displayed in all three shops and the servicemen responded to it.

There were a couple of pinup things from Jerry's designs that I got from Zeke. There was a biker design that was slammed from an Ed Roth image, a guy with a beard, long hair, and shades on a Harley busting out of a skull. Nobody else in San Diego had this kind of stuff. There were a couple of Marine Corps designs—fairly standard pork-chop stuff—but there were a couple of dragons, too. I was anxious to promote the Asian designs.

I developed good business and was getting friendly with some of the sailors, going out occasionally and drinking with them after the shop closed at the sailor bars in the area. I started to develop a following.

As soon as I got into town, I wrote another letter to Sailor Jerry and confessed my sins. I told him I had no idea of his history with Hong Kong Tom when I wrote him before, but that Zeke had subsequently explained. Jerry, it turned out, had a habit of gleefully polishing grudges. He reserved special ill will for Hong Kong Tom and his stepbrother, Don Nolan, a gifted artist and skillful tattooer himself. But Jerry saw them as arch enemies and by dropping Hong Kong Tom's name in my original letter, I had immediately gotten off on the wrong foot with Jerry.

This time, I used Zeke's name and included some photos of tattoos I had done. Zeke was an artist Jerry respected, so his endorsement meant something. So did a clipper ship I put on a Canadian sailor that Jerry had seen and admired for its innovative "water shading" in the sails, an unusual effect in tattoos at the time.

In late February 1969, I found a letter waiting in perfect Palmer penmanship postmarked "Hawaii."

Thank you for your kind remarks, and I have consistently tried to elevate tattooing out of the gutter into

78

respectability status, with some degree of success as far
as my own clientele are concerned—as for the ones who
get marked up (like I did) and do not know the differ-
ence between good work and scratching, I have dam
little time for them, or the "animal markers" who suck
their blood to stay alive. . . . To attempt to emulate the
Japanese in their work style without extensive study of
the oriental mind and culture is utterly ridiculous as
evidenced by some of the so-called "Japanese-style"
work coming out. . . . Anybody can copy somebody else,
but to originate something with impact is where they all
seem to fall short. . . . Always be Ed Hardy and don't
ever make the mistake of trying to be somebody else—
Then you will find the copycats picking your trash pile
and the only way to stay ahead of them is to keep on
originating so fast they can't keep up. Ha Ha . . . I
enjoy doing big work but I am particular who I put it
on. As you realize there is no money to be made on the
big body work and some guy who lets somebody else
scratch up his arms & legs just doesn't get body work
from me as I have neither time nor interest for it . . .
Time is too valuable to me to waste it on people who
don't appreciate it.

He included photos of some of his own work and we struck up
a correspondence.

He was the king of tattooing in the world. He corresponded
with tattooers from all over, England, Australia, Japan. I eagerly
assumed the role of student to the master. Jerry enjoyed playing
teacher and spiritual guru. We sometimes exchanged as many as
three letters a week (work could get slow in the shop some days),
some many pages long. But Jerry demanded fealty.

Early on in the correspondence, Jerry insisted that I not have
anything to do with Hong Kong Tom. He didn't go into specifics.
He just had a big bone to pick with the guy.

*I could put you on to a few things that I think could help
you, but again I want to be dam sure it doesn't get into
the wrong hands . . . helping those birds is like selling
bomb sights to Soviet Russia. They suck your brain and
laugh at you for being stupid enough to help them in the
first place . . .*

I used to go up to Long Beach and party with Hong Kong
Tom and his stepbrother Don Nolan, who had moved down from
Alaska, where he and Tom had a shop. Once working together at
Bert Grimm's, they started doing collaborative work: Don originating the image, Tom outlining it, and Don finishing the color
and shading. I had them do a big dragon on my left upper arm,
covering earlier work by Sparrow other small souvenirs. We would
take whites, smoke dope, and talk tattoo. They would come down
and visit me in San Diego. But now, because I was so intent on
brown-nosing Sailor Jerry, I cut off all contact with them. I was
dedicated to getting close to Jerry and hoping even someday I
might work with him. Jerry created enemies, picked enemies, invented enemies, invented conspiracies. He was an ultra-right-
winger; even Nixon was too liberal for Sailor Jerry. He didn't want
to pass on anything of note to me, if he thought I might share it
with those guys. Being a completely opportunistic turncoat who
would hide his own pseudo-hippie, dope-smoking persona from
Jerry, I wrote that I wouldn't have anything to do with them.

Don Nolan called and asked why I hadn't been in touch. I
cold-shouldered him on the phone. What a fucking rat. I would
do anything to get next to the king.

Jerry and I started corresponding heatedly. He proved to be an
extremely intelligent, wonderfully articulate, totally self-taught
guy. He read heavily and was really into Asian culture. He was
trying to take tattooing to new heights.

I was making good money for Doc Webb, even though he
was skeptical about my insisting on only working a five-day week
(instead of six). I was also building a good client base, guys

who were super-gung-ho, and I was starting to do some big tattoos.

I tattooed one guy from the flat-top aircraft carrier *Kitty Hawk*, who was peppered with tattoos from all over his Westpac cruises. I was picking up this whole education on navy life by osmosis, tattooing all these swabbies. I got tight with a lot of those sailors. But this one guy, Jesus Christ, what a character. I met him at Doc Webb's. We were about the same age. He'd been in the navy for six or seven years. He was an Italian from Philadelphia and a total wild man. He had an Irish buddy and they were a Terrible Two, total degenerate alcoholics and hell-raisers, Old Navy. Whenever anybody asked him what he thought of the navy, he would always say the same thing: "Every day's a holiday and every meal's a feast."

He loved to tell the story about sending a roll of 8mm movie film home to the family at Christmas. He told them it was scenes of the famous sights in Hong Kong and urged them to gather the whole family around, Grandma included, and watch it. When they rolled the film, it turned out to be their swabby son, peppered with crazy tattoos, having group sex with a bunch of Chinese prostitutes. He laughed uproariously when he told the story. He really didn't give a shit.

He loved those Westpac tours, which meant the whole circuit of the Pacific—Honolulu, Hong Kong, Sasebo, Manila. Olongapo City, on the Subic Bay in the Phillipines, was Sailortown: all whorehouses, sailor bars, and pussy shows. He eventually married his favorite prostitute and brought her back to the United States. Then reality set in after she dragged her whole family along and he realized that she had used him as a meal ticket.

His tattoo collection included a big San Miguel beer label tattooed on his sternum, right in the middle of his stomach. He was sprinkled liberally with tattoos, a lot he had gotten from Lyle Tuttle. He'd been around and he was such a hell-raiser, I couldn't help but like him.

I did a bunch of work on him and we would go drinking

together at sailor bars, most with Asian décor and bar girls. These guys wanted to smuggle me onto the *Kitty Hawk,* which is like a floating city. Those carriers are so huge, they said I would never be found. They thought I should set up in Olongapo. "Ed, you can make so much money and get so much pussy," they said. I told them that, as attractive as that was, I actually loved my wife and son and thought I would rather stay in San Diego with them.

I was putting tattoos on sailors by the dozens, but I was also showing off the Asian work. I ran across Tom, a sailor from Oklahoma who had several of Doc's pieces on him. We spent some time together drinking and he saw my drawings. He asked if I could cover up some older tattoos. I drew up some Japanese-style designs of dragons with black clouds and lightning bolts, which turned into big upper-arm pieces. He decided to have me do a back piece, my first. Doc Webb had put a butterfly woman on his back, a late-nineteenth-century design of a woman's face coming out of elaborate butterfly wings. He wanted me to frame the whole thing out. I did a lotus at the base of his spine with waves breaking out from that, and a large dragon emerging from the lotus and covering his back, reaching toward a rainbow that went over his shoulder—like the Taj Mahal song. Nobody had ever seen a rainbow tattoo before. It blew Jerry's mind.

When I got into tattooing, I wanted to make it more like painting. Most tattooing was simple black outline, a solid color in each field. I was after blended colors, gradients, a more extended palette. My whole sense of color came from the more sophisticated perspective of a trained artist. I brought things to tattooing that nobody else did. The back piece got the big thumbs-up from Jerry and I showed the photo off to everybody I could. At the same time, I was still trying to downplay all that with the day-to-day work and not get too fancy at Doc's. Zeke taught me the phrase "Rembrandting," which is when you put extra stuff in the design. The rule of thumb was that you painted the basic flash, and if you wanted to add stuff to a design, if you had the time and the inclination and you liked the customer, you could maybe make it fancier when you tattooed it on him. But all the customer could expect was a straightforward rendition of the flash on the wall.

When I got to Zeke's in Seattle, the sign across the front of the shop read, EIGHT BRIGHT COLORS. Eight colors, a full palette—only a very few shops in the world offered that. I wanted to go even further. The guys in Long Beach had turned me on to a really good blue. You had to sleuth around to get the pigments. The tattoo suppliers had some okay stuff, but you really had to contact pigment manufacturers. But if you said you were using it to tattoo, they wouldn't sell it to you, so you had to lie to them. Some guys had stationery made up for bogus sign-painting companies. You would buy dry pigments, mix them with various ingredients in a blender, and cook them on the stove.

So I had a good blue and I got this purple from Zeke, which he got from Sailor Jerry. Jerry was the only tattooer in the world with purple. It was a striking, true purple, a majestic, royal color and Jerry used it like a secret weapon. Zeke gave me a bottle and I brought it down when I came to San Diego to Doc Webb's. "I have a big jar of that in the back that Jerry sent me," Doc said. "I don't go for that much."

Doc would do a good job, talk to them, and be friendly, but he wanted to get the sailors in the shop and out, with as little extra bullshit as possible. But his wife knew I was in there Rembrandt-ing, and they didn't see any reason to slow down the production line for some extra details or more painterly colors.

I could do fifteen tattoos, maybe more, in a four-hour night shift. Big tattoos took longer, obviously, but I could put on a Hot Stuff devil, "Born to Raise Hell," with his little trident, in less than ten minutes. Some people tattooed really fast—Zeke, Al Miller, *bing-bing-bang.* In fact, one day a sailor wearing his summer whites, short sleeves, came in with a friend. I looked over and saw a Hot Stuff I'd put on him the night before and I'd left the tail off. I finished the tattoo I was doing on his friend and told him to sit back down. I put the tail on—it's just one line with a little point on the end—but I realized I needed to watch myself a little more carefully.

I didn't take speed when I was tattooing, but I would get revved up. There's an enormous amount of energy involved, both the human energy of working a tattoo into someone's skin and the electric energy of the machines. You get into it and get cooking; slap it on, bandage it up, get him out of the chair. When Zeke was in Guam, he would tattoo around the clock. He would have people lined up, sitting on the bench in his shop, and they'd have time to get drunk, fall asleep, completely sober up, and start drinking again. He would tattoo for twenty-four or more hours, probably with a little help, but it was legendary.

I was working in Doc Webb's when I saw my first epic Sailor Jerry tattoo in the flesh. One of his key masterpieces was on a submarine commander, Doug Fletcher, who Jerry virtually covered; after the guy already had a bunch of existing tattoos. Jerry made a large cohesive piece that covered his legs, back, and torso and tied together all the small tattoos that I eventually finished. Before I met Fletcher, Jerry introduced to me through the mail a pediatrician in San Diego, Jim Orr. He had been writing to Jerry about getting a back piece. Jim came into Doc Webb's immediately after flying back from having Jerry finish the work. He took off his shirt and showed us his back, covered with a dragon and all the background. The colors were fresh, dazzling, and the tattoo was mind-blowing.

Jerry did the tattoo in five days. A properly done tattoo is a light abrasion. You can't do an outline and come back the next day and fill it in with the color. The skin is too sore. Jerry approached the epic tattoos in quadrants. He did a prep drawing of the whole tattoo and made rice-paper stencils. He would tattoo the design, totally finished, block by block. He figured out how to do these things like a jigsaw puzzle.

8.

Sailor Jerry

The letters with Sailor Jerry grew increasingly intense. He warmed to the role of sage and freely dispensed wisdom and opinions to me. He was suspicious, almost paranoid, of classic tattooers. He hated Bert Grimm, but Jerry reserved his most dedicated ill will for Lyle Tuttle and, since he knew I planned eventually to settle in San Francisco, he may have seen me as a torpedo he was personally building to sink the SS *Lyle Tuttle,* or "lyleturdle," as Jerry called him in his letters. Whatever his motivation, we rapidly fell into a detailed dialogue. He resisted my many suggestions that I visit him in Hawaii, before finally caving in. "It's your dime," he said.

I lied to Doc Webb about needing a week off for some invented family event. I didn't want him to know what I was doing. If he thought I was laying plans to split, he would fire me. I flew to Honolulu in October 1969. Jerry met me at the airport. He was a big guy, a little over six feet, with crew-cut white hair, pencil mustache, and glasses. He dressed in his daily outfit of a white long-sleeve shirt over a white T-shirt and black Frisco jeans. The Compass Rose tattoo on the back of his left hand was the only one showing.

We went for a drink—although I didn't know it, Jerry had stopped drinking, but he felt the ceremony was important to our meeting—and we adjourned to his shop on Smith Street to talk.

We talked all week. He had the keys to the kingdom. His

87

correspondence with tattooers around the globe amounted to the single biggest storehouse of information in the field. There were no books, no tattoo magazines. There was only a slender grapevine between tattooists, and his was the most important. He was a great tattooist—his work was smarter, more elegant, had a greater color range, involved more sophisticated use of the tattoo machines, and completely different imagery. He was inspiring the few of us who were paying attention. He was a fountainhead of knowledge.

He was known as one of the premier tattooers in the world for the strength, beauty, and clarity of his work, both with his strong Americana—this bold style, heavy-outline style, clear, heavy shading widely recognized throughout the tattoo world as American—and for incorporating some of the elements of the epic Japanese tattoos in his work.

Jerry and I discussed everything from the velocity of whirlwinds in tattoos to arcane Asian mythology. He was a big, tough guy, a brawler and a hell-raiser. He was also a voracious reader and a keen intellect with a curious mind, what the Buddhists call a "monkey mind." He didn't drink anymore, but he told me about waking up in a rowboat a mile and a half outside Waikiki, totally hungover, with no idea how he got there. He told me many tales that week. Sailor Jerry liked to talk story, as they say in the islands.

In his tiny tattoo shop next to a strip club, we instantly launched into the highly charged dialogue we had already established in our letters. We talked about Chinese and Japanese customs, art and philosophy, Western tattoo tradition, technical matters, and the unrealized potential of the practice. I could tell that he had few, if any confidants to share these things with. We sketched different energy vectors of the spiral whirlwind designs that are the basis of classical Japanese tattooing. We talked over many formal and psychological possibilities to expand our crazy old art, including the daunting prospects of getting customers to respond to new ideas.

Philosophical discussions about tattooing were interwoven with Jerry's stories about his travels, other tattooers, both alive and dead—either admirable stand-up guys or scumbags who couldn't be trusted—and a healthy dose of Jerry's fanatic right-wing obsessions that included the hated liberals, the international Jewish banking conspiracy, and various racist paranoia. I kept quiet on these matters and only hoped he wouldn't make me for the dope-smoking/Commie/Jew-loving bastard I was. He leavened his tirades with wonderful stories of old Hawaii. He loved Hawaii with the smitten devotion of a true romantic, and had no desire to even visit the mainland again since first setting foot on the islands in 1931.

He was born Norman Kieth Collins in Reno, Nevada, in 1911, and was raised on a farm up in the Sierra Nevada foothills. He started riding the rails as a teenager and that was where he first tried tattooing using the ancient practice of hand tools. During a stint shipping on the Great Lakes, he came to know the prolific and eccentric Chicago tattooist Tatts Thomas, who showed the ropes to young Jerry. He trained Jerry on the machines and, although Tatts customarily found guinea pigs in the local skid row willing to get a couple of tattoos for the price of a half-pint, Jerry loved to tell the story about the time Tatts took him down to the morgue, where Tatts had a friend working. They showed Jerry a corpse rolled out on a gurney and peeled back the sheet, excusing themselves and leaving Jerry to set up his battery-powered machine and load the ink. When Jerry picked up the arm, the body sat up and shouted "Hey, what do you think you are doing?" Tatts and his friend burst out of the dark corner, laughing.

When Jerry first arrived in Honolulu in the early thirties, he went to work for Valentine Galang, a well-known Filipino/Hawaiian tattooer originally from the Big Island of Hawaii. Filipinos operated many of the shops in Hawaii, often paying tattooers an hourly rate. Since their income did not depend on the price of each tattoo, the shop owners would sometimes slash prices to stay busy. Jerry came to hate that kind of ruthless competition and was determined to attract customers based on the quality of his designs and craftsmanship, not prices.

At Galang's, he worked alongside Galang's brother-in-law, Al Miller, who I knew years later from San Diego and Tahiti Felix. They were part of a tattoo dynasty, extending from Valentine's uncle, Domingo Galang. Al's six brothers and their father all tattooed and his younger brother, Eugene, started in the business when he was nine years old. He was later advertised on the shop's sign as THE WORLD'S GREATEST & YOUNGEST TATTOO ARTIST, 15 YEARS OLD. Al himself started tattooing when he was twelve years old and alone in the shop one day when a sailor in a hurry to get a tattoo came in and Al went ahead and started putting it on. His brother-in-law returned before Al was finished, but realized the youngster showed talent and trained him. Al worked in the shop until Pearl Harbor, when he enlisted in the army. He and Jerry used to travel twenty miles upcountry to the town of Wahiawa on paydays every month. They would hang flash over the edge of the lanai and tattoo sugar cane field workers and soldiers from nearby Schofield Barracks.

Although he had served in the navy, a heart condition kept Jerry out of World War II. He took out Captain's papers in the Merchant Marine instead. The Sailor Jerry name was no joke; he held master's papers on practically every vessel afloat and was a stickler for details such as ship's rigging and nautical symbols in tattoo designs. After the war, he operated shops in a few locations on Hotel Street, the sleazy heart of Sailortown in Honolulu, while he lived with his fourth wife on a boat moored in the Ala Wai Yacht Basin. Known as Shit Street during the war, when Hawaii was under martial law, legal whorehouses lined the block. The tattoo parlors were in the penny arcades. Jerry and a partner ran a place for a while where gobs could pose for photos in front of a photo backdrop of palm trees with a hula girl (who happened to be his partner's wife).

After the IRS came down on Jerry, he closed his tattoo shop in 1950 and left the trade rather than submit to government interference in his business. Among other odd jobs, he captained tourist dining ships and other, different vessels, including a large catamaran, always dressed in full captain's whites. He ran a boat tour of Pearl Harbor, an event that held profound meaning for Jerry, and was portrayed leading a tour in a Dennis the Menace comic book. He met his fifth wife while captaining a Pearl Harbor cruise.

It took California transplant Bob Palm to convince him to get back in the business and open a shop with him in 1960. I had seen Palm when I was a kid and he ran a place on the Pike at Long Beach. He had been introduced to Jerry through one of his closest correspondents, Brooklyn Joe Lieber, and had studied science at Columbia University on the GI Bill. He moved to Hawaii in 1957 and managed to rekindle Jerry's interest in tattooing. Soon after they opened, Palm sold his part-ownership in the shop to Jerry for one dollar, after having to beat a hasty retreat to the mainland following some compromising incident involving a young Marine.

Jerry, who never went further in school than the fifth grade, became an earnest correspondent who kept in touch with tattooers from all over, trading information, sharing designs, acting as a conduit of information between a loose network of tattooers from around the world. This kind of knowledge was life's blood in a tattoo world that operated on hearsay and secondhand evidence. He traded long letters and designs with Pinky Yun, who ran a real blood-and-thunder tattoo shop above the Neptune Bar in the Wan Chai Sailortown district of Hong Kong. Many of the pinup designs in Jerry's shop came from Pinky. His correspondence with mentors such as Tatts Thomas, Brooklyn Joe Lieber, or Paul Rogers in Florida cemented his growing understanding of techniques and history of the tattoo trade. Lieber shared designs with Jerry. Their drawing styles, the way they laid out the flash and painted the designs was almost identical.

Jerry did some work on one Mr. Kida, a Japanese businessman who often traveled to the States. He had one arm covered in rocks, waves, and peonies by Horisada, one of great tattoo masters of

Japan, and Jerry covered the other arm in American-style roses. Mr. Kida was a rare direct connection to some of the Japanese masters for Jerry, an opportunity to open lines of communication and garner information. Another contact was John O'Connell, an American businessman based in Tokyo. He only had one tattoo, but it was a masterful coiled dragon covering his whole belly by the legendary Kuronuma—Horiyoshi II. Westerners with Japanese work, especially from the reclusive Horiyoshi, were practically unknown. This guy would come back and show it off around tattoo shops in the States, belittling Western tattoos and trumpeting Kuronuma as the only real tattooer in the world. Even though there was some truth in it, he was barely tolerated when he walked into almost every shop—a little bit like art collectors bragging about work they bought but didn't create, in a craven attempt for reflected glory. I met the blowhard in San Diego, as he knew I was keen on Japanese work. But through him, Jerry found some connections with Japanese tattooers and started trading photographs and letters. When Jerry returned to tattooing, he was determined to forge an epic American tattoo style that would rival the Japanese tradition.

When I arrived in Hawaii, he was obsessed with his broadcasting career. He had started an all-night talk show the year before on an ultra-right-wing radio station in Honolulu, where, under the name Old Ironsides, he would rant about everything: the Rockefellers, the Jews, the hippies, anything he saw as dragging down America. He would also read his florid poetry in his honeyed baritone voice. The poems were frankly romantic, old-fashioned rhymes, written very much in the style of Don Blanding, the poet laureate of Hawaii in the twenties and thirties. Nobody would have ever guessed that this smooth-talking, romantic all-night deejay was the king of tattoos in Sailortown during the day.

We would sit in his tattoo shop with the air conditioner turned way up, drinking endless cups of coffee, and talk tattoo. We drew together. I watched him put tattoos on customers. I was nearly levitating. This was the powerhouse, the center of world tattooing.

Jerry would get impatient. His radio show didn't start until midnight, but he would want to go down to the station early. I would listen for a while, and then fall asleep on the studio couch. He would sign off around dawn and we would crawl out to eat a hamburger. I was staying with him and his wife Louise, a nurse, and their seven-year-old son, Davy, at their place in Waipahu, about twenty miles outside of Honolulu. We went back to their place where I would try to get some more sleep before we would go back to the tattoo shop around noon.

Jerry was backing the movement to get actor Richard Boone from television's *Have Gun—Will Travel* to run for governor of Hawaii. "Paladin will fix it" was his attitude. Jerry loved anything to do with the Wild West. He was very much a nineteenth-century man—he just didn't understand how the world had changed. And he didn't like it. His racism extended to pretty much everybody except the Chinese. He loved the Chinese. He was in awe of classical Chinese thought, culture, and arts. And even though he loved Japanese-style art, his viewpoint was that the Japanese got everything from China. He was also still leery of the Japanese because of Pearl Harbor. But he really liked the Chinese. He listened to Chinese opera in the shop, which drove people crazy.

Jerry kept a pet chimpanzee named Romeo in the shop. He ingeniously tattooed AL on one side of the chimp's ass and HA on the other cheek. He taught him to bend over and look through his legs, rewarding the viewer with ALOHA. Returning to work one day, Jerry found Romeo had broken loose and wreaked havoc in the shop, including drinking a bottle of black tattoo ink. No sooner had he made the place shipshape, when one of his loyal navy customers showed up, crisply turned out in tropical white uniform for the evening's shore leave. "How do I look, Jerry?" he said, as Romeo bounded into his arms and unleashed a burst of black ink diarrhea.

For me, working with Zeke the previous year had been electrifying. He had an inspired vision of modern tattooing, way ahead of his time, but he was also running wild with testosterone and the instability of youth. Sailor Jerry was a worldwide beacon to anyone who knew about or cared about expanding the field. To sit with him in his tiny Chinatown tattoo shop and experience this intense rapport set my mind sailing. He saw the possibilities of tattoos and he thought I could be a part of it. I understood his vision. It was my vision, too. We were tuned in to the same wavelength. It was like being invited to share a studio with Picasso as he was on the verge of inventing cubism. We both sensed that tattooing would never be the same again. The future opened up to us.

On my last day, I told him I wanted to get a tattoo from him. My flight was going to leave around six o'clock. There was a dragon design I wanted him to put on my upper arm and also cover up with clouds some old, little tattoos. He slammed that dragon on in two and a half hours. He tattooed fast. He slapped a bandage on me and his wife drove me to the airport. When I got on the plane, my arm hurt like hell, but after three or four drinks, I passed out. I woke up landing in San Diego with a hangover and sore arm, but with indelible proof of my pilgrimage to the art's future.

I went back to work, all fired up from meeting Jerry, although I couldn't say anything to Doc Webb. The fresh, bold tattoo glowed on my arm from where it peeked out from under my sleeve, but I told him I got it from Hong Kong Tom in Long Beach.

9.

Ichiban

I made twelve thousand dollars that first year in Sailortown with Doc Webb, all in cash, and, of course, I didn't prepay a cent in taxes. I spent everything as it came in. The Internal Revenue Service came down on me and it was a jolt of cold water. I didn't have the money. I went to see an IRS agent, walked into his office, saw he had sideburns with hair that was a little long and thought I had a chance. I told him I didn't have any money. "We'll take your car," he said. "What kind of car have you got?"

In desperation, I called my half brother, who I almost never had contact with, and he loaned me the few hundred dollars I needed. But, after that, I started paying attention to my business and I began to think about opening my own place. I had been hearing from Zeke, who had left Seattle. Chris, Doug, and I had gone up to see him our first summer in San Diego. His shop had moved to a different location. We stayed with him outside of Seattle. He tattooed a heart with my wife's and son's names on my arm, a sacred Jesus-like heart with wiggly rays coming out of it. I thought that sort of vaguely mystical Catholic imagery might be cool as flash, something new to develop. We had a great visit, talked things up, but he was getting restless. When I mentioned that I was thinking about starting my own shop, he encouraged me. "You should open your own place," he said. "You give Doc half of what you're making."

After two years with Doc, I found a location and, like a

complete dummy, I told a few sailors that I knew. That didn't take long to get back to Doc. He came in one day and fired me. "I think you should pack up your stuff," he said. "I know you're getting ready to move on."

That served me right, Mr. Loose Mouth. I scrambled to get my tattoo shop built. With the help of a friend, I framed out the one big room. I got somebody to plumb a sink and put up a wall with a doorway for a private area on one side and a small workroom on the other. It was close to the other three shops. I was half a block off Broadway, but opposite the servicemen's YMCA and Locker Club. The sailors would come off duty in their uniforms, and keep their civvies at these locker clubs. They would come into town and quickly transform themselves into what they hoped looked like regular citizens, cool guys, to attract some girls. And then there were their military haircuts. They bought these things we called hippie hats, like leather hats with big brims and some kind of stuff sewn around the edge. Bell bottoms—not the navy kind—completed the look.

Civilians had started coming into the shop, guys who were collecting tattoos like art collectors, asking for me. Some had been tattooed by Sailor Jerry. I had been written up in a mimeographed and stapled newsletter sent out through the mail to seventy or so members of the Tattoo Club of America; "Sailor Jerry alerts us to Ed Talbott"—I was still using my two middle names—"working at Doc Webb's in San Diego." Most of these people made enough money that they could travel and collect tattoos from well-known tattooers in Europe and the East Coast. One of these collectors was Scotty MacNaughton, an executive for DuPont, based in New York, who had been collecting tattoos since he was in the navy. I tattooed him some. He went over to get a piece by Jerry. He had work done from a variety of places, big pieces, kind of a mismatch of everything. But he was a walking history book. You could ask what it was like in Cap Coleman's shop in Norfolk. The only way you could learn this stuff was from people who had direct experience with it, oral history.

I continued tattooing some of these guys when I opened my own shop, Ichiban Tattoo, which means number one in Japanese. It was a real buzzword. All the service guys knew what it meant; they all spoke a little chop-chop Japanese. I was really pushing the Japanese thing. I had calligraphy done for my business card that spelled out Ichiban Tattoo Studio in Japanese characters. I made regular trips to Little Tokyo in Los Angeles to see swordfight movies, to go to the stores, and to soak up the culture. I still traded lengthy letters three or four times a week with Jerry, discussing everything from the manufacture of tattoo needles to obscure Japanese mythology.

Ichiban opened in early 1971 and there was a lot of business right away. I worked a straight eight-hour shift from two in the afternoon until ten or later. When I wasn't doing tattoos, I was surfing like crazy. We moved to what's called North County, north of San Diego, a little beach town called Leucadia, about thirty miles up the coast. An old high school friend, Bob Hagstrom, the same guy, actually, who took over our apartment in San Francisco when Chris and I moved to Canada, had relocated to nearby Encinitas, one of a string of surf towns along the coast. He was an enthusiastic surfer and it was good to have friends away from Sailortown.

Zeke reappeared. He had been out to Guam again, adventuring around, and worked his way back to Southern California. I told him I would split the shop with him. There was enough work for both of us. We put in another sink and went back to working together. I was starting to do bigger Japanese pieces on people and would put them on for almost nothing just to do the work. Sailors would come in peppered with tattoos, collectors who came back every payday for another tattoo. I began to suggest planning out larger designs, something that would tie the other tattoos together. We could do a portion every payday until it was complete. Jerry, Zeke, and I were really pushing this Japanese-style work. That was what we wanted to do.

It's not only the scale; the more unified, larger forms fit the body better. I had been immersed in books about Japanese mythology, Taoism, and Buddhism since I'd been in art school. I was flipping over the work of the artists who spurred the Japanese tattoo craze in the nineteenth century. It was all arcane knowledge. Jerry corresponded with a couple of Japanese tattooers and would swap photos and trade pigments, but the world of Japanese tattoos remained remote and exotic, shrouded in the mystery of the Orient.

On the other hand, having Zeke in the picture was a mixed bag. He could be fun. Sitting around waiting for jobs to walk in, he would muse about things like cars in the future being remote-controlled or inventing an instant freezer that worked like a microwave, only made things cold instead of hot. He combined rare talent and unique perceptions with street wildness and low-level larceny. He was always looking for an angle. One day he walked in, worked up about word that Crazy Eddie from Philadelphia was aiming to move West. Eddie had a reputation as being on the heavy, old-school side of tattooing, and was rumored to want to control the West Coast tattooers, wetting his beak like some of the eastern big-city scenes. I immediately freaked out.

"Don't worry, I know how to take care of this," said Zeke. "I'll get friendly with Eddie, play along, then invite him up to L.A. and go out fishing on Captain Jim's boat. We'll shoot him and dump him over the side."

With Zeke, you never knew how much was real. Nevertheless, this scenario caused me to lose sleep for several days, until it turned out Eddie was not coming to SoCal.

Painless Nell retired and shortly after that, she died. We heard that she and her husband Huey had saved a lot of money and were going to travel the world. She pretty much worked all the time, but when she died a few months after she retired, she and Huey were living in a trailer.

Jerry told me a story about Painless Nell and her sister when I was in Hawaii. He asked about Nell and I told him about her and her sister in their hairnets, working with sponges and buckets to clean up the tubes, needles, and fresh tattoos. Jerry asked if I knew how her sister got the wooden leg. I did not. "When Nell was tattooing at the World's Fair, making big money, as practice she put a tattoo on her sister and it got infected," Jerry said. "She had to have the leg cut off. So out of pity, she taught her sister how to tattoo so she'd have a profession."

Painless Nell's space was vacant and the arcade owner was anxious to get somebody in the back doing tattoos, when Zeke moved all his stuff over there one day without warning. He wouldn't talk to me, stonewalled me, packed up all his shit, and wouldn't tell me what he was doing. I figured out that he was pissed off because I had taken somebody out of line. When you're working in a shop with someone and splitting the nut, you take every other customer. Your partner always takes the next customer. A woman came in while Zeke was off getting lunch. She was the wife of a well-known figurative painter in Los Angeles, whose work I knew. You almost never tattooed women. Every once in a while a prostitute would come in for a tattoo, but that was about it. This woman wanted an astrology sign and her husband was a famous painter, James Strombotne. I was starstruck for any kind of art world connection. I told her I would put the tattoo on. When Zeke came back in, he saw I was tattooing somebody out of turn. When she left, he packed up his stuff, went down the street a block and a half, and became my competition in the old Painless Nell spot. Although this was obviously an excuse to get his own game going again, he was right according to the old, unwritten laws of the game. I couldn't be angry about it, but was chagrined.

I took Chris and Doug with me when I went back to Hawaii for a couple of weeks in spring 1972. I applied for and got a Hawaii state tattoo license—took the written test and answered a lot of questions about diseases, how to work clean, and all that. I worked at Jerry's shop. I put some regular wall flash on people and did a big shoulder and over-the-chest dragon on a sailor who already had a matching piece by Jerry done on the other side. He also balanced out my chest with a complex design of a chrysanthemum that he insisted I draw up myself. That went on my right pectoral opposite the shoulder dragon he'd done in 1969. I insisted the flower be green, opposite to the deep red of Zeke's *hannya*. Jerry grumbled about it, saying I only wanted to tell people he was over the hill: "The old man is really losing it, he made this flower green." But I knew there were green mums. We went to the beach a bit and generally dug the Hawaiian scene. Jerry put a Tibetan mantra on my leg, a Sanskrit good luck prayer that he wore on his arm during the war. In our letters he and I had been talking up the idea of opening a shop together. He was scouting locations. We were planning to call it the Mid-Pacific Tattoo Institute. I could see myself living in Hawaii. I went back to San Diego, planning to move to Hawaii and work with Jerry.

More of the wealthy tattoo collectors began coming around, including Scotty MacNaughton from New York City. He was in the closet sexually and was also in the closet with his tattoos, although he already had a ton of work on him when I met him. He loved it. He was one of the first guys who told me how much he liked to sit at board meetings, knowing he had an entire secret life under his clothes. From DuPont, he had developed an enormous business, patenting a type of leather book-binding, which became used by major encyclopedias, and most bibles. This especially cracked him up, as he despised the "holier than thou" church folk. He always laughed about what they would think about his tattoo collection and his wild private life, when he met them at high-level business gatherings. He loved shocking people with his tattoos and had rafts of great stories.

Scotty took to getting tattoos in more and more visible places, and he discovered a heavy stage makeup that could mask his obsession. His hands already had a fair amount of work on them when I first met him and the other work began creeping up from his collar, and into his hairline, like a Technicolor tide. He laughed about being in expensive limos with pious business contacts and how he would "accidentally" swipe his hand against the luxurious interiors, leaving a mysterious tan swath. There were few tattoo enthusiasts in his economic strata. He introduced me to Mike Malone, a northern California hipster from San Rafael who was living in New York City and documenting tattoos.

Malone, whose fascination with tattoos went back to some teenage experiments on friends with equipment stolen from Lyle Tuttle, was helping curate an exhibit called TATTOO! at the American Folk Art Museum in Manhattan. He had been involved in the early days of light shows at the Fillmore Auditorium in San Francisco and moved to New York to help run the light show at the Electric Circus in the East Village. He quit that post to pursue a career in fashion photography and started documenting tattoos and tattooers in photographs with a book in mind.

Malone had a sense of tattoo history. He also recognized that the contemporary tattoo world was beginning to emerge. Bert Hemphill had an enormous collection of American folk art, which he eventually donated to the Smithsonian. When Hemphill wanted to mount an exhibit of old flash and tattoo equipment at his American Folk Art Museum, Malone contacted me about setting up a tattoo shop as part of the exhibit and was also looking to include Sailor Jerry. Through my referral, Malone started corresponding with Jerry. The old man and I agreed it was a good project—it would help advance the credibility we craved—and loaned Mike drawings and photos of our work. The upstairs gallery had a neon TATTOO sign and they set up a typical Sailortown shop—probably the first time tattoos had ever been featured in any kind of museum exhibit. At the opening of the show, the cops spotted the neon in the window and raided it. Tattooing was made illegal in all five New York boroughs in 1961 after some kind of witch hunt following a hepatitis scare. No public shops existed in the city until the ban was lifted in 1997.

Malone was not alone in telling me there would be a lot of work for me in New York, if I were to come to town and work out of somebody's apartment. Another captain of industry who I had tattooed in San Diego was Nils, the vice-president of a large New York firm. All these guys were characters, another world from the servicemen, and it was interesting hearing about the lives they led. They were also really excited about the work I was capable of doing, kind of the first wave of what would develop later with clientele in San Francisco. In San Diego the first primary piece I put on Nils was a large version of a famous erotic Hokusai print, commonly known as *The Dream of the Fisherman's Wife*. It showed a naked woman reclining among rocks at the seashore with two octopi pleasuring her, one small one on her mouth and a large one between her legs. It took up one side of his large ass. He was a dramatic guy, with a strong Danish accent, and loved to show off his tattoos. This was in the days before conventions and semipublic gatherings. At private show-and-tell tattoo parties he would display various works covering his arms, torso, and limbs, then turn around, bend over, and dramatically declare "This . . . is *The Dream of the Fisherman's Wife!*" We couldn't figure out if it was mooning (what we used to call "brown-outs" in the old surfer days) or an invitation to anal sex. It cracked up me and Malone.

(A weird development with Nils came several years later, when I was having brunch with friends. The husband, a physician, had just returned from an early morning autopsy. He started talking about the deceased—a thoroughly tattooed older man who died of a heart attack—and wondered if by any chance I might know him. When he began describing the tattoos, I knew who it was. Although still a New York resident, Nils died in San Francisco for some reason. No more show and tell.)

Anyway, Nils was a key person in the circle of New York tattoo enthusiasts. He offered me a friend's Washington Square apartment, vacant for the summer, where I could stay and tattoo. So not long after our Hawaii trip, I went to New York. My host picked me up at the airport in his big, new Oldsmobile—of course had to tell me what it cost, not a subtle guy—and took me to see a movie at Radio City Music Hall, *Butterflies Are Free*, a sappy film about Goldie Hawn and a blind guy.

After the movie, he took me upstairs to the Rainbow Room. My idea of New York was formed from movies in the thirties. I bought a seersucker suit—I knew it would be hot—and a Panama hat from a good clothing store in La Jolla. I finished the outfit with a pair of bad-ass wingtips. We walked into the place and it was like a *New Yorker* cartoon with tiny tables with little lamps, super well-dressed guys with babes half or less their age in furs. There was music playing. I looked up and there was the one and only Lionel Hampton, elegant in a starched white shirt and tuxedo, his bright smile lighting up the bandstand, playing his vibes in front of an equally well-turned-out set of black gentlemen musicians on top of a skyscraper above Rockefeller Center. I felt like a spy in another country. I'm in New York City. I'm here to do custom tattoos, staying at this elegant Greenwich Village pad full of antiques. I'm on top of the world. After that, we went over to somebody's apartment, and there were a bunch of people there to meet me, including Malone and his girlfriend Kate. They introduced me to a mysterious-looking older guy in the room, Thom deVita.

DeVita was a unique character. He was raised uptown in Spanish Harlem; his father was Sicilian, his mother Jewish. He grew up tough on the streets, but had a fantastic art sensibility and had made art his whole life. He drank at the Cedar Bar and rubbed elbows with Franz Kline. He was on the scene. Thom hung his art along the fence at Washington Square at outdoor art fairs. He was really big on mail art, sending things back and forth. He made a lot of art with things he found around the city— assemblages, montages, drawings, not so much straight paintings. Willem de Kooning and Robert Rauschenberg were also making things with stuff they found in the city, and Thomas Cornell was creating his intense little world using found objects, so deVita was in good company.

I'd been receiving some enigmatic things in the mail from Thom, and Mike had talked him up in our correspondence. Malone took me to deVita's tattoo shop, underground of course.

He called it a "tattooeasy." The scary Sixth Street and Avenue D neighborhood where he lived looked like Berlin after the war. Thom met us at the street door and took us down a long hallway. He had set up shop in his kitchen. He had flash on the walls, but it wasn't like any flash I had ever seen. It was like his improvised take on tattoo designs and a lot of heavy Japanese-influenced stuff.

"This is your flash?" I asked.

"This is what I put on people," he said.

"What if they want Hot Stuff?" I said.

The little Hot Stuff devil was the number one hit cartoon of tattoos. It was made famous by Richard Speck, who raped and killed eight Chicago nurses in 1966, and was caught after being turned in by somebody who recognized him by his tattoo. He had a Hot Stuff and "Born To Raise Hell," on his arm. In the public mind, those were the kind of people who got tattoos—psychopaths, rapists, and killers. Hot Stuff. I could put them on in my sleep. It bought me a lot of lunches in San Diego.

"I don't do Hot Stuff. I don't do cartoons," deVita said. "I tell them they have to get his big brother."

He pointed to the wall, where he had his version of a big Japanese *hannya*, the demon mask on my chest. This big lightbulb went on in my head—like, you mean you could draw stuff you wanted to draw and that's what you'd put on people?

I wanted to do custom tattoos, but I always figured you had to do them in the context of a street shop, where you still served the basic menu. If you wanted to get fancy and whip up something special, maybe somebody could be talked into ordering that, but strictly off the menu. DeVita had his thing set. He was the only game in town, literally the only person that we knew about who was tattooing in New York City. Most of his customers were Puerto Ricans and it was all word-of-mouth. He was unlike anyone I'd met, or heard about, and he started me thinking.

I loved New York. It was warm all night. The bars were open until the wee hours. Malone and I sat at a table, tossing back beers in the Village and I was like, gee whiz, Bob Dylan started out around the corner. I did a lot of tattoos in the Washington Square apartment, including a large Kuniyoshi diving woman and dragon on Malone's upper arm and some work on deVita's legs.

We also made a side trip to see the Bidwell Collection in Springfield, Massachusetts. I had turned Malone on to Utagawa Kuniyoshi, the artist who had fired up the entire mid-nineteenth-century Japanese tattoo tradition. His work was not well known in those days, and we all jealously guarded our sources, passing info on to a very tight circle of fellow tattooers. Malone proved worthy of the trust when he found out about a big Kuniyoshi collection at a museum in Massachusetts. He bullshitted his way into an entrée to visit and photograph the prints. He, Kate, and I went up there and spent all morning spreading the prints on the floor and shooting photographs, until the staff finally figured we were just long-haired types who weren't affiliated with any establishment and asked us to leave. But, before they did, Malone took slides of a couple of hundred prints, a spectacular collection. Duplicates of these were then shared with Jerry, Zeke, deVita, and Cliff Raven. They became the key reference base for us to transform Western tattooing.

Initially, Malone didn't let on to me that he was tattooing people in his apartment. He was embarrassed, but it finally came out. Later, when I was back in San Diego he called to tell me about this crazy Italian secretary who was fascinated with Japanese-style work and wanted a big back tattoo. He was completely honest, told her that he was new to the profession, and that the only two people in this country who could do that kind of work right were Ed Hardy in San Diego and Sailor Jerry in Honolulu. "I think she's going to come out and see you because she hippies around the country," Malone said. "She's got a van and goes around with her girlfriend. She's good-looking."

Francesca Passalacqua showed up with her girlfriend on the Fourth of July weekend. As it happened, Scotty, the bookbinding businessman who introduced me to Malone, was in the chair, wearing a pair of swimming trunks and getting a big cover-piece dragon on his leg. The shop was full of sailors, because they had money left from payday. These two girls from New York, tan, barefoot hippies, walked in. "Mike told me about you," she said. "I want to get a big Japanese tattoo."

She told me the story. She had been working as a secretary, making good money, and living a wild life in New York. One of her roommates was Andy Warhol transvestite superstar Candy Darling, and she partied with that crowd, doing a lot of psychedelics and going to clubs.

A friend took her to the Thalia, a downtown movie house where they showed foreign films, exotic stuff in New York, and they saw a 1946 black-and-white Japanese film called *Utamaro and His Five Women* about the famous *ukiyo-e* artist Utamaro. There was a scene where the most famous tattooer in Edo—as Tokyo was then known—was supposed to do this big tattoo on the back of the most beautiful courtesan in the city, and he can't come up with a design. He is practically ready to commit *hara-kiri* because he can't do her justice when somebody grabs Utamaro, who's slamming down the sake nearby in the geisha district. He comes to the rescue, runs over and draws a design on the back, and the tattooer puts it on her. In the movie, they used a famous Utamaro print for the tattoo image.

When Francesca saw that movie and the lights came up, she went, "I've got to get a big Japanese tattoo on my back." She knew nothing about Japanese culture, and little more about tattoos. She was raised in a town with one of the few tattoo shops on Long Island. Stanley and Walter Moskowitz used to tattoo on the Bowery, where they learned from their old man, tattooing in a barbershop—a standard setup often seen in the early twentieth century. When the city made tattoo parlors illegal, they moved out of the city and opened S&W Tattoo on Long Island in Copiague, Francesca's hometown. The Bowery had been tough, a guts-and-thunder environment. There was still dried blood from fights in the shop on the flash on their walls. The only tattoos Francesca had ever seen were standard-issue American tattoos on older guys. She had no interest in tattoos.

She watched me work for a while. "I think I want to get something done like that," she said, looking at the dragon in progress. She had an interesting story: her first little tattoo from Malone was a Japanese koi (carp) on her hip. Soon after, she called him and told him she had dreamed that she had a dragon on the other side. He told her that was the Asian myth: carp who successfully scaled a sacred waterfall would transform into dragons. So she went back and he balanced it with a dragon on the other side.

She and her girlfriend hung around a little and we talked about it. They left, but said she would be in touch. They were planning on settling down for a while and getting jobs in San Diego.

None of us had actually completed any large pieces on women; I'd only started that aborted tiger on the crazy chick from S.F. It was kind of a goal. We thought it would definitely be cool to put some great piece of art on a good-looking woman and wondered when it would really happen.

I told Malone that she had come into the shop and that I thought she was going to have the tattoo done. She and her friend tooled around in their van and came back to San Diego after Labor Day, got waitressing jobs, and rented a place. We went through some of my sources and found a small black-and-white image in a Japanese book of a dragon entwined around a seated woman in a voluminous robe. The book was all in Japanese; I couldn't see the image detail, but drew it up and put it on her back.

I kept in touch with those guys in New York. I went back during the summer and stayed with Malone and did some more work on deVita's legs. Soon after, he came out for a visit. DeVita got tattoos from both me and Zeke. He had a lot of big individual tattoos and was well on his way to being covered. I filled in his legs and Zeke did a wild Japanese scene on his chest. That fall, Malone moved to San Diego to work with me. He needed to learn more than he could tattooing by himself in his apartment. He was at the same stage I had been in Vancouver. He was green and needed to get his chops up on the machines. We got along. He was full of blarney, had a great way with stories, and we shared a lot of the same sensibilities. I split the shop with him. I figured I would be moving to Hawaii and going into business with Jerry soon. I could turn over the shop, sell it to him or whatever. He took his tattoo name from the fat, rich kid in Ernie Bushmiller's *Nancy* comic strip, Rollo Banks.

He and Kate moved out to San Diego and found a place to stay in Cardiff-by-the-Sea, near where I was living. I was taking classes in Chinese brushwork, bamboo painting, and classical Chinese painting from a woman in town. I was really working on my Japanese connection.

It was a rough time. I was drinking too much, kind of going crazy, not knowing how to handle things. Chris and I split up. I moved out, rented a place down from the rental where Doug and Chris were living. I was at loose ends. I didn't know quite what I was going to do. I was burnt out on San Diego. Everything was just flying around, up in the air. I was ready to move to Hawaii.

10.

Summit Meeting

One of the guys Sailor Jerry corresponded with, Kazuo Oguri, tattooed in a central Japanese city called Gifu. Horihide was his tattoo name. He exchanged letters with a number of Western tattooists. Jerry set me up with him and he and I traded letters and photos, mine full of all these earnest, squinchy questions like "If the cart goes this way, what does it mean?" He took photos of everything he did and had a terrific translator, although that didn't occur to me at the time. I assumed he was proficient in English. He was one of the few Japanese guys to reach out to Westerners and he had an avid interest in Americana.

Jerry arranged for him to come to Honolulu that Christmas 1972, and made something of a summit meeting out of the event. He invited an Australian tattooer named Des Connolly, another pen pal, more of a machine guy than an artist. Malone and his girlfriend Kate came over. I was on the island less than a week, but it changed my life, even though we quickly discovered that Oguri spoke almost no English and none of us knew a word of Japanese.

We all planned on getting souvenir tattoos and Oguri brought over his hand tools, but he only brought his outliner tools because he didn't want to get involved in some big, elaborate, filled-in thing. I was staying at Jerry's house and was going to get a Chinese lion design on my leg. The first day Oguri tattooed at the house, Malone went first. He stretched out on the floor in Jerry's living room on some towels and Oguri put a dragon with chrysanthemums across his whole chest, upper pectoral, and upper arm down to below the elbow.

It was a huge moment. We all had spent so much time thinking about, studying, and talking about the Japanese tattoo tradition and here we were, in its living presence for the first time in our lives. A quiet came over us as Horihide started work on Malone. He didn't even lay out the design first. He would draw a little with a toothpick dipped in India ink, tattoo it in with a needle assembly attached to these chopstick-length tools. He picked up *sumi* ink (rubbed to the correct density on the ink stone) from a brush held in his skin-stretching hand. Then he would draw the next section and repeat. The guy was like a superman to us. Malone looked down at Horihide tattooing him.

"Five thousand years on the head of a pin," he said.

I was overcome. My brain was boiling and I thought this might be the only chance I would ever have to get a genuine Japanese tattoo on my back. I was going nuts over what I was seeing. It was the only thing I could think about. I asked Oguri if he would outline my back the next day.

Jerry happened to have a photo of an image that Oguri had drawn from a famous Japanese print that I knew well. It was in a book I owned from the Victoria and Albert Museum on Kuniyoshi, the famous Japanese printmaker and *ukiyo-e* artist in the nineteenth century whose prints Malone and I photographed at the Bidwell Collection in Massachusetts during my second trip to New York. It was Kuniyoshi's introduction of tattoos into a lot of heroes and bandits in his print work from the 1820s that started the big tattoo craze in Japan in the early nineteenth century. He was the godfather. Oguri had drawn it up and sent Jerry a picture of the drawing. I had always been obsessed with that print, a great chilling image of a ghost. Jerry had the picture there. "Would you do this on me tomorrow?" I asked Horihide.

I had been planning to have Jerry do my back. He had proposed a couple of things, but we couldn't really come up with a design.

We were going to do this shop together, only we were having trouble finding a location. We were like this father-son team. He watched me become entranced as Horihide tattooed Malone. Jerry couldn't resist making a snide remark. "It's been nice knowing you," he said.

The next day, as he did with Malone, Horihide drew out the first part of the tattoo, put the toothpick down, and tattooed it in, freehand with a hand tool. It was impressive enough to see somebody nail a freehand piece, either hand-drawn or with a machine, with a little Sailortown design, but he was doing fearless, epic work across whole portions of people's bodies. He worked his way down my back starting at the top. It took nine hours. The lower he would get on my back, the worse it hurt. I thought I'd never get another tattoo again. He outlined this ghostly demon with long hair and a kimono all across my back, down to the top of my butt.

Meanwhile, my marriage was down the tubes. Jerry and I couldn't find a suitable location for the Mid-Pacific Tattoo Institute. Hawaii suddenly seemed like only a stepping stone to Japan. I was done with San Diego. My Japanese obsession, growing for years, burst open and I asked Oguri if I could come to Japan and work with him.

When we had traded letters and photos, he praised my work. He knew how serious I was and he thought I was good enough to work with him. Or, at least that was my naïve assumption. I knew the art, but the Japanese character was something I did not yet understand. There are extremely complicated, subtle ways that you communicate with people in Japan, even if you speak Japanese, and you have to be aware of nuance.

In general, the Japanese will tell you what you want to hear. They will not contradict you. Language problems aside, I did not fully appreciate the position I put Oguri in simply by making such a presumptuous request. Of course, he accepted.

I went back to San Diego, feeling like king of the world. I was going to move to Japan and tattoo. I would be the first Westerner who ever went over there to do that.

Malone and his girlfriend stayed in Hawaii with Jerry for another couple of weeks. Everything was going so haywire in my life, Malone and I decided it would be better if he moved out of the shop. We had been having a few disagreements. I had introduced him and Zeke and, when Malone came back from Hawaii, he cleared out his stuff and moved over to the back of the penny arcade where Zeke had taken over Painless Nell's shop.

I got home before New Year's. I was going to Japan in June. I saw myself staying at least five years. It was a big change and I welcomed it. It had been my dream destination since I was six years old and my father sent all those packages. The surfboard went back in the closet. I did a series of ink and watercolors in Oguri's style. I signed up for language lessons at a community college. I also started working with a private tutor. I wanted to be able to fit in over there. I wanted to be able to function. That was my goal.

On January 19, 1973, I was working in my shop solo when Francesca showed for the first time in a couple of months. After I finished her tattoo the previous fall, we used to run up to Los Angeles every so often with another Japan-struck friend and catch a Japanese film or look at the stores in Little Tokyo. She was smitten with the culture and wanted to learn more about it. I was still with my wife. We became friends.

I had last seen Francesca at a party that Malone and Kate threw—Malone introduced us in the first place—but she had split back to New York for an extended stay back east over the holidays. She sauntered into the shop unexpectedly that day. "I had a chance to get a flight back out here," she said.

She was actually carrying drug money for a friend who was a dealer in New York.

She'd been on the scene in New York. She was a responsible, young Sicilian-American gal from Long Island, very sharp and savvy. She made good money working as a legal secretary and, at nights, hung out with a whole different crowd. But she always kept a level head, never lost it, never went off the deep end. She did lead this interesting life.

She would take the dough she saved as a secretary, either go in her van or grab a driveaway car with one of her girlfriends, and head out for adventure. She lived by the Grand Canyon and Yosemite one summer. She would use up the money and go back to New York, pick up another temp job, and make more money.

She never used hard drugs. She smoked weed and did psychedelics, maybe a little bit of crystal now and again to keep the lights bright at night. She was making plans to head back to the west coast when a dealer friend asked if she would deliver thirty-five thousand dollars in cash for him to Los Angeles. He would pick up her airfare and pay her fifteen hundred dollars for the delivery.

Her father, meanwhile, had arranged with a friend at work for his friend's cousin to drive back to California with Francesca, so she felt responsible for the guy. Since she saw her payoff as free money, she told the cousin she would buy his airline ticket and pay for it with the proceeds. Before the airport, her dealer friend laid out the pharmacy. She contemplated her choices. "Acid's the logical thing," she said. The money was packed in a big, gift-wrapped Christmas package. The acid was beginning to take hold when she walked into the airport with the dealer's girlfriend and the cousin of her father's friend. It was the early days of airport security and all packages were now subject to X-ray inspection, something Francesca did not expect. She had never seen luggage screened at the airport.

It was the dealer's whacked-out girlfriend who came up with the idea. They adjourned to the ladies' room, where they frantically rubber-banded wads of money to Francesca's feet inside her snow boots. She flew to California, tripping all the way, her feet swollen into her boots with stacks of cash, sitting next to this guy she didn't knew.

It wasn't until the plane started to descend in Los Angeles that she realized she didn't know how she'd recognize the person she was supposed to meet. The contact found her—how could you miss her, this gorgeous, dark-skinned hippie with hair down to her waist and sparks flying out of her eyes?—and she made the delivery. She and the cousin got a connecting flight to San Diego, where Francesca knew some people with an apartment. The next day Francesca drove the cousin up the coast to his brother's house in Laguna Beach. They walked in the house and she saw a vivid painting of a dragon and whirlwinds. "That's Ed Hardy," she said. "He tattooed my back."

His brother was a good friend of mine from Laguna Beach, a bad-boy surfer, ceramic artist, and shoemaker who I traded the painting to for some ceramics, although there was no way Francesca would have known that.

When she walked into my shop that afternoon, I hadn't seen her in more than three months. I told her Chris and I had split up, that I was living on my own and moving to Japan. A pal was throwing a birthday party that night up the coast near where I was living in North San Diego County and I invited her to come along. She didn't have anything better to do.

At the party, I had too many beers and there was no way I could drive back to San Diego. I was renting a four-hundred-square-foot bungalow in Cardiff-by-the-Sea. I told her she would be welcome to stay the night. That was when that all started.

She didn't have a job, so she started helping out at the shop and stayed with me. Neither of us had any expectations. She'd been through a bad marriage that lasted about four months. I was getting divorced. It was nice to get along with someone, but neither of us thought it was serious. I was moving to Japan in June, so it couldn't be anything permanent.

I was focused on going to Japan. Sailor Jerry and I continued to correspond. He was happy that I was going to Japan. We all knew how ground-breaking it was. No Westerner had ever tattooed there.

While I was getting ready for Japan that spring, I needed to go to San Francisco to finish a back I was doing on a woman I had started in San Diego after Francesca moved out. I still kept in touch with my Art Institute pal Richard Shaw, who was teaching ceramics at the institute by then. When I called him to say I was coming, he asked me to give a talk about tattooing to his class. I hadn't delivered a lecture about tattooing since the one I did when I was in school. Shaw went with me that first night in Oakland looking for Phil Sparrow, came back with me a few times, and got a couple of tattoos. He suggested I bring some tattoo equipment. I wanted to show San Francisco to Francesca. We rented a car and drove, checking in at a motel off Lombard Street near the Golden Gate Bridge.

It was a big deal for me to go back to the alma mater and address a class. There were about twenty students and I showed them slides. I set up my portable machine and tattooed a bunch of people in the classroom. Shaw got another tattoo, a steaming cup of coffee with a saucer and spoon. He knew other people who wanted to get work done. One of them wanted a pair of scissors. A light went on in the back of my head. I realized that I wanted to develop clients with more of an art sensibility.

The next day I finished the back tattoo, a classic Hokusai image from the early nineteenth century of two turtles with mossy tails. I was back in San Francisco—where I started out putting tattoos on my friends on my back porch, not really knowing what I was doing—tattooing bootleg out of a motel on Lombard Street. There was something really cool about the whole deal. We went back to San Diego, where I finished up my business and closed up my shop. I actually sabotaged the place, with Malone's help, to keep anybody from opening another tattoo shop on the premises. Zeke and Malone thought that would be best. I said good-bye to Francesca and took a plane back to San Francisco.

The plan was for Oguri to visit the United States and we would fly back to Japan together. He flew into San Francisco, where he met another correspondent of his, a fellow from Portland named Steve Gilbert, a medical illustrator who was very keen on Japanese tattooing. He was a great student of Japanese culture in general and was studying the language. He also was planning to visit

Oguri in Japan, although not for a few months. Gilbert had gone to Reed College, where he was a classmate of beat poet Gary Snyder. When I met up with him and Oguri in San Francisco, we were going to visit Snyder at his place in the Sierra Nevada foothills, a hundred-acre piece of mountainside that he bought with Allen Ginsberg and named Kitkitdizze, after the aromatic tarweed that filled the hillside. I was pumped to meet one of my beat poet heroes, but, when we arrived, Snyder had gone off to do something with Ginsberg. His wife and his two young sons were there. His wife was Japanese so she and Oguri could powwow a lot. We stayed for a couple of days. Steve brought us back to San Francisco where Oguri and I boarded a plane to Japan.

11.

Japan

Gifu was a medium-size city in south central Japan. It became something of an industrial center during the war and, as a result, it was the target of a searing American firebomb raid that destroyed more than twenty thousand buildings and caused more than thirteen hundred casualities on one night. As a manufacturing center after the war, it was known for making paper fans. The city was also known for the replica of an eleventh-century castle overlooking Gifu from the crown of Mount Kinka and ancient cormorant fishing still practiced at night on the Nagara River, where the fishermen used the diving waterfowl to catch fish, but kept them from swallowing their prey with rings around their necks.

Our eleven-hour flight was met in Tokyo by Oguri's apprentice, a tall, cadaverous young man my age named Matsunase, who wore a close-cropped haircut in the style, I would soon learn, of the *yakuza*. Also at the airport was Mr. Kida, Japanese businessman and tattoo fancier who served as translator. Mr. Kida was one of very few middle-class Japanese men to wear tattoos. He had one arm that was done by Horisada, a traditional Japanese artist, and the other arm was covered in American roses done by Sailor Jerry. We ate dinner at the underground shopping arcade under Tokyo Station and boarded the Shinkansen, the bullet train, for Nagoya, where we transferred to a smaller train to Gifu. I stayed the night at Oguri's apartment with his wife and three children. I was already overwhelmed by claustrophobia from the small rooms, narrow roads, and crazy drivers.

The next couple of days were spent sightseeing around the city. We visited a phallic shrine, Takata Jinja, and the Gifu Castle. It was immediately obvious that my pathetic attempts to prepare myself for the language and cultural barriers, now staring me in the face, had been useless.

On the third day, we went to the shop, about a ten-minute walk from his apartment. It was in a nondescript apartment building in a residential neighborhood, a studio space with no bath, but with a small kitchen and toilet. There were two six-mat rooms, one of which had been functioning as a kind of waiting room. His workroom had a sliding door to the outside that opened to a view of greenery. The walls were covered with photos from the tattoo artists around the world he corresponded with and his beautifully painted designs, almost all taken directly from Kuniyoshi prints. In the other room, he had assembled a small table in the corner where I could set up my gear. I assured him that I did not need to work out of a chair. He regarded me as an accomplished and established Western tattoo artist who wanted to learn the Japanese ways. He expected that we would learn from each other. How long I would be staying was never discussed.

Three customers came in that first day, who were absolutely astonished when they slid open the door, muttered their formal greeting to the tattoo master, and looked up to see this *gaijin* face. They were planning on discussing a possible tattoo project. There was much chatter over my presence, but Horihide was the *sensei*—the master—and they accepted his word. These three flashy *yakuza* decided they wanted to take me out for beers. Oguri didn't think this was a good idea, at first, but eventually agreed. My eager hosts finished the afternoon by throwing a beer in the bartender's face, a horrific insult staged, at least in part, for my benefit. The few other patrons in the bar fled, leaving their unfinished drinks behind, fearing a *yakuza* rumble was about to take place. These Japanese thugs knew little of legends and demons and the stuff of woodblock prints. They wanted to know about American automobiles and small-arms manufacture. They wanted to know how fast the cars went and how much they cost. They wanted to know if I owned any guns and if I brought any with me to Japan.

The next day, we went to visit a friend of Oguri's named Kawada in nearby Ichinomiya City, who was an *oyabun*, or gang boss, of a *yakuza* subchapter. The parking lot was stuffed with black Cadillacs. The clubhouse had a gold emblem on the door like a family crest. Inside there was a rack on the wall holding little wooden signboards with every gang member's name. The names of the members currently in jail were printed in red. There was a section for members who were on duty that day. Kawada was actually Korean, a much discriminated-against class of people in Japan. He wanted me to buy him a Mustang. He told me he would give me the money, and let me drive it for six months before I turned it over to him. He and his guys were hot-breathing me to buy them guns. After all, I was American. While we were there, a couple of guys in uniform came in to have some tea, hang out, and watch the big-screen TV. When they left, I asked if they were mailmen. "No," the boss said. "Those are the beat cops."

The *yakuza* impose severe discipline on matters of duty and honor. If you screw up, you slice off a finger. It is an established ritual called *kubikiri*. They cut the finger, place it in a carefully folded handkerchief, and present it to the boss. The more you screw up, the more sections of fingers you lose. Kawada was missing both digits on both little fingers and the outside digit on his third finger. Oguri made a joke to me in English about it.

Tattooing was underground. There was no sign outside the apartment where Horihide worked. You had to know somebody who knew somebody to be introduced. It was very formal. Oguri had insisted on renting an apartment for me close to where we worked. We were in the shop seven days a week. In San Diego, I'd adopted a Japanese tattoo name from a story about a sumo wrestler in the book *Zen Flesh, Zen Bones,* a compilation of stories first published in 1957. The name, Hori Onami, meant Tattooer Great Wave.

It was a struggle, just sitting on the floor to tattoo, which most Caucasian people can't handle as well as the Japanese, who are longer in the thigh and shorter from the knee to the ankle than Westerners. Japanese are able to sit cross-legged more easily and have been doing it since childhood, but I was having trouble working on the *tatami* mats. I was doing mostly coloring work. Horihide would outline and shade the tattoo and leave it for me to color in.

Oguri spoke only a minimal amount of English. He grew up around an American army base after World War II. He had driven a Jeep for GIs when he was fourteen years old. He loved American culture. He saw Japan as a small country of small-minded, small people and he thought everything about America was big. In many ways, Japan was still on its knees from World War II.

Our clients were overwhelmingly *yakuza,* the Japanese Mafia. The few others were tradesmen, carpenters, and such. We could only communicate in limited pidgin English. As for the Japanese I'd been studying, textbook Japanese with careful pronunciation and slow speech, what these guys were talking could have been Martian.

I shipped over a huge load of books—a Japanese dictionary, collections of myths, art books, philosophy tracts, language texts—and I was reading them. But I kept coming back to something Oguri had told me in one of his letters: "You have to come to Japan and see the dark places."

I was reeling from culture shock. As much reading as I had done, nothing could have prepared me for what I found. Any delusions I nourished about fitting in or finding a place for my art and spending a few years working in the country were quickly dashed. Within no time, I was reduced to trying to figure out how the fuck was I going to deal with what I had gotten myself into?

I missed Francesca badly. I hadn't thought about that before I left. I simply assumed I would go to Japan and she would grab another driveaway car—which is what she did—and head back east. But I quickly came to realize that, although I had finally reached Japan, which had been pretty much a goal of my life since I was six years old, I may have let go too easily a woman who was truly special. I wrote to her at her parents' address in Long Island and invited her to Japan. I offered to send her money to buy an airplane ticket, if she wanted to come, and we could share the small apartment I rented. Oguri was skeptical—he didn't like the idea of my girlfriend coming over—but he would never say anything directly confrontational. I still didn't understand how the Japanese communicate.

I hadn't been in Gifu two weeks when a letter came for Oguri from Hawaii. It was Sailor Jerry's wife, Louise, writing to say Jerry had died of a heart attack. She knew where I was and that she could reach me through Oguri. She asked Oguri to have me get in touch. She wanted to sell me Jerry's tattoo business. Those had been Jerry's instructions.

The Big Kahuna was gone. I was stunned. He was sixty-two years old. He smoked and lived on a terrible diet, but I never expected him to die. The day before he died, Jerry wrote a long letter to Paul Rogers in Florida, one of the great tattoo artists of the east coast, and a close friend and correspondent to Jerry for many years.

> *Well I done it. Was down buying some tools and oil for my big Harley and had a heart attack in the store. Knocked me on my ass and I poured out cold clammy sweat until I stunk like a wet dog. Got on the bike and rode out of there and went home after a few minutes but laid in bed for 36 hours with a coronary spasm that made me fight for breath. Kept taking scalding hot showers and got clean for once anyhow, and then on the third day I got up and went in and saw a Chinese Dr. and got some*

nitroglycerine pills in case the thing came back again,
then slept three days and nights straight with hot showers
to take the ache out of my body. Sixth day got up again
but hadn't eaten in all that time so was pretty weak and
couldn't stay up very long. Eighth day back at work
again with Louise as my chauffeur as I was too weak to
ride the bike . . . If I had went to a Dr. with this I would
still be in the hospital and too scared to work besides paying
a month's salary for the bad news. I don't need these
croakers, believe me, not at their prices. A few $ worth of
Chinese herbs is enough and I will live to piss on all their
graves . . . Just came in today to get my medicine and
the Chinese herb Dr. told me I have been drinking too
much cold water and that I have to stop and use hot tea
or coffee, nothing cold for a while. Got me a package of
medicine that cost me $7 so will go home early and boil it
up. Stinks bad and tastes worse but it works and that's
the main thing. Makes me think of when I was a kid my
dad used to make up a pot of sheepshit tea every Spring
and we all used to have to down a cup of it.

Jerry mailed the letter, went home, had another heart attack, and died the next day. His wife was a nurse and knew nothing about his tattoo business, but he left instructions to contact me. In order to place an international call, I had to go to a central telephone office in downtown Gifu and make an appointment for later that afternoon, to account for the different time zones. Jerry passing the torch to me was deeply touching, but I couldn't leave Japan. This was my life's dream. This was my time. I couldn't drop everything and run to Honolulu just because Jerry died. That was not my destiny. I called her. "You're going to have to find somebody else," I said.

She told me the next on the list would be Zeke Owen and Mike Malone in San Diego. I told her to call those guys. Zeke didn't want to move to Hawaii, but Malone bought the shop. He went over there and took over Jerry's shop, and we kept in touch.

By the time Francesca showed up, I had been there about a month on my own. I was feeling squirrelly because I hadn't been talking English to anybody. Francesca seemed exotic to me. This olive-skinned New York Sicilian beauty looked more native than the blond beach bunnies I grew up with in Southern California. We found a soul connection. We have been together since the night she showed up in Japan.

We passed the summer, hotter than hell. Oguri and I worked every day of the week from noon to midnight. He worked continually. If there were no customers, he would work on filling in my back piece that he outlined in Hawaii. We only stopped for dinner, when we would drive over to Oguri's apartment, where his wife made a home-cooked meal. She was cold but polite with us. She clearly didn't like foreigners, but there was nothing she could do about it. We were her husband's guests and she had to take care of us. We didn't understand the Japanese well enough to politely decline the dinner invitation in the first place, which is what would have been expected. Oguri took off only one day a month and would take his wife shopping in Nagoya, a huge population center about an hour away.

In an effort to mend the country's image with the rest of the world, the government made tattooing illegal in Japan shortly after Commodore Perry opened the country to Western trade and visitors in 1854, a ban that lasted a hundred years until General MacArthur lifted it during the Occupation. One of the officers on MacArthur's staff was introduced to Horiyoshi II, the great tattoo master of Tokyo, whose father had studied with one of the great nineteenth-century printmakers. MacArthur's associate, who recognized the rich tradition and artistic value, convinced MacArthur that tattoos were like pottery or printmaking or any of the great Japanese folk arts.

Illegal or not, Japanese tattoos in the nineteenth century are what kicked off decorative tattooing in the West. There was no decorative tattooing tradition in this country beyond a few sailors getting little souvenir tattoos onboard ship, or out on some far-flung Pacific Islands. The Japanese introduced the geishas to Western flash, once the practice took hold, along with exotic images like dragons, serpents, and demons.

Charles Longfellow, eldest son of the poet, arrived in Yokohama in 1871, intending on a short visit, but stayed two years. He stocked his apartment with Japanese courtesans, dressed in silk kimonos, sent home trunks full of curios and artwork, and covered himself in tattoos.

Another one who went over was George Burchett, the great English tattooer. As a cabin boy, he saw the Japanese tattoos and determined to learn how to do it. He returned to England, and soon established himself as one of the premiere tattooists of the great city. A vogue developed among European aristocracy for tattoos in the Victorian era. Burchett tattooed England's King George V, among other royalty. Another British tattooist, Sutherland Macdonald, was a member of the Royal Watercolor Society. There are only a few photos of his tattoos, but he had a delicate, nuanced style. These guys would set up in swanky ateliers and charge big money. Some of the enthusiasts in London and New York even started importing Japanese tattooers.

Japan was a world that had been sequestered for hundreds of years. To people who first experienced the country's rich gifts, it was an incredible fairyland. The revelation of Japan had incalculable effects on Western art. It kicked off Impressionism, Art Nouveau, and, essentially, all of Western modern art. It inspired the Arts and Crafts movement, buildings, designs, and Frank Lloyd Wright. Tattoos were merely a small piece of this vast, fully evolved society revealing itself to the rest of the world all at once.

The firemen of Edo—ancient Tokyo—wore protective blankets of tattoos, over which they would wear embroidered robes with the same kind of strong imagery: strong men, heroes, people kicking ass on violent mythological beings, dragons, and evil spirits. When they would fight fires, they'd throw off their coats and the tattoos would protect them from burning up. Covering their bodies with tattoos of dragons and water was an amuletic application that spread to the criminal underclass in Japan. By the time I arrived in the country, a hundred years later, those criminals were the majority of people getting tattoos.

The Japanese tattoo tradition came out of the *ukiyo-e* world, the Japanese woodblock prints with extraordinary workmanship that made them a high point of world visual culture and art history. *Ukiyo-e,* loosely translated, means "floating world" and the prints concentrated on subjects drawn from the realm of transitory pleasures—geisha, sumo wrestlers, entertainers. *Kabuki* was an important part of *ukiyo-e* culture. *Kabuki* was the people's theater. The high culture theater was *Noh* drama, which is slow and esoteric. *Kabuki* was more explosive, with a more overtly expressive style of acting. A lot of woodblock prints featured *kabuki* actors. The *yakuza* also developed around that same time.

Originally the *yakuza* started as a kind of neighborhood protective association to help ordinary people against corrupt and oppressive feudal governments. They saw themselves as Robin Hood guys. Of course, it evolved into something else. The *yakuza* came to control the gambling and the Japanese are avid gamblers. *Yakuza* groups grew to be involved in every kind of nefarious activity, from assassins to insurance scams, on down to the innocuous little games people play at temple fairs on Buddhist holidays. The *yakuza* are deeply ingrained in Japanese society. They were our customers.

These guys worshipped American gangster movies. They memorized all the lines. Oguri was really into *The Valachi Papers,* which I had never seen. There were also Japanese gangster movies, which glorified the *yakuza* and played up their image as protectors of the community. Oguri also loved *yakuza* novels. The *yakuza* dressed well and kept a beneficent, gentlemanly façade—in their minds, they lived the *bushido* spirit or the warrior way—but a lot of them were rough characters and didn't care who knew it. Flashy guys who spoke in harsh dialects, intimidating in manner. The classic image of the *yakuza* is a particular kind of severe haircut, certain type of clothes, gradient tint sunglasses, a scar and, always, the tattoos.

Those were the guys we tattooed. We were accepted because we did the tattoos that were so important to them. They treated us with respect. I learned a great many interior things about the role of tattooing among these people.

We witnessed some amazing scenes. We went to a ceremony where Oguri's *oyabun* friend Kawada, headed to a stretch in jail, handed off the reins of power to his wife. The *yakuza* were like a family and the boss was like the father. We watched as the lady boss delivered a ritualistic speech to the troops. They all answered her in unison.

Another guy came in fresh from doing five years in prison, although he was still a fairly young man. He had a tattoo that Oguri had started on him before he went to prison, and he wanted to get it finished. Oguri did the shading. I did the coloring. The guy's skin was in terrible shape. It was tricky to get the ink in right. Oguri explained that when you're in the joint in Japan, they don't believe in rehabilitation. They want to make you so miserable, you'll never do anything bad again—minimal food, terrible rations, not enough blankets in the winter, hard-core jail time. You could tell by this guy's skin that he had not been living right for the last few years, not getting the kind of nutrition that healthy thugs should have.

He came along with some of the other guys we had been tattooing to take a day trip to this old mountain village, Takayama, where they filmed a lot of the samurai movies. Oguri was in love with the town, and it was a beautiful drive into the mountains. Oguri drove. They were going to meet us and take us to gang headquarters, when this red ragtop Porsche comes roaring up. All these guys were yelling and the guy with the bad skin was sitting up on the back, waving a short sword, all of them jacked up to the teeth on speed.

Speed was definitely the drug of choice for *yakuza*. A lot of their business was meth labs in the Philippines archipelago, where they would take over a small island and cook meth without drawing attention. They were all shooting speed and it could get a little scary when you have guys with edged weapons, a bad social attitude, and a hair trigger, full of crank.

In our apartment, Francesca and I would lie on the *tatami* mat in traditional Japanese bedding and look at the ceiling, where there were these strange, triangular marks that we couldn't figure out. When we asked, Oguri explained that the previous occupant was a young speed-freak who would fly into rages over the people upstairs making noise, jump up and stab his short sword into the ceiling.

I never got it straight what Oguri's background was, but it looked to me like he had been in the gangs as a youth. I saw some photos of him when he was young, and he looked like a tough. He also had a gimped-up hand. His little finger was curled under and I don't think it was a birth-defect thing. I suspect he decided to get out of the gangs. Quitting the gangs usually involves the loss of a digit. Starting with the end digit—the little finger—if you chop that off as atonement, you can leave the gang. Of course, you can never fully return to polite society.

He had about thirty different back pieces painted on the wall like flash, a lot of them full color. Most of his flash was images of heroes taken directly from woodblock prints by Kuniyoshi. He is the god of all Japanese tattooing, and everybody copied his images verbatim.

Horihide loved drawing. He would project images from a book, make a pencil tracing on a sheet of board roughly the size of a back, and paint them up in classical tattoo style, with a background of whirlwinds or chrysanthemums or whatever. He learned the style of doing these things and even still had designs from his teacher. There were certain themes—carp, dragons, flowers of the seasons, *Noh* drama masks—that were always done. They were the staples, like ships and anchors in Sailortown. He would sometimes paint up new things, but he would never invent a hero. They had to be properly vetted, specifically rooted in traditional art.

It actually turned out to be a surprisingly limited range of images. Once I got over there, I realized the whole astonishing breadth of Japanese history, mythology, and visual art, but the tattooing was as limited and codified as Western tattooing. In Japan, they were pretty much getting a rote vocabulary of images. Like the sailors in San Diego, they could only select from a limited menu. They would choose from whatever Horihide painted up. Or he would make suggestions. Sometimes they would even ask what he thought would be good. That didn't make much sense to me—especially with the big, crazy, complicated, colorful work they were having done—but I could see that I wasn't going to change that.

I was with Oguri once in a store looking at an art book with him. I saw a Kuniyoshi woodblock print where the leg of the warrior went outside the frame of the print. Oguri was obsessed with Kuniyoshi. He collected everything he could on him, including some original prints. When I expressed my enthusiasm for this particular print, however, Oguro disagreed. "It's no good," he said. "You don't see where the leg is going." A bulb went on in my head. *Aha*, I thought. *If this guy can't copy it, he can't draw it.* Oguri drew a carp the way his teacher drew carp and he drew dragons the way his teacher drew dragons. He treated drawing like calligraphy, a carefully proscribed and ordered, almost ritualistic rendering. The first line starts here and the next line comes in, then this line here, that line there—the same way it's been done for thousands of years.

I wasn't crazy about Horihide's personal style. I respected his work, but all the inventive Western tattooers considered Tokyo's Horiyoshi II the greatest tattooer in the world. Sailor Jerry had a slight connection with him and had a few photos of his work. He was a much more sophisticated artist, more nuanced. He was the one I really was hoping to meet at some point.

We ran into a young *yakuza* one night at this place we used to go, down by the train station, called the Night Kitchen, a late-night eating joint. They had wonderful crab croquettes. We'd knock off about midnight and go have a bite to eat. A young thug came in while we were eating. He spoke to us about having a tattoo done on his back of a *kappa*, a mythical water creature somewhat like a monkey with a turtle shell on its back. He had seen such a tattoo in one of the flamboyant *yakuza* movies that were popular in Japan. In the movies, tattoos were invariably painted on, often by Oguri's friend, Mr. Mori, who worked for the popular Kyoto film studio that produced all the gangster epics. Oguri immediately told the young man it couldn't be done, that it would not be appropriate. In my mind, I could see how the tattoo would work and said so, and even offered to do the tattoo, but Oguri shot me a dark look. After the hood left, Oguri told me in no uncertain terms that the *kappa* was simply not a subject suitable for tattoos. He offered no explanation. He simply said he would not allow the tattoo to be done in his shop.

The next day the young *kobun* (soldier) came into the shop to begin work on an armpiece. He was wearing a bandage around his little finger. He proudly explained that since we had seen him last night, he had to cut off his finger.

He came into the shop almost every day while we finished his tattoo. Every time he came in to have us work on the tattoo, he would show off the stump. He would unroll the tape so we could see where they stitched across the stump with black thread. He was laughing about it, like it was a badge of honor.

We worked fast on many of these tattoos, getting them done within the space of a week, if we could, because a lot of these guys were nomadic. Oguri started tons of work he never finished. These guys would often have to leave town suddenly and move to another city. He would show me countless photos of tons of stuff that was only outlined. "Did you fill that in?" I would ask. "No, he disappeared," Oguri would say.

You had to be careful around these people. Oguri understood, for instance, that he could not put the tiger design on the young soldier who wanted it because his boss wore a clumsy version of the same image and it would not be good for the junior to have a superior tattoo. Oguri told me about one poor tattooist who put a poorly executed tattoo on a boss and had to cut off his thumb and presented it to the *oyabun* at his apartment, rather than lose his life over a bad tattoo. Without his thumb, he could no longer hold the tattoo needles, so he became a house painter, Oguri told me, because he could hold the paint bucket by the wire handle with his four fingers.

I might have had brushes with outlaw kind of people tattooing in the States, biker gangs, some of Zeke's pals in Seattle, but I wasn't hanging out and partying with gangsters. As intriguing and unlikely a sociological experience as it was, I grew tired of it quickly.

I know there were Westerners working in some kind of nefarious activities with those guys, probably with drugs or construction or whatever. One American customer I had put a full arm dragon on at Ichiban shortly before closing, traveled to Japan on some kind of business that he implied was underground. He wore a *haramaki*—knitted bellyband—adapted from armor in the old days. The garment was supposed to keep your belly (*hara*, the seat of all spirit and emotions) warm, but worn by almost all *yakuza* with the practical advantage of holding your guts in if you took a sword there in a fight. But nobody I'd ever encountered had been in on the interior workings like we were. As the men who did their tattoos, these guys treated us like we were a trusted part of their scene. We were in the *yakuza* life.

However, like everything Japanese, that proved to be slippery. Nothing is what it seems. The *yakuza* really came to power in modern Japan after the war when they ran the black market. They were like armies, with generals and lieutenants, very organized, very hierarchical. As incredible as it was to be witnessing these things close-up and personal, it finally dawned on me. If I wanted to hang out with lowlife and dangerous thugs, I didn't need to go halfway around the world where I don't speak the language and I don't really know what the fuck's going on. I was not a bad boy. Cherry bombs in a gas station toilet when I was a kid were one thing, but not anything like this.

It became apparent that it was too difficult all the way around. It was obvious I was never going to be accepted, despite my naïve dreams. My usual hustle and glad-handing that worked for me so well in the States was not cutting it in Japan and my language skills were hopelessly inadequate. I could catch only a small percentage of what people were saying.

I got tired of these guys looking at me like some exotic aquarium species and their constant quizzing about the Mafia, something that I could not care less about, but that we may have tacitly encouraged when we let slip Francesca was Sicilian. They were dialed into the same racist simplifications as many Americans.

Francesca was really a fish out of water. As much as she was interested in the culture, she was shocked at the realities of life in Japan. Japanese women were far behind their American counterparts and Francesca caused a stir with her relationship with the wife of Oguri's apprentice. Between pidgin and sign language, Francesca and the guy's wife became friendly and she may have conveyed some things about the way women live in the U.S. that caused some tension with the apprentice. He was a fully old-fashioned macho Japanese, the-woman-should-walk-five-paces-behind-the-man kind of guy and Francesca had no use for any of that.

It was just a crazy way for us to live. Francesca was out walking one day while I was in the studio and this car full of *yakuza* pulled up. *Beep, beep, beep.* She didn't speak any Japanese, but they communicated with her largely through hand signals. They managed to get across they were looking for me and she took them to the apartment where we were tattooing, but it was clear we needed to make other plans. I was at a low point. Gifu was too small and we weren't fitting in.

Oguri had taken us to some classic tourist spots. We visited Kyoto. We saw some temples. I picked up some great books. We got to see some great deep-in-Japan things, but not to the degree I had hoped. I was still wound up about the classical history, mythology, and philosophy, but this environment was not right. Business was slowing down. It was going to start getting cold. I decided I had enough and it was time to go back to the States and see what I could do there using this experience.

Every fall, like the harvest, the cops would stage a ritualistic crackdown on the mobs. The *yakuza* accommodated the police and many would take their families and go underground or leave for Korea. They would cool out for a couple of months, while the cops "cleaned up." A lot of our work dried up, although I wasn't really sure how much that had to do with not wanting to be tattooed by the *gaijin*. There were vague hints, nothing cut and dried or out front. No white guy had gone and tattooed there, ever. I had seen behind the *shoji* screen.

Before I went over, I left enough money with my mother for a return flight. To save face with Oguri, I told him there were problems with my ex-wife and child back home. When I first asked him if I could come over and work with him, I don't think he ever intended for me to move to Japan and set up shop. We took our leave as gracefully as possible.

When I got back to Southern California that October 1973, I called Zeke about a job working with him in Painless Nell's old place in the penny arcade. I was so happy to be back, I celebrated by having Zeke stick a tattoo on the back of my arm. He had a sheet of flash on the wall with really cool designs he made up for all the different states. They were like those decals you used to collect on the wing window of your car. Zeke put a piece on my arm of the Santa Monica skyline, a palm tree and a ribbon that says "California."

I graduated art school with my lofty ideals and told everybody

I was going to be a tattooer and turn this into an art, but found myself in relatively short order stamping Hot Stuff on sailors in San Diego. Now, once again, after I'd gone broke in Japan, I was back in San Diego, totally spaced out. Two weeks before, I was deep in Japan. Suddenly I'm sitting in the back of the penny arcade with the machines clanging and banging and Outdraw the Marshal bleating all day long "Think you're fast enough?"

But the word got out in the tattoo community: "Ed Hardy's been to Japan."

store were in front on the street and a driveway ran down the side of the building to several parking spaces in the back. A gas station was next door on the corner, and down the block was the Silver Platter, a liquor store and deli. I had a window that looked out on the driveway. A couple of blocks away, guys in bell bottoms and Panamas were picking up girls sipping piña coladas at the world's first fern bar, a joint called Henry Africa's. The seventies were in full swing in San Francisco.

I put out a small sign on the front of the building that said simply ED HARDY—TATTOO ARTIST. Realistic Tattoo Studio opened for business in June 1974.

It was strictly by-appointment-only. There was no neon TATTOO sign outside. The door was locked when I was seeing a client. The walls were not stuffed full of flash. I kept a few books of Japanese woodblocks for people to look over for ideas, but I was never going to tattoo another Hot Stuff again.

I was uneasy about opening a private shop, hidden away where nobody could find it, some appointment-only tattoo speakeasy. We could be screwed. If I put out a big neon sign, I ran the risk of getting inundated again with people walking in off the street wanting the same old thing. I didn't know how this was going to work. It was only one long room, covered in funky carpeting, the walls painted white. A buddy helped me put up a partition. I wanted everything to be real Japanese, so it was a sliding *shoji* screen. I kept my sterilizer and coffeemaker in the back. I covered some of the walls with grass-weave wallpaper and bought wicker furniture at Cost Plus. I painted up and framed about eight back pieces, and hung them on the walls, neatly spaced, more like an art gallery. I had a desk with a book of big, glorious tattoo designs, all Japanese. No flash on the wall. I used essentially the same machines, the same pigment range as other tattooers, although I did do some breakthrough work on blending colors. I always pushed for a more painterly look.

Horihide, the Japanese master I studied with in Gifu, felt that the soul of a tattoo was seriously affected by being drawn on the skin. It was the great tradition of the Asian spirit of the brush, where you really feel the dragon or the carp or whatever you are doing and let that spirit into the drawing. I drew every tattoo free-hand with a toothpick and India ink. I worked on straw *tatami* mats and cushions, sat cross-legged on the floor and really fucked up my back. But I was worshipping at the altar of all things Asian. I would draw elaborate, full-arm pieces, some really intricate dragon design, while they were lying down. They'd stand up and it would be an inch too far down. Wipe it off and do it over. Eventually I realized this was stupid. It was not making the tattoo appreciably different or more soulful. I should go ahead and make a transfer image for it. Francesca, highly qualified, easily found work as a temporary legal secretary. When she wasn't working for some lawyer, she would work as my receptionist at a desk in the studio. We rented a nice flat on the cable car line on California Street in nearby Polk Gulch. We had to pass muster with a suspicious Chinese landlady and bring eight-year-old Doug over to her St. Francis Woods house to be inspected. Doug was one of the few non-Chinese students enrolled in Commodore Stockton grade school in Chinatown. He'd ride the cable car running in front of our apartment with Francesca in the morning when she continued down to the financial district, and return home in the afternoon as a latchkey kid.

The first person I tattooed was a guy who called himself Captain Colourz. He was an artist and complete acid head, nice guy. Thom deVita gave me his number and I looked him up. He was very much a part of the psychedelic scene, close with Hot Tuna and had painted a noted mural in some local nightclub. He had tattoos and loved Asian exoticism. Some of his work was from Lyle Tuttle. At a party, Lyle had signed his name on Colourz's wrist without asking him. Tuttle has a very registered, stylized signature with stars on each end. They were probably all higher than kites. Colourz asked me if I could cover it up. My first tattoo in San Francisco was covering up Lyle Tuttle's signature. I saw that as talismanic.

Everybody knew Lyle Tuttle was the San Francisco tattoo man. He was full of blarney and had a way with the press. He put a little heart on Janis Joplin and she talked about it on *The Dick Cavett Show*. I could tattoo rings around him. I was twenty-eight years old and ready to cut everyone in the business a new one, but especially Lyle Tuttle. I had been primed by Sailor Jerry to hate the guy. Sailor Jerry poured an unending stream of vitriol on Tuttle. He hated all tattooists who talked to the press, but he reserved special disgust for Tuttle. He also hated Bert Grimm, who was Lyle Tuttle's mentor. Jerry was a great one to carry a feud, deserving or not. That is the way of the tattoo world. I first met Lyle when I was eleven years old, hanging out in Bert Grimm's place on the Pike. Lyle's prices were maybe the highest in the country. I met the wife of an artist friend, who, when she found out I was going to open a tattoo shop, told me she had a tattoo—real unusual at the time to meet people with tattoos—of a bumblebee that Lyle put on her. I asked her how much it cost. Fifty dollars, she told me. In San Diego, it wouldn't have been more than fifteen dollars. He was one of the best-known tattoo artists in the country and his work was pedestrian. I knew he was a great raconteur. I respected that he had collected an enormous archive of antique tattoo material. He had what he called his tattoo museum on display in his shop, next to the work area. Although I couldn't admit it to myself, I was envious.

So when I opened the shop by covering Lyle's name on Captain Colourz, it was like, all right, now we're going to rock and roll.

Right away, I started doing my back pieces. The tattoo world was small. Word got around. People began to fly in for four or five days. I'd do their whole back like a jigsaw puzzle. You can't do it like a painting—lay in all the dark areas and come back the next day to color in everything. You don't want to go back over all that tender tissue. I developed this approach, which was pioneered by Sailor Jerry. He only did a few of these signature big, developed pieces. He wanted to push the form, but he was mainly stuck in Sailortown. What you do is split a back in four or five parts and do them as sections. I tattooed really fast, so I could get a lot of work done in three hours.

I knew San Francisco had a wide swath of alternative consciousness people. Even if they looked square, they were after something different. I built a large gay clientele right from the start. Gay guys, many in the closet, came to me for big tattoos. The options open to them at other tattoo shops were only the standard designs. In San Francisco, there were all kinds. One kid about eighteen years old came in off the street for his first tattoo. He always thought it would be cool to have a big lobster on his back, he told me. He wasn't talking about a nature portrait, either, but something off a big red seafood restaurant sign. The guy even drew a picture of what he wanted it to look like. I actually went out and got a plastic lobster to draw the thing from.

People were coming in and laying on me a whole arm, their legs, their back. I dove into epic tattoos. That was what I always wanted to do. I was living the life I imagined as a boy. I was doing every day in my shop something only I had thought possible. I printed up my first business cards. WEAR YOUR DREAMS, they said.

Frank Robertson was an old friend and surfer I knew in high school who moved up to San Francisco. We hung out some in my Art Institute days. Frank had become a writer and musician. He was in a band with another friend of mine from the Art Institute, ceramicist Ron Nagle. Frank had gotten married and his wife, Mary, worked at *Rolling Stone* magazine. I contacted Frank to tell him I was back in San Francisco after being in Japan and that I had opened a tattoo studio. He told me he was working for Francis Ford Coppola, who had started a bi-weekly arts and culture magazine in San Francisco called *City*. Frank worked up an article, and came over with a photographer to take shots of me holding a machine sitting on the floor at my Japanese-style setup.

About the same time, a soft-spoken gentleman with a trace of a Southern accent rang my bell while I was actually doing a tattoo and introduced himself as Armistead Maupin, a reporter for a Marin County weekly, *Pacific Sun*. He was also interested in writing an article; he didn't start writing his series, *Tales of the City,* for the weekly until later that year. I was putting an arm piece on somebody I knew through surfer friends. Archie was a free-spirit, part of an industrious consortium of Southern California psychedelic warrior/businessmen, and he had a little *om* on his hand that he got in India. Armistead interviewed both of us. The two articles appeared in September and my phone started to ring, even if the *City* magazine article printed the wrong number.

By fall, everything was rolling. I was doing a lot of big and unusual tattoos. Dennis Cockell came over from England in October. He was a real hip, live-wire British tattooer with a thick accent. We visited for less than fifteen minutes when he told me he wanted to get going on a tattoo. I knew he wanted a souvenir, and assumed it would be a small piece. "I've saved me whole torso for you," he said. "I want the dragons, Ed." He wanted three dragons on the back and two dragons on the front, an interlocking design that made me race home to the drawing table. We started the next day, freehanded it all on, and it took weeks to tattoo. He would lie there for marathon sessions on the *tatami* mat, stoned out of his brain on Percodan, listening to music at full volume on headphones and every so often breaking into song, singing along at the top of his voice to the Rolling Stones or whatever he was listening to. I worked on that tattoo through November, when he took a sidetrip to Hawaii to make the pilgrimage to Sailor Jerry's shop and hang out with Malone, and we finished it in December. This was the first epic and totally spontaneous piece I put on. It really extended my capabilities and Dennis became a lifelong friend.

We drove over to meet Pinky Yun, the great Hong Kong tattooist who had opened a shop in Alameda, a small island on the other side of the Bay Bridge, next to a huge naval base. In the back of my mind, I carried a whisper of Jerry's great fear that if the Orientals ever got into the trade, we'd all be finished. Jerry felt we couldn't match their entrepreneurial skills, work ethic, esthetic reach, or vision. Pinky was one of the most famous people throughout the tattoo world. He ruled over an empire at his shop above the

Neptune Bar in Wan Chai, the Sailortown of Hong Kong. He always wanted to come to the States and made the move when he discovered there were no tattoos shops in Alameda. He greeted me like an old friend. He knew my work and admired it extravagantly. He couldn't have been more friendly and welcoming.

Also at Pinky's shop that day, I met Chuck Eldridge, who would become one of the great tattoo historians and a close personal associate. He had just gotten out of the navy and was already peppered with tattoos. Chuck is the only guy I've ever met who has a lot of tattoos and not one is a cover piece. He kept every tattoo. He did Westpacs on the *Oriskany*. He would take acid and watch the jets land. He had worked in circuses and carnivals. An old-time music fan from North Carolina, he used to race dirt bikes in Texas, and then became a dedicated bicycle enthusiast. He was working with Gary Potts, another crazy guy who was building bicycles he rode up and down Mount Tam that would soon sweep the world as mountain bikes. Chuck asked for my card and told me to expect a visit. When he did come over, I finished his arms, a quasi-Japanese background of flowers, leaves, waves, and lightning, threading everything together with what was already there. We chipped away at that for about a year, while he was working at the bicycle store with Gary Potts. Tattoos and cool bikes were both still underground.

I started tattooing people that I could relate to more than swabbies or soldiers, which is what I wanted to happen. When these people would show off the tattoo, their friends would be astonished at what they saw. Nobody had seen tattoos like what I was doing.

In December, Peter Coyote came in. He was a budding actor who had been one of the Diggers, kingpin hippies from the Haight-Ashbury scene. He had seen the *City* magazine thing and got a coyote head in the middle of his chest. He referred a guy to me who wanted a Tibetan *vajra*. Crossed *vajras* on the middle of his chest—Buddhist imagery: right up my alley. This gentleman arrived to get the tattoo wearing his colors. He was Sweet William, secretary of the Frisco chapter of the Hells Angels, a poet, and a close associate of the Grateful Dead, not any ordinary motorcycle club thug.

He only had one leg, lost the other in a motorcycle crash. I told him my story—that I had been working all my life toward opening this shop and was dedicating myself to one-of-a-kind artworks. There was no flash on the walls, no ready-made little devils in sailors' caps. I showed him my photo albums with some of the big, Japanese-style things I'd done in San Diego. I had some design books I painted with different ideas. "No offense to you or your brothers," I told him. "I am into Tibetan Buddhism. I'm happy to tattoo you, but, please, if any of your brothers come in, it's got to be something different. I'm not going to do death-head skulls for them." He understood and started sending some of the brothers my way. Every so often one of them would come in and say, "I want the Death's Head" and I would tell him to talk to Sweet William, but a lot of my best customers when I first opened were Hells Angels.

That was how it started growing. Word got around that there was this hipster in town doing tattoos. That's how Jorma Kaukonen, of the Jefferson Airplane and Hot Tuna, found me. He and his first wife, Margareta, already had some work done by Lyle Tuttle, but they came looking for me as soon as they heard about me. They were a fun-loving couple with a great sense of humor, but they could get revved up. She was a large Swedish woman and would beat up Jorma when they fought. I partied with them a little bit at their big house in exclusive St. Francis Wood. I did big, Japanese-style back pieces on both of them. I was very proud of the one I did on Margareta. It was a giant Japanese witch with catlike features, flying through the air. She wanted the witch carrying a cut-off head with Jorma's face. I wasn't sure that was such a great idea, so I did a generic Japanese face with the cut-off head trailing blood. She could really sit well—we did it in a few long sessions. That piece went down to her butt and thigh.

Jorma's was a tough one. I didn't know what to do on him and he wasn't much help. "Just make it far out, man," he told me.

I don't like to work that way. I always felt that since these people were going to be wearing it forever, I would really rather tailor something specific for them. Jorma kept saying he wanted me to do whatever I thought would be good. I did Margareta's piece first. I went home and feverishly listened to Hot Tuna records to get some inspiration, as I was not into the psychedelic bands like the Airplane or the Dead. I liked Steve Miller a lot, but he played the blues. I knew the Airplane's hit records like "White Rabbit" from the radio, but I didn't follow his music. I needed to get some kind of clue who this guy was. I absorbed his guitar solos and came up with a crazed skeleton wearing a fluffy, animal-hair vest, playing sort of a futuristic-looking guitar that wasn't really a guitar, and surrounded by a dragon. I had seen a picture of Jorma with a furry vest. It was an okay tattoo, but I always felt it could have been better with some input from him.

For most of the big stuff, I did a prep drawing, usually dye transfer rice-paper prints that I could position where the tattoo was going to go. Customarily, I would tattoo for a couple of hours at a time, maybe three hours. Sometimes, if they wanted to get it done, I'd go longer. With people who lived in town, you could get the whole thing outlined, and a week later, you could start doing some color, section by section. Some I would build up like a painting, where you do all the dark, shade it in, over a period of weeks, sometimes months. Within a few months, I couldn't hold a consulting appointment with someone and schedule the tattoo for the next day. It quickly started getting to where it would be three weeks or more before I could start the tattoo. If someone was having a big tattoo, I would book sessions every week for three or four weeks. I could do small tattoos in a single sitting, but mostly I was doing those big, full-scale epic deals.

Many of my customers were tattooers like Cockell. I started getting tattooers coming to see me in San Diego after I first returned from Japan, but word continued to spread. Tattooers always wanted unique stuff. Doc Forest came over from Sweden and got some big Norse mythology on his leg. People kept coming in with their own ideas. Wear your dreams, right?

More women were beginning to get tattoos. A lot of the early women's tattoos were small things, exotic birds. I loved to draw fantasy birds, not so much phoenixes or identifiable things, but crazy creatures I imagined with swoopy tails and bright feathers. I did tons of those, often really small. They weren't all large, epic tattoos; there were many tiny flowers or dragons. I got into the miniatures—a dragon, two inches long, all detailed out. The challenge was trying to do something different. I would offer design source books, not flash. If you wanted a butterfly, I would give you a Chinese book of a thousand butterflies.

I worked six days a week at Realistic. By the end of the year, I was busy. I was getting people from around San Francisco and I was getting guys with the means and capabilities to travel and get tattoos. They were telling their friends. Other tattooers sent people to me. I was building clientele. The whole thing grew. More people wanted more and bigger tattoos. Francesca kept working so we could count on a steady paycheck, which was good. Rent was cheap on that place, but tattooing is a very up-and-down business. Lyle Tuttle has a coat of arms tattooed on his sternum with a rooster bearing the Latin inscription for "chicken today, feathers tomorrow."

But interest in the epic tattoos continued to escalate. People would get some work done and come back for more, like Archie, who was only having an armpiece done when Armistead Maupin watched him be tattooed for that article the first month we were open; he ended up getting a big Japanese deity on his back. The bar slowly, gradually, started going up for the volume and intricacy of tattoos that people were getting.

In the early days at Realistic, a woman came in and got a really cool leaping Japanese rooster I drew from a print. She was a highly accomplished graphic designer and came back, talking about wanting to get a bigger tattoo. She was looking through my books—I kept a lot of source books of Japanese prints at the shop. She found something in a small book of Hokusai prints of ghosts and demons. It went across two pages. On one page, a real weird-looking witch is blowing out a stream of what looks like little black specks. On the other side is a samurai, reared back in revulsion. It is a stream of rats—the black specks grow bigger as they go across—and they're draped all over him with their tails dripping down. She came back a couple of times and kept saying she thought it would make a great tattoo.

I was never one to push, but I told her, if you like it, I am the guy who can do it. "Where are you thinking about?" I asked. "It would be perfect across your shoulders."

"I was thinking about right across here," she said, placing her hands on her loins. Both thighs. Big, tall, shapely woman. It was a hell of a tattoo. She had a great sense of humor and soon became the live-in girlfriend of underground comic artist S. Clay Wilson, the guy who drew the ground-breaking underground comic, *The Checkered Demon*. He drew some of the most gory, smutty comics you could imagine. I got to know him a little through mutual friends. He was one of those guys—great, crazy internal life; incredible, crazed art—who could not conceive of getting a tattoo. Her tattoo bothered him. "Wilson has a hard time with it," she told me.

There was a doctor from Southern California in the early days at Realistic who wanted me to put a giant squid on him. He had seen me in San Diego before I went to Japan and had a few tattoos on him. At the time, it was the biggest single-image tattoo in the world. The tentacles went over his shoulders and ended at short-sleeve length, in case he had to scrub up for surgery. I had the squid spitting ink on his chest to cover up a big, dopey tattoo he had there. The really long tentacles went down his legs and ended with these pod things on his feet. The eight shorter ones all wrapped around. We worked on that for quite a while. He would come up from Los Angeles. It wasn't earthshaking art, but it was highly unusual illustration in the medium of tattoo. There was no background other than a few sweeping waves. It was like a giant squid had crawled on his back.

Another one of my more unusual early commissions came from a gentleman who owned a bank and other businesses in St. Louis named Charlie Lazier. He loved anything that moved fast. He was into motorcycles, cars, custom bicycles, everything. He especially loved hot-air balloons. He broke a record once for crossing the English Channel in a hot-air balloon. He was probably about sixty years old when I started working on him. He already had quite a few tattoos and was referred to me by Paul Rogers, one of my "uncles" in the tattoo business, who lived in Jacksonville, Florida.

This guy brought me the menu from the Concorde. He did a lot of business in Europe and always flew the Concorde. On the menu, they had a hand-colored engraving of the first manned flight of the Montgolfier Brothers in 1783. The balloon was tethered in a courtyard. I copied it, put it up in the sky, flying at an angle over his back, which I covered in clouds. I showed one of the Montgolfier Brothers in his powdered wig in the basket looking down, and buried a pinup nudie that had been on his back under the landscape, turning her curves into anthropomorphic forested hills, a trope you see in some early Renaissance paintings. He came out from St. Louis and we knocked it out in five days. I did the whole blue balloon in one day, which was quite a piece of tattooing, and went back and did the sky and ornate basket the next day. People pick these tattoos, especially the big ones, to sum up who they are. *This is who I am,* the tattoo says, *what I really care about or what I think of myself as.*

There was another fellow, Forbes, who was originally from London and lived in San Francisco, who I did a couple of arm pieces on first. He was an artist who did these extreme, crazy, cool figurative paintings, a gay man with a thing for Japanese guys. He always had some Japanese boyfriend, various happily married men, so to speak, who would come over on business. He wanted sumo wrestlers in waves. They were taken from traditional prints, and the holds that they would have been grappling, but it was like these totally beefy boys with all these crashing waves around them were having sex all around his upper arms. He always spoke about wanting to go to Japan and, I thought, this will give them a jolt when they see it.

Eventually he decided to go for a back piece and painted the watercolor for it himself. It was a Buddhist priest on a lotus throne in the midst of crashing waves, cherry blossoms at the top of his back and falling through the sky. He had the priest committing *seppuku,* cutting his belly open, and at the same time, having an orgasm. He drew the hard-on and the ejaculation. Off to one side of the priest's head floated a black orb, surrounded by a corona of energy. It was supposed to represent the next state, nirvana or whatever. We didn't do his ass. We did it down to the beltline and then we had the water and blood drain down to where his cheeks started. I called it "Coming and Going."

We lived for two years at the flat on California Street. My mother came up to visit us. She accepted the fact that I was tattooing, but she didn't love it. When I was a kid, she put up with it—"It's a phase Donnie's going through." I knew better. I told people it wasn't a phase. I don't know how I knew that at that age, but I did. She was always so proud of my art and was thrilled that I was going to go to Yale. When I decided to become a tattooer, she was not thrilled. When we stayed with her on our return from Japan, I was laying in the sun on the lounge chair in the backyard patio with my shirt off. She could see for the first time all the work I had done on my arms and chest. "Oh, Donnie," she said, "you've got all those tattoos. I bet you have those things all over."

"You're never going to find out," I said. That was final. We were not going to talk about it.

She continued to support us emotionally. She would visit us until her stroke. I was on the phone with her when it happened. It was like something came unplugged when we were in the middle of a conversation. The next day we found out that she had been hospitalized. She had graduated from shitty factory jobs making half what men did to a career with the post office in our hometown. She had good government medical insurance. She was co-matose for some time. For a few months, we went down and stayed for periods of time, and I would come back to San Francisco to work. Her doctor despised me, thought I was trash. You could tell by the way she talked to me and looked at me. Francesca was too dark to fit into the conventional Southern California role model, either. The doc said little to us other than something along the lines of "We're doing all we can." Eventually, a younger doctor, about my age, took me aside and told me I didn't have to leave my mother in ICU. It was obvious she was not going to recover. He told me I could take her home, that he could supply me with enough morphine to keep her comfortable, and that she could die with dignity. Of course, her primary physician was furious, but that is what we did. We checked her out, put her in the ambulance, and took her home. I called all her friends I could locate within driving distance, and they were able to say good-bye. We hired a night nurse so we could get some sleep. During the day, the sun was shining. She was in her bedroom, with music playing on the radio. Friends came in to see her. After less than a week, she just slipped away.

She would have been sixty-five and was planning to retire. She had already, several years earlier, taken care of business, and put me on the deed as co-owner of the house. So my mom died. We inherited a paid-off house and a 1972 Chevy Nova with a V-8 engine. We drove back to San Francisco with the Nova. We sold the house in Corona del Mar and, with the proceeds, bought a big, old house on Clayton Street in the Ashbury Heights. I was partying heavy and developing an interest in cocaine, but Fran, who was still working secretarial jobs, insisted we buy a house with the money. Left to my own devices, I probably would have pissed it away.

So we had a house with reasonable payments. Doug was in school. Fran was working, I was tattooing people. It was a new era.

13.

Reno

The Reno tattoo convention in January 1977 was the first good look we got at how rapidly the tattoo movement was expanding. There had been a small meeting the year before in Houston where about fifty people showed up, but Tattoo '77 at the Holiday Inn was shaping up to be an entirely different matter right from the start.

The International Tattoo Artists Association started in Europe, with a lot of English members as well as people from around Europe. Once they connected with National Tattoo Supply in Long Island, they cooked up this convention. They were the same people who had circulated the mimeographed newsletters that discovered me in San Diego when I was still working for Doc Webb. We heard about it and knew people would be coming from all over the world, so Mike Malone and I decided to attend and make our presence known.

We reserved a booth in the name of Chuck Eldridge. Nobody in the tattoo world knew him. Malone and I flashed out the booth to look like a classic American tattoo parlor. We built a special dummy rail with a front on it that I painted with a snake twined around the word "Tattoo," its letters made of branches. On the top rail, we glassed-in a bunch of "hell money," which the Chinese burn at funerals. Sailor Jerry was fond of the stuff. We had a bunch of bogus bills and fake coins, playing off the luck thing, Reno the gambling town, divorce capital of the world, all that stuff. I stayed in character the whole convention, wearing a green celluloid eyeshade. Every time I was on the convention floor, whenever I walked into the hotel, even if I wasn't in my booth, I wore the eyeshade. Mike and I painted up some special convention flash. There was a tattooed cobra rising over a pile of money. Gambling images are always good tattoo material—hands of cards, pairs of dice, race horses—and we played that up. The three-day event was a smash. More than two hundred tattooers showed up. People came from all Europe. Tattoo Ole from Denmark had a shop on the harbor in Copenhagen that had been in the same spot for more than a hundred years. George Bone came from London. A lot of the people came through San Francisco first and stopped off at Realistic.

What Sailor Jerry, Malone, and I had done had really hit the tattoo world. I had been tattooing professionally for ten years. The tattoo world was small. They knew about me. They traded photographs of the Japanese-style work I was doing at Realistic. We put quite a buzz through the convention floor simply being there. And we were slammed at the booth, putting on tattoos right and left.

Tattooing was still illegal in New York City, Oklahoma, Indiana, Massachusetts, and several other states. In Florida, it was only allowed with a physician on the premises. The convention barred piercing, although it caused a stink at the time, because it raised the sinister specter of S&M at a time when we were trying to gain a little respectability for tattoos. Most of us pushing to expand the work didn't buy the argument that piercing and tattooing were on the same level. They both took place on the body, skin, but in very different ways. This was the coming-out party for new tattoo. It wasn't a wild party, although there was plenty of drinking and people going off to their rooms to smoke weed or engage in various sexual liaisons, licit and illicit. People dressed up. One guy from Long Island brought a bevy of beauties he had done extensive Asian work on and had them tricked out in filmy, sequined gowns. Tattoos were no longer only for sailors. Malone and I were surprised at all the one-of-a-kind Japanese work we saw. We had no idea how much of that was going on. A lot of people were wearing masterpieces they wanted to show off. They held a tattoo contest and people paraded up and down a runway. Judges voted and they handed out little plaques. I won "Tattooer of the Year."

There was a lot of media coverage, way beyond the front-page article that ran in the Reno paper. Many photographs were taken. Photographers came from the *San Francisco Chronicle*, *Parade* magazine, all over. My picture appeared in *Time* magazine. *Playboy* ran a photo of me in my green eyeshade putting a colorful fantasy bird on the ample breasts of a good-looking young Asian-American woman.

Our friend Emiko Omori showed up with a documentary film crew. Emiko first came to me at Realistic shortly after it opened, having read the Armistead Maupin column. She and her partner got small dragon tattoos and she started shooting film of the process almost from the start.

But the most important thing for me that weekend was meeting these guys from East Los Angeles, Good Time Charlie Cartwright and Jack Rudy. They walked in with a whole squad of people and the first really new tattoo style that any of us had seen. They were doing these exquisite single-needle, fine-line monochromatic tattoos, the sort of work you couldn't find outside prisons. A lot of photorealism, fancy lettering that came from gang writing, a more naturalistic image bank. The whole thing was drawn largely from Chicano street culture.

Charlie was born in 1940 and came out of Kansas. His father was a fundamentalist preacher and he grew up with a hard-core fundamentalist Christian grounding he never lost. He married a Chicana and immersed himself in Latino culture. He tattooed in his car, drawing designs in ballpoint pen on the moleskin headliner. He put the tattoos on in the backseat of the Chevy.

He and his brother bumped into Zeke Owen in a tattoo shop on Main Street in downtown Los Angeles, when Zeke was doing a guest spot at the shop where he had learned to tattoo in the mid-fifties. Zeke and Charlie started talking and Zeke told Charlie to take the machine and put a tattoo on his brother. Zeke watched. "You can do this," he told Charlie, and sent him down to the Pike to find a job with the same guys who owned the Main Street shop.

When Charlie and Jack met, Jack Rudy was fresh out of the Marines and was obsessed with "jailhouse" style tattooing. He was raised in a Mexican-American home—his adopted father was Chicano and Jack grew up in Chicano life. He knew how to gangster write. He could really draw and loved that highly detailed style of drawing.

Instead of doing sweep things with something more akin to a brush, an assembly of needles, they developed the intricate style of dot shading. For this, you use a single needle—it was like pointillism. They'd build up tones in the skin, dot after dot after dot. Insane amounts of time went into some of these tattoos.

People in prison have nothing but time on their hands, and tattoos have always been a big part of prison life. As with the military, prisoners have minimal opportunities for personal expression and tattoos were a way of individuating yourself. A tattoo also said you can lock me up, but you can't control what I put on my body. Tattooing in prison was always forbidden, but that simply made it more desirable. They couldn't take it away from you.

Cons would jerry-rig tattoo machines from all kinds of things. I heard about guys who swiped the windshield-wiping mechanism from the warden's car. There can be a certain drama attached to prison tattoos—tears coming out of the eye, etc. One ex-con showed me his tattoo. "That was put on with Bible ashes," he said. Prison tattoos cross all cultures. The Russian gulag tattooing only came to light about twenty years ago when drawings made by some warden, careful, exact renderings of the sophisticated, complex iconography and sentiments, came to light.

Jack and Charlie opened a shop together carefully located in a neutral zone between warring gang territories on Whittier Boulevard in East Los Angeles, Good Time Charlie's. Some of the flash was classic street-shop stuff that Charlie had painted up when he first started, but most of it was black and gray, very Chicano-centric. Big sheets of lettering samples in various Old English faces, big, block *Ben Hur* letters, and florid, almost delicate gangster writing. A lot of their customers were big on getting names; the name of their gang, the name of their neighborhood, a dead relative or friend. They painted up stuff from Mexican restaurant calendars, heroic Aztec warriors rescuing maidens and all that.

Shortly after Reno, I made my way down to their shop. Those guys put an electric charge through me that weekend and I wasn't the only one. I flew down to Los Angeles to meet up with Bob Roberts and go out to Good Time Charlie's with him. I had only recently met Bob when he came up to Realistic to have me do some work on him. He was a real interesting guy—a skilled keyboardist who played saxophone in a doo-wop band called Ruben and the Jets, who were produced by Frank Zappa. He was a hell of a painter, and knew art history. Initially, Bob learned to tattoo from Colonel Bill Todd and Bob Shaw, who, at that time, owned Bert Grimm's shop. Bob Shaw was Bert's nephew, a great street tattooer and raconteur. By the time Roberts and I met, he worked in Hollywood at Sunset Strip Tattoo, which Lyle Tuttle opened but had been purchased by Cliff Raven of Chicago. Raven, an out-of-the-closet gay man, was the only other guy besides me who Phil Sparrow taught to tattoo. He also had an art school background and was focusing on the Japanese-style tattoos at the same time as Jerry, Malone, Don Nolan, and me. Roberts and I became buddies right away and we were both struck dumb at Reno by the barrio tattoos of Good Time Charlie.

Bob got a tattoo from Jack Rudy and Charlie put one on me. I always wanted a skull tattoo. My favorite skull tattoo comes from the nineteenth century, a naked woman bent backward to form a skull. Her breasts are the eyes. I have a photo of some World War I doughboy with it tattooed on his forearm. The same image was used in the Milt Zeis tattoo supplies flyers that I sent away for when I was a little kid. I loved it. I thought that was as bad, albeit corny, as it gets—a naked woman who's also a skull. Sex and death. There are certain tattoos that are the high-water mark. It can't get any better. It can't get more succinct, any more of a big Zen slug to the side of the head. You see an image like that and you go, "Of course, I want to wear that on my body." I painted it up on one of my first sheets of flash, before I went to Vancouver.

My first wife asked me not to get a skull tattoo. Francesca had a pretty good sense of humor about most of my tattoos. She already had to see my ex-wife's name in two different languages tattooed on my arm (although I eventually had them covered). I didn't get the naked woman skull, but I got a nice skull from Charlie—my first single-needle tattoo, something entirely different.

We were smitten with this style of tattoo, like anybody who has ever been pole-axed by art. When you're so drawn to art, to making pictures and looking at art, it's really all you want to think about, besides maybe sex and feeding yourself. To us, this was like a beacon from Mars. It was like, *bang,* and you suddenly see everything differently, your whole perception of what art can look like is changed in an instant. That's how it was for us to see this Chicano art. It was not something either Bob or I had been conversant with; we had only been exposed to it peripherally growing up around Los Angeles. We knew the *pachuco* style, and thought it was cool, a real hipster thing.

I was gone with this. I'd been so deep into the Japanese thing, and this was like stepping into a new world I never knew existed. I wanted nothing more than to try to learn how to do this. I thought I'd like to paint up these designs, see if I could put some of these tattoos on people. I started to think about opening a shop in San Francisco to do that. If you want to do a certain style of tattooing, you have to find people willing to get it. It is not like you see some guy painting with oils and you can decide to go to the store and buy some oil paints and canvas. That is one of the complicated parts of the tools that we use. It's a matter of getting the attention of people who might get this kind of stuff.

Bob Roberts moved to San Francisco and went to work with me at Realistic. We continued to talk about the prospects of opening a place to do this kind of work. I decided to take the plunge.

14.

Tattoo City

I knew I wouldn't get people walking in out of the blue to get these *cholo* tattoos in my private, appointment-only tattoo studio on Van Ness Avenue. I figured the shop needed to be in some highly urban, heavily Latin neighborhood and that meant the Mission District to me. It seemed like the San Francisco version of East L.A. I didn't know that it wasn't.

I rented a vacant store beneath a flophouse hotel in the heart of the Mission District at Twenty-fifth and Mission, a block from the BART station. It was a nice, deep place with large display windows on the sidewalk. We painted the front room black and built a closed-off area where we had one work space with some stations, another work space behind that, and a back room that opened to the alley. We stocked the front windows with cactus and succulents that came from a trendy store on Market Street called Red Desert. On the wall in the front window I airbrushed a woman's head with a snake curled through her hair, soaring eagle, and rose. They were all in black, my version of *cholo* style. It was finished off with gangster writing that said TATTOO LOCOS—TOTAL. There was no conscious graffiti tradition developed in San Francisco at that time.

We opened Tattoo City in high style in September 1977. Bob and I had become friendly with Jorma Kaukonen and Jack Casady of Hot Tuna and Bob had been sitting in with those guys on saxophone. They offered to play the opening, practically insisted.

I might have gone to some gig that they'd done, but generally the psychedelic world was not my musical taste. I liked those guys—they were fun—and I didn't want to insult them. I warmed to the idea of Hot Tuna playing the opening.

We did want a big blowout and invited everybody we knew. Even my mother-in-law came out from Long Island. A huge crowd showed up. We set out nice food in the back and the place was overrun. You couldn't hear yourself think with everyone shouting to be heard over the band. God knows how long they played. You could hear the band a block down Mission Street. The cops showed up and told us to quiet things down, which, of course, was impossible.

With Bob and me doing the appointments at Realistic, we needed more people to work at Tattoo City. Chuck Eldridge was eager to learn to tattoo, so we started training him. We also brought in Jamie Sommers, a conceptual artist connected with the Art Institute. Her husband was a teacher there and she was studying for her master's degree. She and her husband, Bob Rasmussen, were intellectual artists who were intrigued with tattoos from the art/ sociology/ culture angle. They were really smart people, the first people like that I'd encountered, who sensed the bigger picture behind my obsession. Francesca and I first met them on our visit to San Francisco before we went to Japan, and they came down to San Diego and each got an intricate tattoo of their own design. I didn't realize at the time it was a forerunner of what my work would soon become. When we returned to the city after Japan, they helped us put together Realistic. Eventually, Jamie wanted to tattoo. She was trying to work tattoos into her artwork, often strange assemblages made out of all sorts of stuff. She wanted to tattoo chicken skins, dry them out, and make them part of these sculptures. I set her up with a machine. I told her that was like toy tattoos, that real tattoos had to be done on a living person. The tattoo wasn't complete until the person wearing it responded and took it out in the world. That is what makes it a tattoo, not just ink and needles.

Bob and I started training Chuck and Jamie, and also brought in a guy nicknamed Horse, who had been corresponding with me from San Quentin Prison, where he was finishing up doing some time for armed robbery. He was a young, white biker from a wealthy district of Los Angeles who'd developed a heroin problem and become a stick-up guy. He sent me some talented drawings and I was so keen about jailhouse tattoos after meeting Charlie Cartwright, I thought I might give him a try after he got out. Bob and I went over to visit him in prison. I had never been through anything like that. After I vouched for him, he was accepted by a halfway house program so he could work a shift at the tattoo shop. He did have a style and did very precise, skillful drawings. The problems developed later, of course.

Throughout my career, I've never really taught people to tattoo. I've helped some get started a little bit, but not much more than to give them the fins and shove them off the dock. Sometimes I'll tell them what to do when they're learning to swim and already in the water, but I've never taken anybody for a formal apprenticeship.

Tattoo City was rolling. Bob and I were tattooing out of both there and Realistic, splitting shifts, working the appointments at Realistic and then going across town, sometimes the same day. I was doing big ongoing back pieces at the private space, and would sometimes make an appointment to work on them in Tattoo City. Chuck was doing fine and Jamie was cultivating unusual images of her own. We had the crew. We were doing the deal.

Not long after Tattoo City opened, I got a call from Jack Rudy. He and Charlie had come up from East L.A. for the opening. We had gotten to be big chums and spent time hanging out, celebrating, working this style, digging tattooing. It was a very heady time, because tattoos were fresh and new, and the things I was getting to do were unprecedented. I had made a success with Realistic. My dream of appointment-only, one-of-a-kind tattoos had come true. Bob was busy. Riding high.

Jack told me Charlie had a religious vision and was giving up tattoos. God spoke to him and told him he could be more effective spreading the gospel. "Charlie's going to quit tattooing. He wants to give up the shop and I don't know what I'm going to do," Jack said.

He was totally dependent on Charlie—he only worked on percentage, and was not a partner. I took it on myself to save this great historic tattoo style these guys created.

Their shop was unusual in East L.A. for a number of reasons. In addition to the tattoo work, the shop itself was housed in a stand-alone building, some ice plant around the front. It was a dangerous neighborhood that didn't look like a slum, but was in the middle of gang territory. There was no phone in the shop because Charlie's attitude was "You can't put tattoos on over the phone." They were open long hours—basically they ran all night and it could get pretty lively when the lowriders were out. A lot of people were full of drugs and booze, and were ready to rumble.

Some of the tattooers were enthusiastic pot smokers. They put an extra-large exhaust fan in the back room and, between customers, would go back and toke up, smoking these big, Uncle Billy briar pipes. I've met people who could tattoo well when they were loaded on weed. I wasn't one. I tried a couple of times and immediately realized that I was paralyzed, tripping on how the machines sounded, my concentration scattered. I don't know how those guys did it, but they did. Who knows where visions come from? But Charlie had this vision and now was ready to move on.

I had some money remaining from the inheritance my mother left me. It seemed like a great idea to buy the shop from Charlie and let Jack run it. Francesca grudgingly went along with it. As in many other instances throughout our long relationship, my heeding her objectivity and common sense could have saved us a lot of grief. But I was full of myself. Owning a shop in East L.A., I could go down there and hang out, soak up the culture, maybe do some tattoos. They had a crew running the place—Jack and three other people.

It didn't take long for things to go sour. Jack was at odds with Lady Blue, who was tattooing at the shop. Charlie had known her from the Pike and she never got along with Jack, who could be stubborn. The way he saw it, she was a troublemaker and didn't fit in the shop. A young guy came in one day, an ex-gang banger from San Gabriel named Freddy Negrete, who worked out of his home using homemade machines. Jack thought he was brilliant. On his recommendation, I agreed to him firing Blue and hiring Freddy. She immediately went back to Captain Jim's, where she had worked on the Pike, and told him that I'd bought the place, how busy it was, and that Jack didn't know what he was doing. Jim did some quick research—which I could have easily done before I bought the business—and found out there was not even a lease on it, only month-to-month rent. He bought the building.

Two weeks after she was given the heave-ho, Lady Blue walked back in the shop with the title to the real estate and gave us until the end of the month to get out.

Rather than fold my tent and flee, I decided to stand and fight. With what little savings we had left, I bought a building two blocks down the street. It was a large paved lot with a small building in what they called Hansel-and-Gretel-style architecture that had most recently been a used-car lot. It had been built in the twenties as a real estate office during the Southern California land boom when they were practically giving away land. An old Spanish-style fountain sat in the front. The car dealers put up wires across the lot with spinners hanging from the wires and large outdoor lights. But the auto dealership moved and the place was for sale for only $25,000 because it was such a bad neighborhood.

We got a bank loan and bought the property. Chuck Eldridge, who was handy with building skills, came down to help with the remodel, along with his North Carolina friend Psychedelic (or Psycho) Joe, an ex-roadie for several Southern bands. Jack didn't show up once during the construction. We built a tattoo shop in the little building with four stations, plumbed sinks, the whole bit. In a nod to that Southern California landmark, Disneyland, I decided to call the place Tattooland, and had a giant banner painted that hung across the entrance to the lot.

I was starting to find out the hard way that being smitten with different tattoo art styles was one thing, but the people and scenes they're part of may not be so tidy or enticing. In the case of this art style, it was largely supported by gang culture. It was like being in Japan, hanging out with the *yakuza*. It was colorful and exciting, as long as you didn't get your throat cut. It slowly dawns on you that you are in the middle of violence. There were shootings. There were stabbings. Angel dust was the drug of choice for the neighborhood. All kinds of gang stuff was going on. The later at night, the more likely it was to happen.

One of the first hints came when I showed Freddy Negrete around the new location for the first time. He was a charismatic, good-looking young guy who could really tattoo. He had credibility with people because he was from a certain gang, although not right in that area, and he brought a lot of those people into the shop. But I could tell he was nervous when I first showed him the setup. It was a tiny space. The sinks were at the back and the tattooers faced the street. "Do you have to have those set up like that?" he asked.

The little building was no more than fifteen feet wide and we had three stations going across and a little toilet on the other side in the back room. There was a Dumpster behind the building, and a chain-link fence at the alley. I didn't understand his problem. He finally confessed. "There are people with grudges against me," he said. "I'm afraid if I'm sitting there, they could just drive up in the alley and blow me away right through the wall."

I told him there was not going to be any metal plate installed in the back of the building or anything like that, so he would simply have to deal with the situation, but I started to wonder what I'd gotten myself into.

The last night at Good Time Charlie's, of course, there was an incident. Since it was the final night, we were all there and people were coming in for tattoos. It got later and later, they often worked until dawn. Between the pot and a general laid-back attitude, they took their time. Jack was the worst—a very decent person, but that guy would make you wait and wait.

That night was the end of a brief era, but nobody was bummed out. We were building the new place. In two weeks, we would be open for business down the street. In the middle of the night, some gang bangers came in, and we closed the door. That was it. We were closed. These would be the last guys to get tattooed in the original GTC location.

Around three o'clock in the morning, I heard yelling outside. There was a guy with a finished tattoo out front, and some guys from another gang who heard we were closing and came around to get some work. The guy who already had his took it on himself to send them away. "Hey fuckers," he said. "They're done."

That set off a chilling cacophony. These rival gang bangers sounded like animals yelping. "What the fuck's going on?" I asked.

"Oh, shit, man," said Jack. "They're calling out their gang, making their presence known."

Somebody pulled a knife and somebody else got his throat cut in front of the shop. All hell broke loose. There was no phone in the place. Somebody ran for a phone booth and called the cops. The ambulance came to take the poor guy away.

When we realized that the cops were going to be descending on the place, Freddy suddenly got real nervous. "Shit, I've got a piece on me and some weed," he said.

A sober realization swept through me. I have a young son. I'm a San Francisco property owner. I have commitments. I've got a nice wife who has been putting up with all this shit. And here I am in the middle of the ghetto, blood on the sidewalk. It's turning very dark.

The cops came and they didn't search the place. They didn't find the weapon. They didn't find the weed. Outside on the sidewalk, there was a spray of blood in front of the shop. RIP Good Time Charlie's.

We opened Tattooland a couple of weeks later. I was so taken with the style of tattooing that when we first met these characters, in the old shop, I got Jack Rudy to do a large photo-realist portrait of Francesca on my leg. Francesca was spooked about the tattoo. We all know it can get dicey putting your loved one's name on you, and some people had the superstition that it doomed the relationship. But I was so taken with the portrait tattoos that were a staple of the work at G.T.C.'s—a tattoo style I'd never really seen—that I couldn't resist. I told Francesca that if we split up, I'd just get it covered with the world's biggest panther head.

The tattoo of her face took forever. The single needle tattoo, all dot shaded, required a lot of time. We did the outline in one sitting that lasted many hours. It took at least two more sessions to fill it in. Jack is a great storyteller and he loves to talk, but whenever he opened his mouth, his foot came off the switch. It was like the joke about Gerald Ford chewing gum and walking. He couldn't talk and tattoo at the same time. After going through this, I assured him that virtually identical graphic effects could be accomplished with a shader needle assembly—and eventually he expanded his repertoire and became, along with Freddy, the premier pioneers of black and gray style.

Once we were settled in Tattooland, Freddy put a sleeping lady's face on my arm and wrote *"Mi vida es un sueno"* (my life is a dream) underneath. I thought it was a great romantic, melodramatic phrase, which came to the tattoo world from a popular Latin song. For me, it also evoked the great Goya etching *The Sleep of Reason Produces Monsters*.

Freddy also put the hawk on my neck on September 10, 1978. I remember because the date was almost consecutive numbers: 9-10-78. On my first trip to visit Good Time Charlie's, I had seen guys in that neighborhood walking around with tattoos on their necks. I thought that was the craziest thing I had seen, a tattoo on the neck. At that time, people rarely even had tattoos on their hands. Almost every shop would refuse to tattoo people anywhere that was visible, and it was against the licensing regulations in a lot of cities. I was in love with the whole dark romance of these tattoos, the poetics, the phrases, and the beautiful, delicate script and calligraphy. Seeing these guys with these huge tattoos on their necks just inflamed the macho, testosterone-crazy appeal. Another permanent souvenir of my dermagraphic cultural tourism.

I flew down once a month, hung out a few days and did some tattoos. Back in San Francisco, I bounced back and forth between two studios. I kept the appointment-only business going at Realistic with Bob Roberts, and was also working out of Tattoo City in the Mission, which I was running with a crew. I was tattooing at Realistic on the summer solstice when the phone rang and it was Horse, from the other shop. "I think you better get over here right now," he said.

"What's going on? I'm putting on a tattoo."

"There was a fire in the building and the shop kind of burned down," he said.

I was in the middle of putting on a tricky design of a Japanese carp underwater in a pond with floating lotuses on a woman's shoulder. I told him I would drive over when I was done. "I've got to finish this tattoo," I said. "The shop's not going to go anywhere."

When I arrived on the scene, the fire was out. The shop didn't burn down, but the damage from both the fire upstairs and the water was extensive. Somebody with a grudge against someone in the flophouse hotel upstairs had poured a five-gallon can of gas under the back door to the building, which opened to our back room. The fire blew up from there. Several people died upstairs, but the luckiest thing of all is that Chuck Eldridge, who had the back room set up as a place to stay, had made a fortunate liaison with a young lady he met that evening and stayed at her place. He would have been killed. It destroyed everything he owned—all his cool bicycles, his collection of tattoo historical material. He served in the navy and was a tidy guy who kept everything shipshape. Mr. TCB, I had no insurance on the place. Nothing. So that was that for Tattoo City.

We lost some flash and tattoo gear. There was a lot of smoke and water damage and some of the flash never lost the smell. We salvaged what we could. The shop had been open less than nine months.

As we were still reeling from this, Bob and I were called downtown by San Francisco police detectives, who wanted to know if anyone had a grudge against us. They said they had a tattoo shop in Daly City, right on the other side of the city line, under surveillance. The owner was suspected of selling explosives and weapons to gangsters who may have been involved in the recent Golden Dragon massacre in Chinatown. In a war between rival gangs, the Joe Boys and the Wah Ching, gunmen opened fire in a crowded restaurant, killing five people and injuring many others. The detectives showed us photos of suspects leaving that tattoo shop. The lead detective was also still investigating the Zodiac killer, a case that had been going on for years. We didn't recognize any of the people in the photos.

I gave up the nutty idea of a street shop in San Francisco. I let everybody go except Jamie Sommers, who was turning out some extraordinary, sophisticated tattoos. She could handle the expectations of Realistic clients and was bringing in her own clientele from the art world. She did high-concept tattoos and eventually started doing psychic readings to determine the right tattoo for the person.

Our paths started to diverge. I understood what she was doing, but sensed a subtle elitism toward those of us tattooing in more traditional genres. She would hold psychic readings with people and thought that was the only way to truly illustrate someone's inner spirit. To me, it was just steering people toward a style of work she wanted to express. Anyway, she developed an avid set of customers and did well. Jamie worked with Bob and me for a couple of years before moving to her own private studio in North Beach, then Marin County, and, eventually New York. She died tragically in a 1983 prosaic accident when, riding her bicycle in SoHo, she hit a pothole and went under the wheels of a garbage truck. I never knew her birth name. She took her moniker from *The Bionic Woman*, a spinoff of the seventies TV show, *The Six Million Dollar Man*.

Realistic was something of a boys' club anyway with me and Bob, who also eventually moved to New York. He had been playing saxophone with the S.F. ska/punk rock band The Offs. In 1981, on a New York tour, Bob fell in love with Pam Brown, a gorgeous young art student who had been Joey Ramone's girlfriend. It was the height of the downtown scene and Bob thrived in it. He kept delaying his return to San Francisco. The final straw came when he didn't show up for an appointment with some guy who had flown in from Oklahoma for the job, and I had to cover for him, and fit in his big job into my already-complicated schedule. I called Bob and told him to not come back to work, and he understood. After that, I was on my own again at Realistic, and Bob and I stayed close friends and sidekicks.

He married Pam, set up a great private studio—Spotlight Tattoo—in their loft in Manhattan, and got involved with the music scene, playing with the New York Dolls and swimming in all that downtown energy. He tattooed the rockabilly revival kids in the Stray Cats when they were young punks from Long Island in a band called the Bloodless Pharoahs. He made up that cartoon cat with a great big quiff that he put on Brian Setzer and it became the band's logo. He never got another dime for it. Those guys went to England and caught the eye of The Clash and hit it big over there with their pompadours and tattoos. The Japanese rockabilly kids worshipped the Stray Cats.

15.

Skins & Skulls

In 1979, what was essentially a long fan letter arrived in the mail from Portsmouth, England, from a tattooer named Ron Ackers. He was older than me and had been tattooing a long time. He ran a classic Sailortown tattoo shop in an historic English port. He introduced himself and invited me to come to England. The letter came on stationery with a fancy design, a big, scrawling handwritten thing. He told me I had many fans over there and that I could make a lot of money. He even told me what he was making, which was a shocking amount of candor from a fellow tattooer. He wanted to let me know he had a jumping shop and we both knew it was a cash business.

Not long after that, a second letter came from Ron, saying he was coming to San Francisco. He knew Lyle Tuttle and had been to San Francisco before in the late sixties. Ron was an interesting cat, a total bandit of the old school, really interested in tattoo history, an antique collector and a hustler. He had done well with tattooing. He brought a friend, Stan Davies, who tattooed in another small English town. These guys had been on the scene, tattooing since the late fifties. We hit it off and when Ron repeated his invitation to come to England, I started planning a trip.

Francesca and I had always wanted to do a roots tour. Her people were from Sicily and neither of us had been to Europe. We decided we would do England, and take a week in Sicily. My father was English. I had a cousin near my age over there with whom I used to correspond when we were kids. I had always wanted to go to England. As it turned out, London proved far more hospitable than Sicily, which came as something of a disappointment to Francesca, who was raised in a very Sicilian New York household.

The address for Ron's shop was The Arches, under the railway arches at the Portsmouth Harbour station, near where Lord Nelson's HMS *Victory* was moored. It had been Sailortown for hundreds of years. With the tiny shop fitted into the arches under the station, the place had a curved shape. It was barely big enough for the two side-by-side stations. The walls were flashed out solid. Ron was a freehand tattooist; he had no stencils. "We've got them all memorized," he said. He could see all his flash from where he sat and he slammed them on.

We stayed at his house with his wife and two daughters. He set up a room in another building, not his shop, where I could work and threw a big party for me, where he presented me with an ornate silver engraved cup commemorating my visit. Ron had a great flare for drama and awareness of history. Tattooers came from around England, and in the days after the party, I tattooed them all. Some of Ron's customers heard about it and came. I met all these people and banged on a lot of tattoos.

Francesca and I went to London to see Dennis Cockell, the British tattooer whose torso I covered with dragons when I first opened Realistic. We'd kept up a correspondence and were very much on the same trip. He was more my age, really into music, an encyclopedia of pop music knowledge. The jungle telegraph of the tattoo world sent my reputation ahead of me. I had been tattooing at Realistic five years and my thousands of tattoos had traveled the world. There were many Ed Hardy fans waiting to meet me in England.

In Portsmouth, I made friends with one London tattooer, Jim Silles, who traveled down there to get a big Japanese chest piece and wanted to get a back piece done, too. Jim, along with Dennis, became one of my main mates in the UK. An Irish Londoner who at sixteen got a job at a funeral home (where his duties expanded to postmortem work), then at an exterminating firm called Rent-O-Kill, he fully appreciated the weirdness of these situations, and moved through a variety of scenes, including the Mods and original (nonracist) Skinheads. Jim was an avid record collector of ska, early reggae, and African music for many years. We share an absurdist sense humor, certain musical tastes, and remain in close contact.

Jim ended up getting a Japanese "hell scene" on his back, from a medieval painting. It was a great theme, but including the tiny human figures being grotesquely tortured made me uneasy, like it would be bad luck. So I made it an "empty hell." Jim was a little disappointed, but went along with it.

After such a positive experience, for the next few years we made the England run twice a year. In London, we rented a place in Knightsbridge, walking distance from the Victoria and Albert Museum, which I knew had an enormous collection of Japanese prints. When I found out about Kuniyoshi, the nineteenth-century god of Japanese tattooing, the only book that had been done on him was written by a curator at the V&A. At the museum, I could go into the print room, look at the actual prints, and photograph them. Every morning, I would walk over to the museum. In the afternoon, I would do tattoos at Dennis's shop in Finchley Road, Exclusive Tattooing.

We also hooked up with my cousin Philip Kear, who lived in London and worked at that time for *The Sunday Times*. Philip was a major league history buff and has a graduate degree in Sanskrit from the University of Edinburgh. His father was Scottish and his mother was my father's only sister, out of six siblings. It was great to connect with my English cousin, and his knowledge of English history and geography led to some great auto journeys around the South and West on subsequent trips.

In England, the Victorian-era romance with tattoos faded quickly. By World War I, tattoos in Great Britain, like the United

States, were largely seen on the working class. There were guys who tattooed on the piers and near the amusement parks, but it wasn't a big deal. Certainly when I first started going over, there were few tattoos on hipsters. In the clubs I went to, almost none of the punk rock kids were tattooed. Dennis Cockell eventually put a tattoo on Steve Jones of the Sex Pistols and some other musicians, but it was rare for people in that scene. English tattoos on alternative social groups were pretty much confined to occasional pieces on Teddy Boys, referring back to bad-boy images of the fifties in their drainpipe jeans and waterfall hairdos.

I had been turned on to punk rock the year before in San Francisco by Leo Zulueta, a Filipino-American graphic designer who was raised in Hawaii and San Diego, a savvy beach guy and nuanced hipster. He was the first punk enthusiast that I had met. Leo was also seized with a passion for tattooing. Bob put a tattoo on him at Tattoo City and told me what a unique guy he was. Leo brought in all this unusual source material and came back to have me add abstracted black flames to Bob's tattoo.

Leo explained the punk scene to me. "The best thing about it is it includes everybody," he said. "If you're unpopular or ugly or whatever, you can fit into the punk scene." That was like a light went on for me. Punk could be a new avenue of social acceptance with some really crazy dress styles to go along with it.

I developed an avid interest in punk, even before I went to England. Leo and I and a few other friends had gone to the Sex Pistols concert in January 1978 at Winterland. That was a thrilling evening. I always liked English music—The Beatles, The Stones, the whole British invasion. The exciting new music scene in London was just another thing to like about the country. We started going to England a lot. I would tattoo to pay for the trip, and travel around. I went out with my cousin. We drove to the countryside. He knew all these obscure churchyards and weird history. We would do the big history soak, have high tea, and then go to the Charing Cross Road bookstores. I hit the clubs at night and sometimes Francesca came along. We saw Elvis Costello, and The Pogues opened for him. I dug the Two Tone ska sound, loved Madness, and went to see the ska rude boys Bad Manners.

I decided to take Doug, my son, to England in 1980. He was fourteen years old, had moved back with Chris, and was going to school in Boulder. He was at that stage of simmering teenage rebellion and wiseass behavior. Although he wasn't in big trouble, I decided to bring him back to live in San Francisco with me and Francesca. I went to Boulder for a visit, and we rode the train from Colorado, aiming for a summer England trip. When I broke the news to him that he'd be relocating to San Francisco he was not thrilled, but my firm stance was that he was a kid and did not get a full vote. We had a grand time on the trip to England.

He met my cousin, who took us to Stonehenge and other historic sights. We visited my uncle and aunt in Bridport, down where my father came from in the West Country, and where we still had relatives scattered in Devonshire and Somerset. When we were in London, we stayed above a Wimpy bar on Finchley Road in Kensington down from Dennis's shop. At night, I went to the clubs (Doug was too young, but he dug the whole thing).

It was on that trip with Doug that I began drawing again. It simply happened. I didn't plan it or think about it. I was so pumped up by what I saw in the clubs, I had to get it down. The skinhead scene at the Two Tone shows was a biracial crowd with a definite sense of style. They embraced the whole ska thing. Working spontaneously with a Sharpie on typing paper in bold, simple black strokes, I tried to get down what I'd seen that night and ended up with a series of drawings. It was the first art I had done for myself since I started tattooing.

Every month, I realized I should do some work for myself. I was running multiple tattoo shops and driving myself crazy. I put a lot of time into drinking. And I was drawing every day, making images for tattoos, and then tattooing them on people, grinding all this color into their skin. I was using my hands, but I wasn't in that ventilated space where it didn't have to be for anything, it could just be art. That's what this series of drawings was.

I came back with a big load of ska and English pop music 45s. I had become friendly with Dean Dennis, who started out working in Lyle Tuttle's shop after Lyle married Dean's aunt. I put an epic bicentennial tattoo on his back—a blonde pin-up girl on an eagle on the American flag. Dean broke away from Lyle's and ended up opening a shop in a former butcher shop on Broadway, Dean's Tattooing and Art Gallery. He liked to put up art on the walls. Greg Irons, just starting out, showed there. Dean saw my drawings and suggested we mount an exhibit.

Leo worked at a copy shop where he could get in at night when they were closed, and make high-quality photocopies. I gave each of the drawings a title and Leo velo-bound it into a little book called *Skins & Skulls*. We sold the book, twenty different drawings, for ten bucks. The drawings all showed the clothing, the leather jackets and whatever, and the hairdos they had, but where there would have been faces there was nothing but skulls. They still had the looks and the attitudes I saw; they were just skulls.

We threw an opening party at Dean's Barbary Coast Gallery on Broadway in August 1980. I made a mix tape of the 45s I brought from London and it was like an Ed's-back-in-town-with-the-latest-sounds-and-his-drawings-from-the-club-scene party. A young couple came to the party who were on the punk scene, Jonny Whiteside, a writer, and his wife, Annie. They published a sporadic magazine called *Beano* that chronicled the music and fashion scene. Because they had been living in London, they recognized people that I drew as skulls. I thought that was pretty cool.

My reputation was beginning to spread. I received a phone call in early 1981 from the producers of the hoary television quiz show, *To Tell the Truth*, about appearing on the show as a contestant. I was going east for a tattoo convention and didn't even think to ask for air fare. I showed up with one of my key clients, Tattoo Charley Bockwith, a social worker from Brooklyn, who displayed his extensive Japanese-themed tattoos, and a handful of pals from the convention in the audience, including Zeke Owen. I stumped all the panelists except Kitty Carlisle and got to meet Soupy Sales, who was also on the panel. It was as famous as I had ever been.

16.

Queen Mary

I t was also about this time that I stopped drinking. Phil Sparrow was the first to suggest I might have a problem with alcohol, after showing up one too many mornings hungover at his shop. He cheerfully admitted he suffered from the same problem, but went into the program in the fifties when he was still living in Chicago and turned his life around. In February, Francesca, after living through countless times where I could only stop drinking for a few days at a time, finally gave me an ultimatum. We had finally married at City Hall on our eighth anniversary. A year later, she had had it. "You can't seem to quit this on your own, so either you get some help, or I'm leaving," she said. "I can't take it anymore."

I got on the phone, found a support group two blocks from our house, and went to a meeting that night. It was a revelation and a relief, especially to learn my penchant for booze was more like an allergy than a moral failing. After I introduced myself as a tattoo artist, one middle-aged guy approached me after the meeting and showed me his tattoo. He told me he got it in the fifties in Chicago from Phil Sparrow. I haven't had a drink since.

As an adjunct to that, my newfound clarity allowed me to realize that Francesca's desire to get a dog might actually be a good idea. I had been rejecting that for a variety of reasons, one of which, I realized, was a childhood trauma from our dog being run over when I was about eleven years old. We got a boxer, a breed she had loved when her family had one during her childhood. My stern statement that the dog and its responsibility would be hers, melted before we even got him home, and Rocky, with his wacky boxer exuberance and outstanding physique, moved into our lives.

Leo Zulueta was also the first person I knew who went nuts for what I called the anthropological tattoos, black graphic designs that echoed the tattoos of the South Pacific islanders. Christian missionaries largely wiped out the indigenous tattoo traditions, instinctively understanding that these indelible marks were somehow the work of the devil. The missionaries wanted the natives to stop running around with their breasts exposed, fucking on the beach, and getting tattooed. Isolated tattoo practices remained in places like Samoa, the hill tribes in the Philippines, and the Sarawaks in Borneo. Outside of that, little remained of the pretechnological tattoo world.

Leo was very involved in the punk scene when Bob and I met him, a genius graphic designer with a deep scholarly interest in island tattoo traditions. He became a good friend, and was so dedicated and stoked about tattoos that I encouraged him to start tattooing. He started doing small work on people in his crowd under my guidance. Right away, he was creating his own vision of the black graphic tattoo, unlike anything anybody had ever seen.

Mike Malone actually was the first modern tattooer to bring back the South Pacific black graphic tattoos. Soon after he took over the old Sailor Jerry shop in Honolulu, he began to see local Samoans with indigenous tattooing, and began to explore the roots of tattooing in the islands centuries ago. Sensing the built-in interest in these traditions, Malone drew up a sheet of Hawaiian tattoo designs based on classic images from old engravings. Among the designs, he also invented wraparound bands of classic black graphic Hawaiian designs. This was the origin of what has since come to be known as the Hawaiian Band. It is about as ubiquitous in Hawaii now as T-shirts.

When the oceanic voyaging boat *Hokule'a* was launched in

1976, Malone had tattooed a black graphic chest panel on one of the crew of this much-anticipated outrigger journey from Hawaii to Tahiti. The goal of this first historic voyage was to duplicate the migratory pattern of the original Hawaiians. It drew a great amount of attention, and Hawaiian Bands took off quickly. Before long they were seen everywhere in the islands. Wearing one became a matter of ethnic pride. Herb Kane, the famed Hawaiian painter, did a series of oil paintings for *National Geographic* that showed natives in outrigger canoes wearing Malone's designs, even though that particular style of tattoo never existed before Malone. They tattooed half of their bodies from the forehead down. They did other things. But there was no such thing as the Hawaiian Band.

The Hawaiians seized on it and built a history from it. Malone did the same thing that Good Time Charlie did. He decided to open up the imagery, and offer people the content and the style that they relate to, that speaks to them as part of their heritage. A few tattooers in New Zealand had developed styles based on the historic forms prior to Mike's explorations, but with renewed interest in tattooing all over the globe, the resurgence of this black graphic work soon spread to every island group in the world. Tattoos are back in a big way in island culture. In Hawaii, every third person has some black graphic Hawaiian tattoo. Even older women embraced it. Malone reintroduced something that had been squeezed out by the invading culture. His Hawaiian Band was a natural because not only did it look cool, it could be hidden under a short-sleeved shirt. Of course, since its inception almost forty years ago, the look has proliferated in size, complexity, and visibility.

Around the same time, Ernie Carafa suggested we put on a tattoo convention together. Ernie owned a successful shop in Toms River, New Jersey, a happening summer spot with a boardwalk on the Jersey shore. He had been in the navy and been tattooed by the great American traditional tattooer Paul Rogers, who introduced us through the mail. A bunch of us—Malone, Bob Roberts, and I—began to go back east and tattoo with Ernie for a week or so at a time. It was still illegal to tattoo anywhere in the five boroughs of New York City, but it was always legal in Jersey. I would go to Ernie's and stay busy as long as I wanted, mainly on other tattooers from all over that area, and then go to Long Island and visit with Francesca's family.

Ernie, who was beginning to branch out in business selling tattoo supplies, thought we should do a tattoo convention in the Los Angeles area. Tattoo conventions had been gaining in size and popularity since Reno five years before. We went in with a friend of mine from San Francisco, Eddie Nolte, who ran a screen printing company that made T-shirts.

When the packet of information from the Los Angeles Convention Bureau arrived and I saw the brochure for the *Queen Mary,* I knew where we were going to have our little clambake.

It was perfect. I knew that the ship once had a room that was called the Tattoo Room, a lounge decorated in tattoo flash. My father had been on the *Queen Mary* when it served as a troop ship during the war. It was permanently moored in Long Beach Harbor less than a mile from the Pike, where it all started for me. You could see the Pike from the decks. We presented a proposal and cut a deal to hold a tattoo convention on the *Queen Mary.*

Ernie also thought a tattoo magazine might be a good idea. He knew my interest in tattoo history and disseminating information. My idea was to make our convention truly informative and educational, a convention where you can learn something besides to not snort that much coke again. I wanted to hold discussions, slide shows about tattoos, various lectures on specific topics. Bring up the consciousness a little. A magazine to sell at the convention went right along with that thinking.

I hit on the title, *Tattootime.* Ernie saw it mostly as a platform to promote his tattoo supplies business. He was also making money with Malone, in a company they formed called Mr. Flash, to sell sheets of flash Malone drew. Malone named the company Mr. Flash because he saw there was a Mister everything in

Jersey—Mr. Pizza, Mr. Video, etc. He loved the whole Jersey deal; it was something unique to us West Coast boys. Nonetheless, I told Ernie we weren't even going to put an advertisement for his business in the magazine. It was going to be a high-quality magazine that would reflect well on the intellectual grounding of this new tattoo movement, without being stuffy.

I drafted Leo Zulneta for his graphic skills and we decided to devote the cover to the black graphic designs we were both flipped over. We tossed around different ideas about what to call it. It was Leo who came up with the title: *The New Tribalism*.

This whole realm of design Leo introduced me to made me think in a new way. It also represented a challenge to me because I had been narrative-driven in all my art. I had no experience consciously creating abstract, or such highly stylized, things. Leo was doing this uniquely personal design work with hearts and crosses—classic imagery—in a heightened black graphic style. It took the art into new realms and I was very impressed.

In early 1982, while we were planning the convention and magazine, a tattooer from the South named Ron Darth came to San Francisco to have me do a set of matching Samoan-style tattoos on his legs. I had done some work on him before, but nothing like this. He traveled a lot and had been to Hawaii, where he saw some Samoan guys with the traditional Pe'a tattoos covering their legs and hips. When he came to San Francisco that spring, he brought with him a book about Samoa that had photos showing people with these black graphic tattoos. In Samoa, they hammer tattoos in with a sharpened piece of turtle shell on the end of a stick. They capture soot in a coconut to make the ink. I went home that night and made some drawings. The next day, I started drawing on him.

He wanted Japanese serpents, so it wasn't a straightforward homage to tribal tattoos, but a cross-cultural concept. I added other elements like trigrams from the *I Ching*. Against a backdrop of geometric black graphics, these twin Japanese snakes—one red, one blue—coiled around his legs over his ass to his hips.

It was a hell of a tattoo. We worked in four- or five-hour sessions. I didn't have any transfer patterns. I made it up as I went and drew it on, piece by piece. I took photos with my SX-70 Polaroid so that when I got to his other side, I would know what to do. It had to form a single, unified design when his legs were together. It was a major tattoo for me, way different than anything before. It took a lot of work, but Darth didn't mind. He kept shooting himself with some kind of painkiller. We used a photograph of the finished tattoo for the cover of the first *Tattootime*.

"This matched set of leg tattoos was inspired by Samoan Pe'a work; two Japanese-style serpents rise through quasi-Polynesian pattern. Tattooed freehand in 75 hours over a nine-week period, spring 1982," I wrote in the caption.

The issue featured a package about black graphic tattooing. We thought it was too important, too cool, ignored for too long. Leo did an article about the swastika, which he felt had been unfairly demonized by the Nazis, in spite of its deep history and significance to Buddhists and Native Americans. I wrote an article on Sailor Jerry, who was not well known outside a few people in the tattoo world. We used lots of good photos and presented the material in a lucid, intelligent manner. It was the first tattoo magazine.

Leo introduced me to Vale, a North Beach writer, musician, and avid social documentarian who used to work at City Lights Bookstore and who belonged to the original version of Blue Cheer. A deep reader, thinker, and alternative consciousness commando, Vale not only published a punk-rock tabloid, *Search & Destroy*, he ran a typography shop out of a storefront and showed us how to set the type and paste up the pages. A tattoo customer from Realistic introduced me to a printer in South San Francisco. We ran five thousand copies of *Tattootime: New Tribalism*.

"Tattoo Expo '82," held on November 12–14 at the *Queen Mary*, the retired World War II ocean liner permanently docked in Long Beach Harbor, proved to be a giant success. The magazine was a big hit. The ship was a fantastic setting. The tattoo floor stayed busy. People were partying, drinking, doing whatever they were doing in their rooms, but we gave them something a little more. We had talks on subjects such as the use of symbolism in Japanese tattoos or a lecture by UCLA art historian professor Arnold Rubin. We found an obscure documentary from the sixties about some alcoholic tattooer in Texas and showed that.

On the convention floor, Leo was tattooing fingernails, because you could put a tattoo on your fingernail and it would grow out. He tattooed Doug on his fingernail, because Doug was only fifteen, and I wouldn't let him get a tattoo until he was eighteen. He wasn't going to fill his arms up with *Star Wars* junk.

Robert Williams put up a display advertising his artwork. S. Clay Wilson, the underground cartoonist, introduced me to Williams, whose work I knew from his days with *Zap Comix* and R. Crumb. I ran into him again earlier that year when Doug and I attended the San Diego Comic Convention. He was starting to do oil paintings he called *Zombie Mystery Paintings*. They came in two sizes—the $500 size and the $700 size—but you had to buy it sight unseen. I thought that was outrageous and immediately ordered one. He didn't have any tattoos, but he understood that we were swimming in shared water. He and his wife came to the show and we were doing coke and smoking bombers, and having a great time.

But the big thing that happened to me at the convention to me was reconnecting with Japan. Early in the planning, I decided to see about arranging for Japanese tattoo artists to attend. I stayed in touch with Horihide in Gifu. He came to visit in San Francisco a few years before and actually put on some tattoos with his hand tools at Realistic. He brought along a customer of his, a nice, well-mannered *yakuza*. His problem was that he was a speed freak who didn't want to risk bringing his stuff with him. Oguri asked me if I could help, but I told him I didn't have those kind of connections. As a result, he kept falling asleep. We would go out to dinner at nice restaurants and this well-groomed Japanese gentleman would fall asleep with his face in the soup. Oguri got a laugh out of it.

Through correspondence, we arranged for Horihide to appear at the convention. We were going to build a special platform for him in the center of the floor. Few people in the West had actually seen Japanese hand-tattoo work.

I still had an address for Kuronuma Tomatsu—Horiyoshi II— that I copied from the back of a photograph at Sailor Jerry's when he wasn't looking. In our minds, Horiyoshi was the greatest living tattoo master. His work was unlike any other Japanese tattoo artist, and exuded sophistication, much more painterly. It had a tremendous amount of energy. In his hands, tattoos were not so much a codified folk art, as it was with almost all the other tattooers in Japan. He made the ancient come to life. Jerry and I knew he was the guy. He and Jerry exchanged some correspondence over the years, after a Japanese businessman and tattoo enthusiast who Jerry had also tattooed made the introduction. So I sent the grand master a letter inviting him to attend our convention as a special honored guest.

I soon received a letter back in perfect English from a Japanese publisher named Kunihiro Shimada about a forthcoming deluxe, coffee-table book on the works about Horiyoshi's work, *Horiyoshi's World*. "Mr. Kuronuma sends his regrets that he can't travel there," he wrote. "However, I could come and visit you and bring along a man with a full classic body tattoo done by Horiyoshi." This was a huge deal for all of us involved.

Oguri ended up ill and went to the hospital. He didn't come and we didn't have the live tattooing, but Horiyoshi's representative came and brought a lot of photos of the old man's work. Nobody had ever seen this many photographs of the great tattoo master's work. It was so important for me to see because he summed up everything that I was trying to do with the Japanese style. He was the living embodiment of the high-art end of tattoo.

He was the son of a master tattoo artist called Horiyoshi and was given the name as his father's only apprentice. Horiyoshi the first was a populist artist in the Tokyo neighborhood where he grew up. He worked on the local festivals—decorating floats, painting kites—and was a gifted, trained artist before he went into tattooing. He studied with a pupil of Kuniyoshi. He was in the lineage. Kuniyoshi, Kunisada, and all the great printmakers studied with a master named Toyokuni, who was the head of a great school. They took the last part of their teacher's name to make the first part of their art name. Kuronuma's father studied with Yoshitora, who took his name from his master, Kuniyoshi.

The publisher Shimada spoke English and was a hip guy, easy to get along with. He called Horiyoshi from the ship and gave me the phone. I babbled in my half-assed pidgin Japanese that he was the greatest artist in the world or something and totally embarrassed myself.

Kuronuma wasn't only the greatest Japanese tattoo artist; he was a key figure in the entire history of tattoo in Japan. At the request of the Allied General Staff, he demonstrated the previously secret ancient art to photographers from *Life* magazine. It was Horiyoshi's work that was recognized by one of General MacArthur's staff, which led to bringing tattoo art out of the underground for the first time since the Emperor made it illegal in the nineteenth century.

The tattoo master was in his late sixties and largely reclusive. He was not known for associating with other Japanese tattooers. He might have tattooed one or two non-Japanese in his life. But that didn't stop me. I still asked Shimada if I could come to Japan to visit Horiyoshi and get a tattoo. I was astonished when he said yes.

I immediately made plans for a spring trip to Japan. I began corresponding with Horiyoshi through the publisher. I told Kuronuma I'd been saving some space, and I knew the image I wanted.

17.
Tokyo

When the wife of Dr. Katsunari Fukushi phoned Realistic that fall 1982, I already knew who her husband was. He was the second-generation guardian of a collection of tattooed human skins at a hospital museum in Tokyo that many knew, but few saw. His father, Dr. Masaichi Fukushi, became interested in tattoos while studying moles. He found that he could more easily track pigment movement on skin that had been tattooed, which led to his discovery of needle-penetrated, tattooed skin resisting recurrences of syphilis, prompting his scientific interest in tattooing. He began his collection of tattooed skins in 1926. His son, also a pathologist who specialized in cancer research, continued the family hobby.

The tattoo skins were the subject of a multipage photo spread in *Life* magazine as early as 1950, during the Occupation when American curiosity about the strange and mysterious Japanese culture was at a peak. The magazine article may have been an influence on writer Roald Dahl's wonderfully creepy short story, "Skin," that I first read as a teen in a collection called *The Graveyard Reader*. The tattoo world was familiar with the collection, which was housed at the Medical Pathology Museum in the University of Tokyo, but nobody I knew had ever seen it.

Mrs. Fukushi spoke excellent English with a British accent and they came to visit my studio. Fukushi was a short, intense man who did not speak a word of English. Both he and his father maintained avid interest in the tattoo community—his father used to sponsor annual meetings of the Tattoo League at a Tokyo bathhouse that was also photographed for *Life*—and he had heard of my work at Realistic. When I mentioned my plans to travel to Japan in the coming spring, Mrs. Fukushi immediately proffered an invitation. "You must come and visit us and see the tattooed skins."

This was shaping up to be an interesting trip.

When I told a Japanese print dealer in San Francisco I knew about the trip, he asked "Do you know Donald Richie?"

Of course, I knew who he was. Donald Richie had been the cultural ambassador to the West for all things Japanese since he got there, right after the war. Richie was the author of the Japanese tattoo book Phil Sparrow showed me the first day in his shop. "I'll give you his phone number," the art dealer said. "You should call him. I think he'd like to meet you."

Donald Richie was the father of Japanese cinema. He quickly moved from film reviewer for the *Stars and Stripes,* the military newspaper, to one of the leading figures in the postwar Japanese movie business. He translated the movies and wrote the subtitles. He was the man who brought Japanese cinema to the West and knew all the great directors and actors. He learned to speak Japanese fluently but decided not to bother spending the enormous amount of time required to learn how to read and write. He could communicate with people. He would be a brilliant contact. All the threads were connecting.

Another hipster North Beach friend, artist Bob Basile, who I met through Leo Zulueta, was into the retro-rockabilly scene and connected with a bunch of Japanese hipsters fixated on fifties American pop culture. Bob had been to Tokyo and seen what was going on. He thought the Japanese rockabilly kids would love to get tattoos. He told me about the rabid interest in old American clothing. Not only secondhand or old, unsold garments called dead stock, they were designing new clothes to look like old American wear. They had the haircuts, the works. Getting a tattoo struck me as different than getting a haircut or putting on clothes that make you look like James Dean or Elvis. Tattooing carried such a heavy onus in Japan. It still was seen exclusively as a *yakuza* thing and stayed almost entirely underground. But, I figured, what the hell? Bob had brought one Japanese friend to Realistic for a small tattoo, and was so convinced it would be a hit, I packed up all my gear in a little doctor bag—it doesn't take much—and took that along.

When I got to Japan in spring 1983, I met the great Tomatsu Kuronuma. He was very welcoming. With his publisher Shimada serving as interpreter, we were able to communicate a lot. Even before he left Long Beach, Shimada asked me to contribute a piece of writing to the book he was producing about Horiyoshi and I was to work on that while I was over there. I told Horiyoshi that I wanted a tattoo of the Goddess of Mercy—called *Kannon* in Japan, *Kwan Yin* in China. She is a major Buddhist deity, sort of the Virgin Mary of the Orient. I saved my left rib for something special and this was that. I'd had Bob Roberts put a fierce protectorate Buddha on my right rib, *Fudo Myo* in Japanese. The two figures are a matching pair in Buddhist iconography. Horiyoshi started work on the outline and he worked slowly. It is a big tattoo—from my pectoral to the top of my thigh. In the three weeks I was there, we managed to get the outline complete and start coloring it in. Very quickly it became apparent I would be returning to Tokyo.

I met the rockabilly guys and they wanted tattoos, just like Basile said. I did the first couple of pieces in a swank mid-century-style apartment on the top floor of a deco-inspired building in one of the trendy youth districts of Tokyo, Harajuku. The apartment belonged to the president of a clothing company called Cream Soda, all fifties American look, and this was their main building. He got a small tattoo far up under his T-shirt. It was a big deal. His staff was impressed. Then they all wanted one. I started tattooing those guys.

What they wanted were classic American forties-style images, real Sailortown stuff—hearts and anchors, eagles and pinups. There wasn't much call for that in San Francisco. It had stayed alive along the eastern seaboard, where people tended to be more conservative about the tattoos they liked, real, no bullshit, strong, American tattoos. The hipsters out in the West were interested in everything but that. To the Japanese guys, these were exotic American trinkets.

There was a rock band, the Black Cats, associated with the Pink Dragon clothing label. All the band members got tattooed. Cream Soda Company owned the clothing company and had stores all over Japan, a big, thriving chain that specialized in Americana. The tattoos were an instant rage. I knew immediately I would be back.

I called up Donald Richie. He was completely friendly and open, a totally down-to-earth fellow who had only recently returned from snorkeling in the South Pacific. He traveled a lot, both for pleasure and on juries for countless international film festivals. For a number of years, he lived in New York and was head of the film department at the Museum of Modern Art, but he missed Japan too much and came back. We met at a coffee shop near where he lived in a traditional section of Tokyo and it was a great meeting, another solid connection.

Dr. Fukushi and his wife lived in a spooky, Addams Family–style house behind walls in a swank, older neighborhood of Tokyo, a big, late-nineteenth-century home that had belonged to his father, full of overstuffed furniture. They may have had some Japanese rooms, but the only parts of the house I saw were all grand Imperial décor. One room was dominated by a bust of his father. In a big glass frame was one of his tattoo skins.

Fukushi was a big fan of Horiyoshi II. He knew what a great tattooer Kuronuma was and felt a special kinship since they were both the second generation practicing in their field. Dr. Fukushi contributed some medical text to the book they were doing. The Fukushis were both gracious hosts and his wife killed me with her elegant, precise English. We went for a meal and then she said, "Shall we go see the wet skins?"

Yes, of course, but only in the interest of science, weird tales and my lurid American appetite for the bizarre, surrealistic aspects of life.

Dr. Fukushi the elder developed a deep appreciation for the artwork and traditions involved and began a scrupulous catalog of motifs and designs. He worked at a charity hospital and paid for many people to finish their tattoos on the condition he could harvest the tattoo when they died. As a pathologist, he conducted autopsies on a number of these tattooed people and developed a method for lifting off the upper dermal layer, flensing these people and preserving their skins. He not only amassed a collection of more than 3,000 photographs of tattoos and extensive notes and records, he acquired the major portion of the museum's 105 tattooed human skins. His photographs and records were destroyed in the 1945 Tokyo air raids, but the skins survived.

His son, who had visited tattoo studios with his father since he was a child, followed in his father's footsteps. During his student days, he traveled to Micronesia and published papers that provide rare firsthand documentation on tattooing among Pacific Islanders. He personally collected more than twenty skins in the collection.

The Museum of Pathology had all kinds of medical curiosities and oddities. There is a famous Japanese film, *Realm of the Senses,* based on a true story about a deranged, sexually raged mistress who cuts off her lover's penis. They have the specimen in question in a jar. We walked into the skin museum and, of course, I remembered every detail from the photographs in *Life* magazine, but especially vividly recalled the guy with the huge demon mask on his back, alive and in a bathhouse, and there it is—in a glass frame on the wall.

They had us put on lab coats and we went in to see the wet skins that were kept submerged in chemical tanks. They scraped the fat off the back and dunked them in some kind of secret sauce to cure them. There were many full-body suits. Mrs. Fukushi took a photograph of me holding a wet skin out of the vat. I think they were a little unhappy when I used the shot that year on a Christmas card, sent out to a small number of friends in the tattoo world.

It had been ten years since I was tattooing *yakuza* in Gifu. We took a single one-day trip to Tokyo then, went to a museum and came back. This time, Tokyo was electric and exciting, *Blade Runner* style, va-va-voom, big Western/Eastern mix. Super high-tech, futuristic society with stores crammed with electronic gear we hadn't seen yet in the States. I was out in the museums, I was scouting Japanese prints. I was running full clip every day, tattooing guys, checking out traditional culture in museums, slogging around, just digging the city, using the subway, taking taxis, on the go. Ten years before, the country was still getting off its knees from the war. In the interim, the yen kept growing stronger. The Japanese car industry had grown into a giant. Sony was selling televisions like mad. The country was starting to take off.

The last week of the trip I headed off to Guam to meet Dan Thome, a merchant seaman I knew through the tattoo shop. He was interested in Pacific Island tattooing, the classical "tribal" stuff. He did a bit of hand tattooing and lived in Guam part of the time with Maria Yatar, a Filipino-Guamanian woman, a musician and writer who was Dan's ticket into that society. I went down, stayed with them a few days and tattooed several people at their place. It was the first time I'd been back to Guam since working construction in the summer of 1965. The island had changed some, but not to the degree it has since Japanese honeymooners discovered it.

Dan and I took off for Palau, a diving paradise near the Marianas, and flew Air Micronesia into Koror. Palau is a series of islands. Koror is the capital, and we were going to another island in the group, Peleliu. It was a good long flight from Guam. When you're out in that part of the lake, everything's pretty far. All the old ladies got on the plane carrying Pepsi cans. I thought they were bringing soft drinks for the flight, but it was so they had somewhere they could spit their betel juice. Most everybody in that part of the world chews betel nut. It gives you a strange, low-level buzz, simultaneously a little spacey and sort of speeded up. The stuff also rots your teeth. They chew it wrapped in a leaf, sprinkled with lime juice, although some people also add tobacco to the recipe. On Guam, the guys would just roll a Marlboro into the mix and chaw down. The women on the plane were spitting bright red juice into their Pepsi cans on the plane. When we landed at Midway to pick up more passengers, the airport consisted of an airstrip and a grass shack, the sole purpose of which was to sell betel nut.

Dan knew a *haole* guy in Palau who had gone native, and he pointed us to Peleliu, which was the site of a two-month battle during World War II that sustained the highest U.S. casualty rate in the Pacific War. There were still wrecked planes in the jungle.

I set up shop at an open-air boat harbor. We took the battery out of one of the trucks to run the tattoo machine. I worked from a cast-cement bench while these guys were sitting in a truck, in the truck bed, or with their arms draped out the window for me to tattoo. The Japanese controlled the islands long before the war, until the U.S. Marines liberated Palau. They worship the Marines. Several of the Palauans I was tattooing wanted United States Marine Corps designs. They were picking them out from a book of old-fashioned tattoo flash I brought to show the rockabilly kids. I tattooed a lot of guys there. They were the first tattoos on the island in a long time.

After a few days, I returned to Tokyo. Japan looked good to me. Tattooing was still totally underground in the country. These kids wanted American-style tattoos and they couldn't get it over there. Find a need and fill it. Plus, it would give me a chance to connect with all my cultural interests, and have Horiyoshi do more work on my rib.

I wasn't simply the first Westerner to tattoo in Japan, I was almost the first non-Japanese. My tattoo "uncle" Pinky Yun from Hong Kong had done some work in Japan in the fifties, but he was mostly tattooing servicemen. My clients dug the fact that I was an American. Even when they began getting tattoos like dragons and tigers, specific Asian imagery, they recognized my style. "I don't want it Japanese style," they would say. "I want it pop style. I want California dragon."

I went back later the same year. Shimada helped me find a place in a low-rent, short-term building, a residential hotel in the Shinjuku 2-Chome, the gay bar district. A lot of Shinjuku is sex clubs and nightlife. The apartment was set up Japanese style, but it also had some Western furniture like a couch that opened into a bed, so I didn't have to sleep on the floor. I had a phone put in so I could make appointments with my customers.

And they would come in. On some days, I tattooed for fifteen or sixteen hours. I had my cassette-tape player blasting and would stamp out tattoos. They'd file in, see what they wanted, or bring me their drawing. I'd do a transfer or draw it on their arm and slap on the tattoo. It was like navy paydays.

At first, I wasn't really getting quite the prices I did in the States. Within a couple of years, the yen began to rise steeply and I tried to figure out how to raise my prices, but it was Francesca who pointed out all I needed to do was charge them the same yen prices, a bit more than the last trip and I would make more money. I gradually raised my price structure in Japan until I was getting pretty good money for tattoos. Exotic imports are always more expensive. I built a lot of business.

On that second trip to Japan, I went to Yokohama to meet Yoshihito Nakano, who tattooed under the name Horiyoshi III. He comes from a different tattoo family than the Kuronumas in Tokyo and his tattoo name is written with different characters. His family tradition of tattoo stretches back to when Commodore Perry opened Japan in the nineteenth century. They tattooed many aristocratic Europeans and wealthy Americans in the Victorian era, when Yokohama was a wild-and-wooly seaport.

Horiyoshi III was almost exactly my age and he had the killer classical, bold Japanese tattoo style. He did only hand work. Horiyoshi II in Tokyo, whose father trained him to do hand work, used machines as he grew older. Nakano proved to be a fascinating colleague—an artist dedicated to the ancient traditions, but with an eye on the modern world. He was a follower of esoteric Shingon Buddhism, an avid reader who was passionate about art history and mythology and understood the significance behind the myths the tattoos represented. We became great friends and, at my encouragement, he even started to make judicious use of the machines in his work. I met his whole posse, all the guys he tattooed. What a fun-loving bunch they were. I was beginning to build friendships and find people I could hang out with over there.

In September 1984, I went over with Doug, who was about to turn eighteen. We went from San Francisco to Hong Kong, accepted an invitation from Pinky Yun to visit him in Hong Kong, where he still owned property. We became great friends after he moved to Alameda, and he made periodic trips back to China. Pinky and Sailor Jerry shared tons of designs and information about machines, etc. Most of Jerry's signature pinups from the beginning of the sixties were slightly transformed Pinky originals. Pinky's shop was one of the most world-famous among navies from every continent, in the heart of Sailortown of Hong Kong, full *World of Suzie Wong*—a lot of sailors, a lot of hookers, a lot of bars, separating those sturdy seamen from their cash.

It was a real treat to have Pinky be our host and he gave us the royal tour. He introduced us to several other tattoo shops in different districts. We did a whirlwind day trip to Macau, the Portuguese colony famous for its gambling. We raised a stink on the bus when the driver suggested that, since time was getting short, they would skip the Taoist temples with these murals that Doug and I wanted to see. The other tourists weren't that interested in murals of Taoist immortals. The driver grudgingly took us to the temple.

I met with our printer in Hong Kong who Francesca had gotten

a lead to, and we had used since the second issue of *Tattootime,*
"Tattoo Magic." They did great work at a substantially lower cost
than in the U.S. I was interviewing Pinky for an article in the
third issue of the magazine and took photographs of his shop.
After a week in Hong Kong, we went to Japan.

Doug was excited to be in Japan because he grew up with the
same sensibility I did. Like my dad leaving for Japan when I was
six and sending back all this exotic Japanese stuff, Doug turned
seven when I went to Japan and started sending him stuff back—
Japanese superhero books, all that crazy Manga culture that was
starting. He bopped around town a lot on his own. He went out
and explored while Horiyoshi was working on my rib. I went back
down to Yokohama to visit Nakano. I brought along a VHS copy
of a just-released documentary, *Signatures of the Soul,* directed by
New Zealand filmmaker Geoff Steven and narrated by Peter
Fonda. Steven and his crew filmed tattooers around the world,
including me at Realistic. It was the first comprehensive documentary in general release. Also, just before the trip, a married
couple from Italy, Giorgio Ursini and Simona Carlucci, had visited Realistic and convinced me to co-curate a giant tattoo exhibit the following year in Rome. I wanted to personally invite
Horiyoshi III to go to Italy.

I knew I needed to appeal to his sense of adventure. "Do you
like pizza?" I asked.

18.

Roma

Back at Realistic in San Francisco, I was doing more and more of the big, elaborate tattoos—still doing small stuff when it came in, but concentrating on the insane, epic pieces. It was beginning to be obvious how far all this tattoo stuff was spreading.

But the first real intimation I had of the velocity came at a tattoo convention that following spring after the *Queen Mary*. A tattoo artist approached me and said, "Ed, I want you to check out the tribalism I'm doing on my girlfriend." Leo and I made up the title as a joke, New Tribalism. When this guy showed me this fine black graphic design he put on the calf of this nice-looking *young woman*, I thought to myself, "Tribalism—We've invented an art movement."

Tattootime really hit home. Circulating a mass-produced representation of information, ideas, and photographs made a huge difference. I always wanted to spread the story of tattoos and their history. I first wanted to write a history of tattooing when I was twelve years old, but didn't have enough information. I always wrote. I kept journals. But nothing prepared me for the success of *Tattootime* and the way it spread the word. It lit the fuse for the explosion of tattooing. It was a struggle to get the product into magazine and bookstores. Francesca would drive all over the city and mostly get turned down, or met with terms so ridiculous that it wasn't worth putting it in the places. In London, we trolled Charing Cross Road, hitting up the numerous art book stores, and were snobbily dismissed. Who would be interested in a periodical about tattooing?

By the next year, biker magazines like *Easy Rider* began to produce tattoo magazines of their own, and they all fed this groundswell of people getting tattoos. It was happening, and there was an audience.

Eventually we took over the publishing and christened the enterprise Hardy Marks Publications. Francesca ran the office, distribution, mail orders, and edited. I wanted big themes. For the second *Tattootime*, we featured "Tattoo Magic" and went into the amuletic aspect. We did articles about Christian tattoos and inventive cover work and ran several pages of full-color photographs of extraordinary tattoos.

Giorgio and Simona were a couple from Italy who made an appointment at Realistic for him to get a small tattoo. They explained that they worked in television and media and wanted to stage a tattoo exhibition in Rome. They approached me about putting it together, said they could obtain government funding. I wished them well and figured there was no chance of them pulling it off, but they got it going.

The Arts Council of the City of Rome funded the monthlong event, to be held at Trajan's Marketplace, one of the big ruins down in Historyville near the Coliseum. They wanted to have live tattooing. They were building a stage for people to show off their tattoos all through the show.

As far as I knew, there were not more than two or three tattooers in the entire country of Italy. Tattooing was still pretty much in the dark ages globally. California was a different story. Tattoos had become a badge of honor among the hipsters and were spreading every day. It was catching on in England and France wasn't far behind, but Italy had no tattoo tradition. We were bringing the wide world of tattoos into the center of ancient Rome.

Horiyoshi III agreed to attend. He had never been out of Japan before. He brought his wife, their infant son, and one of his best friends, who had a crazy/beautiful full body suit, all hand done. Pinky Yun came over to represent China. Through the New Zealand filmmakers who made the documentary I showed Nakano, I made contact with a master tattooer from Samoa. I also connected with a half-Maori man from New Zealand who had traditional-style work from that culture by a renowned tattooer from Wellington, New Zealand, Roger Ingerton, who did highly inventive work.

Lyle Tuttle flew in, which was great. He is a grand showman in the old tradition of sideshow attractions—The Tattooed Man—and always up for showing off his full-body suit. Leo Zulueta came over to demonstrate—what else?—New Tribalism.

My buddy Malone didn't want to be bothered, but he had taught the trade to Kandi Everett in the mid-seventies. She was a sophisticated artist raised in Hawaii and one of the first of a growing breed of talented tattooers. She and Malone had been a couple for several years and had a lot of adventures, expanding each other's outlook. They remained friends and close associates. Kandi was hip to island culture, and she came to Rome to represent Hawaii. The Italians were a little confused to see this big, white gal from the islands, but they didn't know you could be local and not look like a native.

There was a heart specialist I knew from Ohio, virtually covered, who brought his wife. My Canadian friend John Van 't Hullenaar, who tattoos under the name The Dutchman, because he originally came from Holland, flew in from Vancouver. It was a big, monthlong party in Rome.

"L'asino e la Zebra" (The Donkey and the Zebra) drew a lot of media attention when it opened in May 1985. All the papers, radio, and TV from all over Europe flocked to the scene. Nobody had ever seen anything like it before. Tattoos were being treated like art. They ran power lines into the ancient ruin. We were tattooing in the open-air and the place was filled with buzzing of tattoo machines. Every couple of hours a procession of people displayed their tattoos on the stage built in the open center of the historic space. There were display boards covered with photographs of tattoos and tattoo designs. Music was blasting out of loudspeakers—Prince's "Purple Rain" was a big hit that summer.

Almost all the people that came in for tattoos wanted tiny pieces because Italians were still reluctant about tattoos. Tattoos remained somewhat forbidden. I had four-by-six photos of my flash in a display album, mostly fifteen-by-twenty sheets. One had Sailor Jerry pinup pieces made to go on a forearm, about nine to ten inches high. A stylish young Italian woman pointed out a devil girl and said she wanted one of those. "How big do you want the tattoo?" I said.

"The same size," she said. It was about an inch high in the photograph.

I kept putting on these teeny, miniature Sailor Jerry–style tattoos. They had interpreters for us. The communication was fantastic.

One madman I knew from Amsterdam, Henk Schiffmacher, showed up, more or less, on his own. I'd known Henk a bit before, and had tattooed him, in San Francisco. He had his work gear with him and went nuts when he saw the setup. "I want a fucking booth," he said. "I'm European."

Every day, the Italians took a long lunch break and a mob of us would traipse out past the Trevi Fountain looking for a restaurant. We definitely did not look like ordinary tourists. Bill Salmon and his wife Betsy were good friends who I'd done unique work on, which I was keen to see represented at the show. Bill had gone all out for the show and had his hair cut into a Mohawk. I had tattooed the sides of his head, which wasn't too common at that time, with pink and black geometric shapes. We turned heads.

We clocked more than 30,000 visitors during the run, which ended on a downbeat note after running into some problems with local customs. One afternoon, we were told the place was closing the next day for a three-day holiday weekend we hadn't been informed about. Outside of an iron gate about eight feet high, the place was an open historic site.

At night, when we shut down, we wheeled our gear to a locked room, but all our displays and everything else stayed out. They gave us almost no notice and little time to pack away our equipment, but assured us everything would be all right. It turned out the guards took off the holiday, too. Person or persons unknown easily swarmed over the gate and ransacked the place. They stole flash, paintings, photographs. They took some machines. A favorite machine of mine disappeared.

I went ballistic, screaming at the plainclothes security guards—through an interpreter—and they just gave me the dead-eye stare. "Unfortunately, we can do nothing about this," the interpreter said. "All the guards are Calabrese."

What went without saying was that Calabrese make up a lot of the Mafia, the sort of lower-level guys who held down government jobs at important historic sites. They didn't care what I thought. We finished what was left of the show in a somewhat less festive mood.

In the end, there was a beautiful catalog put together by an Italian publisher. Donald Richie contributed a piece. I tried in vain to convince them to make the text bilingual, but they refused out of some misplaced sense of ethnic pride. Like, how many people in the world read Italian? But it was a cool catalog and the show was phenomenal.

Within a couple of years, there were tattoo shops all over Italy. The same thing happened in Japan. Not long after I started tattooing on those rockabilly kids, young people started getting hold of machines and tattooing out of their apartments, which quickly built into the enormous scene it is today with tattoo conventions, magazines, and hundreds of thousands of people wearing tattoos. There are tattooers everywhere in Japan, some upholding the traditional arts, but many doing hipster fusions of Western designs, in every style imaginable.

Tattoos were always global. A Chinese text from the eighth century describing the Japanese people said that the men tattoo themselves with dragons and fierce beasts to frighten away predators when they go swimming in the sea, spearfishing for food. Many *haniwa* clay figures dating from the Kofun era of 300 BCE to 300 CE have striations on them that are probably tattoos. This wasn't anything new anywhere.

19.

The Hamilton

I finally sold Tattooland in East Los Angeles in 1984. I was burned out at last on my East L.A. fantasy. I was still wild about the art, but it was ridiculous to be spread that thin. I was spending more time in Japan. I gave Jack Rudy all the furnishings and the name Tattooland. I wanted to be doing other things. It was Francesca who suggested we take the money and buy a place where I could work.

We found a small studio apartment in the Hamilton Building on O'Farrell Street, where all the delegates who signed the United Nations Charter in 1945 stayed when it was the Alexander Hamilton Hotel. It was a tall, deco building in a rundown downtown neighborhood, but it was secure, twenty-four-hour doorman and all that. We bought the place and walled off a work area with a bookcase. There was a sofa with a foldout bed. We still had the house on Clayton Street that we bought in 1976, but I had this little apartment for work.

I had been working solo at Realistic for some time since Bob Roberts split. Bill Salmon, who had been on the Rome trip, had started tattooing. Bill was a wild and crazy guy who was selling car stereos when I first met him. He had one arm full of a mixed bag of stuff when we met. He had been saving the other arm, which I did solid with him in collaboration. He had some of the most visionary ideas for tattoos—intense, blow-your-mind, wacky work. He was burning up with the love of tattooing. I put a lot of tattoos on him and his wife, Betsy.

She came up with an amazing tattoo design concept. There is a surrealistic Max Ernst painting that she greatly admired called *Angel,* done during World War II, a clumsy, strange figure with a bird head, dancing in an arid landscape, with his arms up in the air in these tattered clothes. She wanted to have him holding up a vintage Wurlitzer jukebox that's exploding and throwing records across her midsection, which would then be caught by something on the other side. I came up with a female figure emerging from a lotus, catching the records in a net made of a musical staff holding the notes to Elvis's "Return to Sender." Her face, surrounded by fire, was a stylized Maori facial tattoo pattern. I called it "Sender Goddess." When we went to continue it on her back, she decided it should be a figure leaping into space with no black in it, only colors, like a vortex of color energy—this large, asymmetrical, abstract thing in the center of her back.

These are my people—people who see tattoos I could have never imagined. Wear your dreams. They were a crackerjack pair.

I was putting all these wild tattoos on Bill. Their apartment was decorated with tattoo stuff. He collected tattoo posters. He wallpapered parts of the apartment solid with commercial tattoo flash. He loved hobnobbing with tattooers. He was just living, breathing, eating, sleeping tattoos.

I encouraged him to tattoo, but he was too green to be left alone running the shop. He needed someone who knew what was happening to be around. I had my new place set, but I wanted to keep Realistic going.

Greg Irons agreed to start working at Realistic. Greg was a genius from the underground cartoon scene. His *Yellow Dog Comics* ranks with R. Crumb's *Zap Comix* as a classic of the era. He had lived in London and worked as an "art slave" on The Beatles' animated movie, *Yellow Submarine.* He drew psychedelic posters for the Fillmore Auditorium and album covers for the

Jefferson Airplane. A terrifically talented artist, he was living on peanuts and decided to teach himself to tattoo after Airplane guitarist Jorma Kaukonen told him what he paid for his tattoo work.

Bob Roberts and I met Greg long before he segued into tattoos and, when he did, he became famous faster than anybody ever had in this business. He had a unique graphic style fresh to tattooing. My work was primarily about introducing new imagery, expanding the medium, making it more painterly, opening it up to more expressive visions, but Irons came out with a strong, instantly identifiable graphic style all his own. He worked at different shops around San Francisco and Seattle, but was never happy with where he was working. He was tattooing out of a pad in Berkeley owned by his Japanese-American girlfriend, about three blocks from where Phil Sparrow lived (Francesca and I still saw Phil for dinner a couple times a year).

But Greg was not happy with the hassle of having tattoo customers come into your home. It got to be like a constant party. He liked to tattoo loaded on weed and strong coffee, which some people know as a weedball. Greg was looking for something to do, and I suggested he come work at Realistic. The idea of having a tattoo artist of his obvious abilities at Realistic made me confident about the shop's reputation and survival.

He was stoked. He drew new business cards and a flyer. He spent about a week working at the place before he left for Japan and Thailand. He told me he had wanted to go to Asia all his life. He was a tattoo star and making good money. He already had a large base of fans, was mobbed at the conventions, and the conventions had gone worldwide. But before he settled into Realistic and took a real run at it, he wanted to take this trip to Asia.

Irons went over by himself in November 1984. He carried a letter for the Fukushis from me. From Tokyo, he went to Thailand. In Chiang Mai, he was able to negotiate a tattoo from a Buddhist monk, a snake that was supposed to be a protective talisman. In Thai culture, however, the snake is one of their symbols for death. In Bangkok, Irons was killed when he stepped into a special lane reserved for buses that ran the opposite direction of traffic. He was thirty-seven years old.

It was a terrible loss and an incredible shock, but there was no way I could leave Bill Salmon alone at Realistic. I needed to find someone to step in. Bill introduced me to Freddy Corbin, a young, hipster guy who had been tattooing around town and had a unique style and a big squad of followers. He was an up-to-the-minute guy with his finger on the pulse. He came to me for a tattoo and ended up going to work at Realistic.

It was Freddy who introduced me to Daniel Higgs, a real live wire—artist, writer, and musician—from Baltimore who had a powerful and highly unusual style. Bill and Freddy thought highly of Higgs and told me I should hire him. Higgs was working at another shop in town and had come for a tattoo at the condo at the Hamilton, so I knew him solely as a customer.

When we met to talk about it, I asked Higgs to show me his poetry. I figured a person's poetry would be a good indicator of what kind of person he was. His poetry was highly whacked out and very original. He was interested in a lot of thought systems, obsessed with the roots of Christianity, especially Gnostic and other esoteric pursuits. He was kind of tormented by larger questions of the meaning of life, which I liked. I prefer my tattooers to have a little something more going on than what time does the bar open.

These fellows mapped out territory I did not know. I was kind of out of the loop. I wasn't running around with a bunch of hipster young people. Even when I went to some of the punk shows, I always felt like the older tourist. With these guys at Realistic, they had things going on. Once again, I had a crew running.

I also had Dan Thome, the guy who took me to Palau, using the place to do a little hand-tattooing, minimalist, linear deep South Pacific–style tattoos, specialty work he did on very few people, when he wasn't shipping out. Realistic had something different going on. But it was still going on. I was renting the space. It meant a lot to me. The place was already like a touch-

stone of contemporary tattoo history. I wanted to keep that going. Plus, I had my apartment to work out of for myself.

I went back to Japan in August 1985 with my friend John Van 't
Hullenaar, The Dutchman from Vancouver. He was hot on the
Asian thing and I had done some large tattoos on him. He was
keen to go to Japan. It was fun to share with friends and show
them around my Japan. Every time I went over, I had work done
on my tattoo and picked Horiyoshi's brain as much as I could
while he was working on me.

In Harajuku, one of the most famous youth districts of Tokyo,
they would close off the roads in Yoyogi Park on Sundays and
thousands of kids would swarm over the place, dressed like cartoon characters with outrageous haircuts, rockabilly fanatics who
looked like Elvis, girls in poodle skirts with petticoats. They blasted
music out of giant boom boxes roughly the size of a small car they
ran off generators and danced their crazed choreography, their
take on fifties hepcat jitterbug. The culture was in full bloom.

Word about me spread from the Pink Dragon store to the
other rockabilly kids. They wanted to get an introduction. They
would come to my rented apartment, very polite, and want to get
a tattoo. Like the way it worked when I started doing unique stuff
at Realistic, word of mouth was all I needed for a steady supply of
customers.

I always saw the Fukushis whenever I went to Tokyo. We would
go to these fabulous sushi dinners and go to the *kabuki* with them.
They were close to Horiyoshi II and they were involved with his
publisher, Shimada. The rockabilly kids looked at me like I was
from Mars if I happened to mention that my wife and I were going to the *kabuki* or my studies of the classical arts. It was like
somebody coming over to this country from Japan and being
obsessed with the details of George Washington's life.

When I returned, Gordon Cook had died. He was a really
complicated guy who pissed off a lot of people because he could
be so abrasive. He tried to instill in me his sense of aesthetics,
which he did, and guide me in my printmaking and making art,

and when I went into the tattoo world, he felt like I had dropped everything.

After the Art Institute, we stayed in touch and he eventually came to appreciate what I was doing with tattooing. When Francesca and I made our San Francisco trip before moving to Gifu, I immediately contacted him. At that point, he was married to Joan Brown, my other big mentor in art school. The marriage to Joan lasted a few years. He remarried, and he and his third wife, an Irish woman named Liadain, had a daughter, Kate, who was the apple of his eye. Gordon smoked and drank heavily his whole life. He was overweight. He was a hard-partying guy. This beautiful daughter gave him a new wind and he was doing everything with her. Kate was allergic to smoke and Gordon was trying to quit smoking, really making an effort to clean things up for the sake of his little girl. He was painting and beginning to receive some of the recognition due him.

We had good times. We went out one night to see Big Joe Turner in some club on Divisadero Street. Gordon turned me on to Big Joe when I was in art school. It was Christmastime and they had a Christmas tree onstage. Charles Brown, who sang "Merry Christmas Baby," was also on the bill. We saw each other frequently. We would hang out, and talk art. He looked kind of askance at my deep interest in the Japanese stuff. He appreciated the core philosophical values, but Gordon could be dismissive. I showed him the book *Horiyoshi's World* when it came out, raving about this great Japanese tattoo master and tremendous level of nuance in his work. "For Christ's sake, Donald, you've got something better to do than make some Jap famous," he said.

Gordon dropped dead from a heart attack at fifty-seven years old. He came back from a trip and died, just like that. It rocked my world.

The next spring, I surfed for the first time since I left San Diego and it flipped a switch in me. We visited Mike Malone in Hawaii almost every year, would do some tattoos in Sailor Jerry's old shop and hang out. This year, I accompanied my friend Yoshihito Nakano, the Yokohama tattoo master, Horiyoshi III, to the San Diego tattoo convention and then flew with him to Hawaii before he was to return to Yokohama. One of Malone's pals and tattoo customers, an ex-military guy who never left the islands after the service, got me out on a long board on Waikiki Beach. The first turn into the first wave and I knew. One go-out and I was back in the game.

When I came home, I called one of my closest old friends, a master board shaper, Mike Marshall, who I knew growing up in Newport, and asked him to make me a board. He put me onto the latest wet-suit technology, and after more than ten years out of the water I started surfing again in the cold waves off Ocean Beach in San Francisco. By fall, I was ready to go back and visit Malone in Honolulu again, this time with my board bag. I surfed Waikiki every day on the soft, rolling waves in the warm tropical sun. My pals took me for a pancake breakfast on my way to the airport to go home. "Shit, Hardy, you should just move over here," one of them said.

"Maybe I will," I said.

On the flight home, I decided I would. I got off the plane and told Francesca. "Let's sell our house and move to Honolulu," I said.

20.

Honolulu

The Hamilton building apartment was already set up. I'd removed the kitchen appliances to make a tattoo room. The tiny kitchen was barely big enough for my bodywork table, an adjustable physician's exam table. I had a steady business built up. People were coming in from all over. You weren't supposed to run a business out of the building, but there was a little-old-lady hair salon on one of the lower floors and I figured, if I kept it quiet, it wouldn't be a problem. I told all my customers, "Don't get in the elevator with bandages showing." With an apartment for me to do tattoo appointments, we had already begun to toy with the idea of moving out of the city. Francesca has had asthma since she was a kid. We had a beautiful home on Clayton Street, built in 1912, but when the fog came in, Francesca called it the death cloud. We were considering Marin County. She was studying the Japanese language at San Francisco State. A late bloomer in her college education, she had been accepted to U.C. Berkeley, to major in Japanese studies.

But we hadn't even discussed moving to Hawaii. We always had a wonderful time in the islands. We both love the tropics. The Japanese flavor in the islands first attracted me when I started tattooing and was planning to move there and tattoo with Jerry. It's halfway to Japan and the surfing is great. I got off the airplane with the salt still in my hair and this spur-of-the-moment bomb-shell I laid on my wife. "All right," she said. "Why not?"

So we got geared up to move to Hawaii. I wasn't going to tattoo over there. Malone and I were great friends, but we would never work as business partners. He nurtured this thing that Sailor Jerry had going and was doing great, important work. I wasn't going to horn in on his scene. My plan was to fly back to San Francisco every few weeks, sleep at our apartment, and tattoo frantically as I did around military paydays while I was there. I would work all day and make enough to pay for the whole thing and then go back to Hawaii.

Francesca went off to Hawaii on a foray to look at real estate and check out the university. I had recently reread *From Here to Eternity*, where there was a scene at a private home in a hillside area of Honolulu I'd never heard of with a beautiful view of Diamond Head. I told her, "Check out this area." She found a place on the exact hillside with a killer view, but she was worried it was too small and too poorly constructed. She was beginning to have grave misgivings about this caper. Visiting "the rock" for vacations was one thing, but setting up our primary life on the island was another. She checked out the University of Hawaii, and found the general lassitude of the students—the kicked-back, "hang loose" pervasive Island attitude—pretty disturbing. If she was going to apply all her efforts into getting a difficult degree, she wanted a top-notch environment among motivated faculty and student body. I hopped a jet, utterly determined to make the move.

The real estate agent had pointed out to her that because, in the parlance of Hawaiian real estate, the house is up on stilts—built on supports from a sloping hillside—it would be possible to develop another level under the existing house. We saw a bunch of different places, but that was the one. Despite her misgivings, Francesca gave in. We sold the San Francisco house and bought the Honolulu pad in a whirlwind deal. All this happened since October. By Christmas 1986, we were living in Hawaii and I was surfing at Waikiki. Early the next year, Francesca enrolled in Japanese at the university and we started remodeling the downstairs, building a spare bedroom, a sewing/office room, library, and a studio for me. If one of my clients wanted to come over to Hawaii to be tattooed, that wouldn't be stepping on Malone's toes.

I stopped drinking after my first AA meeting in 1982, but I still smoked plenty of weed, and did coke once in a while. I finally quit everything in Hawaii. I stopped because of our boxer dog, Rocky. I was giving him some contradictory instructions and he looked at me with the total sincerity that only a dog can project. "For Christ's sake, Ed," Francesca said, "you're high and you're telling him two different things. The poor dog is confused." I looked in the dog's eyes and wondered, why was I tormenting this brute? I stopped smoking weed after that. I was off it all.

Tropical life was good for me. I basically stayed on the island through the first three months of the year except for a week of tattoo appointments in S.F, mid-February. At the end of March, I flew back to the mainland to attend a tattoo convention in San Diego.

It was the longest I'd been away from tattooing since art school. All I did was surf my ass off. I had two buddies, supertalented young longboard surfers from Newport, who worked night jobs in restaurants, parking cars and whatever, and surfed all day. I'd met Steve Farwell and Robert "Wingnut" Weaver through my old sidekick Mike Marshall. They were on the cutting edge, reinventing and reviving longboard style—surfing had largely gone to short boards in the seventies—and kept me motivated. Having regular sidekicks who were hard-charging gave me more incentive to go out all the time. I was forty-one years old, spending my days with kids twenty years younger, and riding hairier, more intense waves than anything experienced in my youth. As Francesca and I settled into living in Hawaii, I started thinking maybe I didn't have to put on any tattoos here. I had been floating on extra money from the sale of the house. I thought, *If I can get away with only going to San Francisco every few weeks and not tattooing when I was in Hawaii, maybe I could start doing some art for myself again.*

I had been doing tattoos for exactly twenty years and nothing but tattoos. The one small exception was the *Skins & Skulls* drawings that I did in London. I had a nice studio space in Hawaii, but all I was drawing were tattoo designs that I had to put on in San Francisco.

Then it hit me. What kind of art shall I do? It was like the blank piece of paper and the typewriter. I didn't have any ideas and I realized that I had become totally dependent on the input of commissions, bizarre scenarios that were fed to me by people who wanted them as tattoos. I didn't have an original idea in my head.

At first, I thought I would do things that didn't have anything to do with tattoos. I tried to rewind the tape in my head to when I first came to the Art Institute and I started painting still lifes. In Honolulu, I started by doing a couple of scenes of the clouds on the hill, a couple of landscapes.

I always wanted to be a painter. I painted flash with ink and watercolor, but I never did a lot of painting. I started doing small acrylics of albino gorillas. There was a famous albino gorilla in some zoo in Europe that Malone told me about, and my Asian zodiac year is the monkey. And, of course, this is me—a white monkey over in Hawaii.

It was a complete Rip Van Winkle thing. I had been out of the art world for twenty years. It is not that I wasn't thinking about art and kind of staying in touch, going to occasional museum shows, but it wasn't my main focus. Tattooing took up all the time. I woke up in Hawaii with a brush in my hand. It was a challenge just to work on my own art and develop something.

I was still somehow laboring under the yoke of feeling that tattoos made you a second- or third-class citizen. It wasn't an accepted art medium, although I kept trumpeting that idea. I was publishing magazines, talking to the press, whatever I could do to help legitimize it, but I realized I was as much a victim of this kind of mentality as anyone. I thought I shouldn't touch tattoos in my artwork, that it would undermine some kind of legitimacy, or purity, that I stupidly felt. But this imagery, that I have been drawing since I was ten years old, was part of my artistic DNA. Once I understood that, I knew I could make art with anything. The subject doesn't matter. It is only an excuse, a trick to get them into the tent, to look at this thing that you made in some way that's going to affect them above and beyond the narrative content of the imagery. You want to hit them with some kind of mystery.

I tried to return to what drew me to tattoo designs in the first place, the kind of beauty that they had, the kind of specific, unique stories that they told, and began to mix those with completely unrehearsed ideas.

When I started doing watercolors, I was still working pretty much with things that had an outline, like a tattoo, but with more subtle tones. I would simply put on some music, start painting, open up my mind, and see what came out. I immediately began having fun. There was no big intention. I was trying to hang on to the purity. I didn't want to turn this into a day job, another way to pay the rent, which had always been my tendency, coming from a blue-collar upbringing. I was simply going to try it out. I thought I might eventually want to show these things in art shows or a gallery, but, at that point, I was just making work. I started photographing them, carrying around little albums of photos, and that began my whole reconnection with personal art.

I started doing the gorilla paintings probably in February. One of the two pieces I did the first day that I painted was called *Nosebleed Angel.* I had the notion to do a cloaked head, influenced, as I was, by late medieval art like Dürer. I'm not into Christianity, but I like the look—people with robes, the crucifixes, all the potent, symbolic religious imagery. What came out on my brush that day was this very delicate flying thing, in subtle watercolor tones. I used a lot of understated shades in the veil that suggested a face or a skull, but it was only blushes of pure, transparent color. From under the veil trailed a crimson line, like a ropey drip of blood. I thought, *If this is an angel, you shouldn't be able to see its face*. It wasn't plotted; that is the kind of crazy-ass scenario that occurs to you while you're making pictures.

Some of my watercolors had specific heraldic Americana tattoo images, like black panther heads and American flags, only done kind of weird. The rule I made for myself was I was not going to draw anything out. I was not going to put down any marks with pencil. I was going to start with the brush and follow what developed. You can surprise yourself. That was a huge revelation. It was like being back in high school when I would sit down and make marks, make pictures, bang it out.

But having that bank of tattoo images, the muscle memory of knowing how to draw not only specific tattoos, but all the Asian stuff, and all the rules of composition, never left me. All my work, tattoos or whatever, had evolved keeping in mind Taoist principles of composition, a yin-yang universe of opposites. The appeal of the images lay in the fact that they were designed with these balances of power. You're putting it together with this hidden architecture.

I started playing specifically off tattoo images, the tattoo designs that hit me with the greatest mystery when I was a kid hanging out at Bert Grimm's, like the *Rose of No Man's Land,* based on a World War I tattoo design that came from a popular song. It was an homage to the nurses at the front—a nurse's head with a red cross on her wimple set in the middle of a rose, often with the phrase in a ribbon, "Rose of No Man's Land." The first tattoo I put on my ankle was a woman's head in profile coming out of a flower—she wasn't a nurse, but it was a woman's head coming out of a flower. I started painting takes on these things, triptych pieces with the woman's head flanked by mysterious objects like these anthropomorphic cactus figures I did in one painting. I wasn't setting out to do something far out or surrealist. It was just the way my head worked.

Since I first started hanging out at Bert Grimm's, I have been consumed with passion for a tattoo called "Rock of Ages," based on a famous nineteenth-century hymn. There were only a few

back piece themes dating from the late nineteenth century offered in shops. There would be a crucifix and angels. Another was
called *Duel in the Sun*, based on a Brooklyn Joe Lieber design (per-
haps adapted from a Japanese example), which showed two eagles
fighting midair over a rabbit. Bert Grimm put that one on Lyle
Tuttle's back. And there was *Rock of Ages*. Out in the middle of a
vast ocean and a sinking ship, a woman climbs from the stormy
sea and clings to an oversized rugged cross on a cairn of rocks.
The original hymn was written by a British preacher, Reverend
Toplady, who took refuge during a rainstorm in a cleft in the rocky
landscape in the south of England about five miles from where
my father was born.

When I was being force-fed Lutheranism on Sundays by my
mother, and spending Saturdays in the tattoo shops, I would request that hymn. They thought it was sweet that little Donnie
was requesting hymns, but I would request that hymn because
when the whole congregation sang it, I could mentally put myself
back at Bert Grimm's, looking at the tattoos.

The first *Rock of Ages* watercolor I did featured some strange,
small cloaked angel heads flying around in the sky and a ship going down in the sea. I was sort of rewinding, going back through
my visual education in tattoos, starting with classical populist
American tattoo themes. I wasn't doing watercolors with the Japanese stuff, although that would come later.

I was making a lot of art in Hawaii. Every few weeks, I would
fly to San Francisco, sleep at the apartment, have dinner with
friends, and tattoo like a son of a bitch during the daytime. Back
on the rock, I would lock right back into doing my art. Of course,
I still had to work on drawings for tattoo commissions, but in
Hawaii, I had plenty of time. I would go back for three or four
weeks at a time and just dig it, go to the beach, and paint.

21.
Beyond Skin

I always knew I would want to show my art, but I started slowly. In 1990, I had a piece accepted for the annual juried show of contemporary work by artists living in Hawaii at the Honolulu Academy of Art.

Time was at a premium. I felt desperate to do as much of my art as I could, but I still had to spend a lot of time off the skin making prep drawings for the tattoos I was doing in San Francisco. There would be as many as fifteen people waiting for tattoos. They weren't all giant epics, but each one required planning, research, and drawing. Putting on the tattoo may seem like the work, but getting the image together was a big part of the deal.

Tattootime put us in touch with all sorts of different tattoo enthusiasts and we were always looking to expand our network. We received a fan letter from an art professor in Green Bay, Wisconsin, Davey Damkoehler, who said he was using *Tattootime* as a textbook in his class. He also mentioned that he had gotten a tattoo from Greg May, a Wisconsin tattooer about my age who I had met out in San Diego when I was tattooing at Doc Webb's. Greg was a wise-ass who learned to tattoo from Tatts Thomas in Chicago, who was also Sailor Jerry's teacher. He had a thriving shop in a resort town called Lake Geneva.

Greg tattooed with me at Ichiban briefly, after he broke up with his wife and came out to the coast. He liked tattooing, but he only had two small tattoos tucked away under his own T-shirt.

Basically, he tattooed because he liked the money. We parted ways when he came in, saw me painting some Marine Corps flash, and said, "You're putting too much color in that . . . It's going to take too long to put that on." I had enough of that shit from Doc Webb's wife: "No blue! No purple! Process them."

(Greg came to an unhappy end many years later when he was murdered by a couple he lived with and they dismembered his body with a chain saw, covered his severed head in a bucket with concrete, and stole his valuable Civil War memorabilia collection.)

I told Francesca that, if I played my cards right, I was sure this Davey Damkoehler would pay for me to give a talk to his class. I almost suggested as much in my reply so when his letter arrived asking me to lecture at Green Bay, I was hardly surprised. I had already been planning to route myself through Chicago and examine the collection at the Chicago Art Institute.

I went to New York on my way to Chicago to see some museum shows and check out the galleries. I occasionally would go to New York and tattoo a little bit in those days. In Manhattan I saw some prints by a Chicago artist named Tony Fitzpatrick, incredible small etchings that included tattoo and circus sideshow imagery, kind of faux naïve. I bought an etching of the palm of a hand with a tattoo. When I told the gallery owner I was on my way to Chicago, he gave me Tony's number. "You should call him," he said.

I went downstairs and called from a phone booth on Broadway. He knew who I was. He had been bagging images from *Tattootime*. He found out I was doing art. He and master printer Steve Campbell had established a small fine arts press and he invited me to come to Chicago and make some prints. He also ran an art gallery he called World Tattoo because he loved the whole idea of tattoos. He also said he would like to give me a show.

In Green Bay, I gave a talk with a slide show. Because I always had been documenting my work, I showed them a lot of the great tattoos that had never been seen outside the pages of *Tattootime*: the balloon man, the squid man, the epic Japanese pieces I had turned out at Realistic. There was something good about being back in academia. I never did want to teach, but it can be cool to drop in, sell some snake oil, and get out of Dodge.

I'd never been to Chicago. The city blew my mind. The people were so straightforward and warm. I knew Chicago tattoo history from Phil Sparrow, Greg May, and Cliff Raven. His original shop still existed, although Cliff had long before moved to Los Angeles. I also admired a lot of mid-twentieth-century Chicago artists, from H. C. Westermann through the Hairy Who, a self-named group of postmodern imagists who first exhibited together at the Hyde Park Arts Center in 1966. It seemed like the Chicago and San Francisco art scenes shared certain qualities of eccentricity, humor, and Otherness. After our initial meeting, I made several trips there and Tony got me making etchings for the first time since art school. He also mounted my first solo show at his World Tattoo in 1992. It got good response and good sales.

Later that year, I got the chance to curate a show on the Rock of Ages theme at a cool Hollywood gallery. Artist and designer Billy Shire ran a small gallery on the hip strip of Melrose Avenue called La Luz de Jesus above a place started by his family in 1971, Soap Plant. Billy expanded with a location next door, Wacko, and basically showcased the unclassifiable mix of art, craft, culture, and pop humor that thrives in L.A. He showed a lot of Mexican folk art, but he also gave a lot of blue-chip artists their first shows. Robert Williams and Manuel Ocampo both had their first shows there. Billy had a great eye.

To accompany the exhibit, we published a prayer book with fake-leather binding, red-ribbon bookmark, and Old English typefaces to look like an eighteenth-century Bible. I invited various people I knew to contribute, both tattooers and artists in other mediums, and the theme took them in completely different directions. It was no longer simply a woman hanging on a cross in the middle of the ocean. That was a fun show. We were beginning to take this tattoo stuff, do something different with it, and take it places it had never been before.

About the same time, I wound up helping put together a photo exhibit of tattoos at a Santa Monica gallery run by Bryce Bannatyne. His family was in the antique business in the Bay Area and he became a specialist in Frank Lloyd Wright material and early-twentieth-century modernism. His gallery mixed paintings on the wall with original furnishings and architectural pieces by Wright on the floor. Gordon Cook's widow had tipped me off to him because he had put on a show of Gordon's paintings. When I went down to see the show, we stood outside his place and talked for three hours.

He wanted to do a show of photographs. He knew that photography was becoming a highly collectible commodity in the art world. We had a couple of shots from Robert Mapplethorpe of a muscled guy with a black panther on his arm. We had some photos by the always-collectible Joel-Peter Witkin, because I'd gotten to know his wife, Cynthia Witkin, who learned to tattoo from Jamie Sommers of Tattoo City. Jamie did a large conceptual piece on Cynthia's back. Cynthia herself was doing interesting tattoos based on Southwest imagery that got her written up in *Tattootime*.

We called the show Forever Yes. Bryce suggested the title emphasize the positive aspects of tattoos and I came up with the phrase after thinking about the sometimes mangled English expressions Japanese customers wanted on their tattoos. We did a blow-out party for the March 1993 opening, got a lot of publicity, and produced a fine catalog. After that, the show traveled to the Honolulu Academy of Art.

Through my Chicago connections I met Ann Nathan, who ran a well-established gallery in downtown Chicago, and put together a show with her, Eye Tattooed America, in 1993, which encompassed not only tattooers, but other artists who used tattoos in their work, including Ed Paschke, one of the most famous Chicago painters, part of the Hairy Who group that first blew my mind when I saw their work in an exhibit at the Art Institute when I was a student. I went to the opening, and did my dog-and-pony show with the slideshow. That traveled extensively. In 1994, I loaned a lot of work to a show of vintage flash, Flash from the Past, for the Hertzberg Circus Museum in San Antonio, Texas.

Meanwhile, around 1992, Mike McCabe, a New York friend, introduced me to Ann Philbin, director of the Drawing Center in New York, a superhip nonprofit space that did fabulous shows over wide-ranging themes. The only requirement for an exhibition was it had to be drawing. It could be a da Vinci, it could be graffiti, it could be anything, as long as it was a drawing. McCabe thought it would be a great place for a show of tattoo art.

Mike had a degree from Columbia in sociology and was one of the first people I met who was thoroughly conversant with street as well as academic culture. He had gotten introduced to tattooing through deVita and Richard O. Tyler on the Lower East Side. Tyler was a unique, complex character who'd been on the underground art scene in the city since the fifties, involved with Claes Oldenburg and others in the Happenings days. Tyler, who went by the name Reverend Relytor (his name reversed) evolved an extremely complicated mix of Tibetan Buddhism, numerology, and his own offbeat outlook. He published amazing mimeographed collages, tracts, and broadsides. He did amuletic tattoos, had a great sense of humor, and was one of the great undocumented underground artists of Manhattan. He and deVita co-owned side-by-side buildings on East Fourth Street. Tyler's was a disused synagogue where he held services of his own devising.

Mike had been tattooing for a while at his own shop, after working at a number of other things. With his great sense of humor, broad perspective, and respect for the deep Western tattoo heritage, he was as eager as I to get broader exposure for the art and the Drawing Center was a perfect fit.

We planned a historic survey, a hundred years of tattoo drawings, everything from nineteenth-century small books by tattooers in Yokohama to the latest designs. Young tattooers were coming up with extraordinary work at an incredible rate. It took a while to raise the funding and I had to help solicit contributions. One of my collectors, Laila Twigg-Smith, who bought my art and wasn't tattooed, made a generous gift. We called the show Pierced Hearts and True Love, from the title of an important early book about tattoos that I read when I was a kid.

When the exhibit opened in September 1995, it was written up in *The New York Times* and the *Village Voice*. The opening was the biggest opening of any kind that ever happened in SoHo. A thousand people clogged Wooster Street, closing it to traffic. John Waters was there. So were David Byrne and his wife Adelle Lutz. We held panel discussions. Academics debated tattoo art. We published another terrific catalog. Having stopped traffic in New York with an opening, tattoos seemed to have finally arrived on the art scene.

That year was one of the most intense ever. My father, at age ninety, had had a stroke. In 1975, he was forcibly retired by Uncle Sam and had flown out of Saigon just as the city fell. Returning to his wife in California, they soon moved to Arizona, where Sam could recapture his lifelong fascination with the Old West. I kept in touch with him and visited regularly. As my father's mental condition worsened, my stepmother ran out of patience. He was moved to a series of care facilities, getting booted out of one after another for his orneriness, until I finally flew down, retrieved him, and that February, moved him to a facility in Orange County, where my half-siblings could keep track of him.

In March, I traveled to Boulder, Colorado, to make lithographs with master printer and publisher Bud Shark. I'd met him and his wife, Barbara, in Honolulu the previous year. They'd seen my work, and invited me to their studio. During the two-week stay, we produced a portfolio of seven large prints based on traditional tattoo imagery, which we named the "Tattoo Royale Suite," the title inspired by the film *Pulp Fiction*.

In early May, Francesca and I went to Japan, where I produced another print project with master printer Paul Mullowney, an American expat who had printed in San Francisco. Paul was fluent in Japanese and headed a team producing intaglio etchings. We completed eight large complex etchings loosely based on Japanese mythology. During my stay, I received word that my father had died. In one of the prints of an ascending dragon, I made the dragon aiming at a cowboy boot disappearing into the storm clouds, and titled it "Cowboy to Heaven."

All the time, I kept doing tattoos full speed on both sides of the Pacific, while I lived in the middle. I made multiple trips every year to Tokyo, which was becoming less of an adventure and more of a regular part of my business. I didn't even notice how insane it was.

After only twenty-four hours in Tokyo on one 1989 trip, I found myself deeply enraptured at the *kabuki*, transported through centuries, watching excerpts from an eighteenth-century musical originally so long and complex, they took several days to present, which is why they only perform excerpts now. These were *ukiyo-e* woodblock prints come to life. I was sucked in by the sheer theatricality. The old myths seemed real and fraught with drama.

The next day I met with Shimada and some other guys in a coffee shop, straining to hear the conversation over a strident TV disaster show booming from the giant TV set behind the sushi bar with burned infants, frantic medics, animals in pain, cartwheeling dragsters on fire . . . a whole picnic of catastrophe. That juxtaposition right there was the signature thing about Japan: all this wonderful stuff, right along with this horrible shit. Tokyo could be hot and sweaty and stink like hell. I would drag myself home at night dead tired through the streets, catching whiffs of gas leaks and puke. I was living in Hawaii and surfing my ass off, with the scent of flowers wafting offshore. I was beginning to wonder why I was coming halfway around the world to be in the middle of *this*?

I tattooed from 10:00 A.M. to 1:30 A.M. nonstop without eating one day on that trip. I would pop cassette tapes in my boom box and go to my zone, while all these guys streamed through. My apartment had two chairs and a table. Whenever somebody needed to lie down for bodywork, I would drag in the sleeping couch. I was well past tattooing on the floor—that is what screwed up my hips in the first place—but my back went out nonetheless. Japan for me has always been kind of heaven and hell.

In March 1990, Francesca and I got to visit Hawaiian music man Martin Denny at his Honolulu home. My friend Vale, the North Beach documentarian/typographer who helped us with *Tattootime,* had conducted extensive phone interviews with maestro Denny for a lengthy article in his publication, *Incredibly Strange Music,* and asked if I would take pictures of him. Denny lived in a cool mid-century modern with all this natural lava rock in exclusive Black Point, right on the cliffs, overlooking the ocean. A weathered wood beachcomber sign announced the name of his home, QUIET VILLAGE, the title of the record that bought the place. We looked through his old photo albums. He had lived in South America for a number of years where he led bands with guys wearing big ruffled sleeves and all that. He had all his old albums with the sexy babes on the covers, and he spread them out on the floor. I got on a ladder and took photographs.

In April, I worked in Japan for two weeks, came back, and, a week later, went to Amsterdam for a tattoo convention put on by my friend Henk Schiffmacher, who crashed our party so memorably in Rome. When I first met Hanky Panky, as he called himself, he came through Realistic and got a tattoo from me before he started tattooing. He was a photographer and had me tattoo a roll of Kodachrome on the side of his forearm, with the film unwinding down his arm. A bit later, he owned a tattoo shop in the Voorburgwal, where the girls stand in the windows. Several years later, there were some complications involving Henk, a woman and her ex-boyfriend getting out of jail and he had to leave the tattoo field for a while.

Henk set up the convention in an abandoned church, famous as a rock-and-roll nightclub called the Paradiso. I agreed to tattoo at the convention and was immediately sorry. All I wanted to do, once I got there, was go to museums. I saw Rembrandt's house. I saw all the old masters at the Rijksmuseum.

Two weeks after I returned to Hawaii, Francesca graduated from the University of Hawaii with a degree in Japanese language, an interest she had pursued since we came back from living in Japan in 1973. She was enrolled in a graduate program in Japanese literature and was offered a scholarship to study for a year in Japan, which would have aided her in her goal to translate arcane nineteenth-century *kabuki* texts. Although enormously proud of her and the herculean effort she put into her studies, I had to be the bad guy. There was no way I could juggle our complex life commitments in two places, solo. I begged her to turn down Japan. It was a bitter blow to her, but she rebounded by immersing herself in classes in clothing construction and reconnecting with a life-long passion for textiles and fashion. In July, I went back again to Japan to work for two weeks. I did another two weeks in October, but the glamour of tattooing in Japan was wearing thin.

Moving beyond Western retro souvenirs, I was doing whole arms on people and starting to do back pieces. I was making better money for tattoos in Japan than I was in San Francisco—I would come home with cash—but my back was killing me. "Romance is gone," I wrote in my journal. "It all seems like why bother. I just want to be home. The novelty is off this. Attitude adjustment time."

But that is the way it is with pairs in Asian culture, always rising and descending. Soon enough, it would come to me. "I remember why I'm here. I'm shoveling imported coals in Newcastle." I was this henchman. I was doing dragons in the place where they were born.

One Japanese hipster brought in a photo of a '49 Ford in front of an A&W Root Beer stand, probably taken around 1956, when he and his friend came in for matching tattoos. He pointed to the flames on the hot rod and said he wanted those flames on his arm. He and his friend wanted tattoos of a large scroll like a pirate's map with an inscription: "Nothing can ever bother me because

Mr. Sumi is always with me. We are brothers under the skin."
They polished it off with one of Sailor Jerry's designs—a little
Hot Stuff in a cowboy outfit twirling a lariat. Sumi was his bud-
dy's name—and the kicker is that *sumi* is the word for traditional
Japanese ink.

Japan was crazy. In the morning, I watched some guy on TV
called Captain George in a show called *Good Morning Japan*. I
was going to a store that sold World War II military-looking ap-
parel called Poop Junior. I would meet friends at a coffee shop
called Fizz. They also had cigarettes called Life. Sometimes I
would listen to Armed Forces Radio just to hear English.

I spent almost the entire month of May 1991 in Japan, and
went back later in the year. In the same year, I made five working
trips to San Francisco. It had become obvious that Realistic was
hardly an ideal place for the young, with-it tattooers on the crew.
I handled my appointments at the Hamilton apartment and these
guys were stuck in the back of an office building without a sign
on the street. I started scouting around for a new location and
rented a place on the block of Columbus Avenue in North Beach
I had my eye on when I first started looking for shops in San Francisco seventeen years earlier. This would be the home of the new
Tattoo City. I did the last job at Realistic on June 20. I made it a
point to call Captain Colourz, who I put the first tattoo on in 1974
when I covered Lyle's name on his wrist. I put a heart on him to
close out the cycle.

It was about that same time that I did one of my most extraordinary tattoos, "Freeway Panther." Don Pugsley was someone I
had tattooed since the late seventies at Realistic. He had served in
Vietnam as a special forces medic, and then studied in the writing program at the University of Iowa. A big guy, he had a Japanese-
style shoulder piece from Cliff Raven in Chicago and made the
pilgrimage to San Francisco for one of my dragons to balance out
his other side. Eventually Don moved to Los Angeles to try his
hand at screenwriting and developed a solid career as a character
actor.

Pugsley watched with interest as tattoos became increasingly inventive and intricate, but he felt that the art had devolved into excessive fussiness in polychromatics and detail, and the real power of American tattooing had been lost. He had been saving his back for something dramatic, a piece that would be instantly readable to someone driving by on the freeway at sixty miles per hour. That's when I came up with "Freeway Panther," an enormous panther head, neck, and bloody claw that completely filled his back.

From its first appearance in the thirties, the black panther had been the signature image in American tattooing. An instant classic with a graceful silhouette on the skin, the primal form that harks back to millenniums-old designs on Chinese bronzes. Sailor Jerry's dream was to develop a new tattoo style that would borrow formal elements of scale and composition from Japan, but utilize uniquely American subject matter. Pugsley wanted to make this a reality and we'd tossed ideas around for years. This tattoo represented the fusion we envisioned.

Grinding black ink into his skin hour after hour, carefully avoiding his numerous small moles with my face inches away from the surface, I felt like I was slogging across a vast epidermal night sky, with the moles as stars. The tattoo was a tarry specter. When he pulled up his shirt to show off the finished piece, people instinctively would back up, recoiling from the tattoo's luminous presence.

Doug went to Hawaii in 1992 to take up Malone's offer to teach him to tattoo. Doug had been around it his whole life and used to help me in the shops. I would paint tattoos on him when he was a kid. But I refused to let him get any tattoos when he started getting interested as a teenager.

When he turned eighteen, all he wanted for his birthday was a tattoo. He picked a scene from classical mythology, *Apollo Slaying Python in Front of the Oracle at Delphi*. I had to research it and draw it up. But he never did express any interest in doing tattoos. Malone had already made the offer to teach Sailor Jerry's son.

Doug had worked at Safeway and, through a friend he met a at work, landed a job crunching numbers with a securities firm.

He had come to Hawaii with his girlfriend for a visit and Malone put a tribal design on the backs of his calves. I told him on the phone that Malone made this offer, certain he wasn't interested in learning to tattoo, but to my surprise, he was receptive. Doug was an alternative culture guy, hung out with alternative people, but he worked in a totally square environment. "At the end of the day, all I have is a bunch of goddamn figures in a drawer," he said, "I think I'd like to get into tattooing."

He moved to Hawaii to work with Malone in the old Sailor Jerry shop. Malone recruited Doug's "practice potatoes" from the multitude of drunks and junkies among the street people in Chinatown, inveigled into the shop with the offer of a free tattoo. They worked together, ass to elbow, in that tiny space, while Doug served a true apprenticeship. He also came to the Forever Yes opening in Santa Monica, and Bob Roberts' son Charlie was there as well. He also was just starting to tattoo. They joked with each other about holding their noses and diving into the same wicked life they'd been raised around.

I went back to Tokyo in October 1991. I was working on the Forever Yes show at Bryce Bannatyne's gallery, and trying to connect with a Japanese photographer who had photographed a lot of Horiyoshi III's work in Yokohama. The rockabilly guys were starting to want me to do less conservative tattoos. One guy brought me a Japanese comic book and wanted a tattoo of some character with a cross on his back and reapers for arms. There were a few more people tattooing around Tokyo—still underground, but tattooing. I was starting to see people with non-Japanese traditional design tattoos they got from traditional Japanese tattooers. I saw a wolf head on one guy and was surprised to learn he got the tattoo from a traditional Japanese artist. Because the youngsters were starting to want this, some of the traditional tattooers wanted to get that market going.

One of my customers was a man who owned a hipster clothing

store in another city and took the train with his wife and infant son for two hours to be tattooed by me. He had a mix of rockabilly tattoos and dragons, but I also lined out a large "Elvis Presley Forever" on his arm with a long, thorny rose branch wrapped around it, a tattoo based on a dream I had. He dressed completely like a fifties bad boy, but would bow to you when he walked in the room.

I always liked taking friends to Japan and, in 1993, went over with Bob Roberts. We stayed friends even though I fired him from Realistic. Everything worked out in the long run. He kept the underground tattoo shop in his apartment near Gramercy Park going for years until somebody figured out that he was making a lot of money, and knocked on his door. "It's me," the customer said. He'd just finished getting his tattoo and stepped out for a few minutes. When Roberts opened the door, the guy was pointing an Uzi at him. He took him for everything. After that, Bob got tired of New York and moved back to Los Angeles.

I took Malone to Japan that August, but I was also spending a lot of time in Chicago, where I had started making prints with Tony Fitzpatrick and held my first solo show at his gallery, World Tattoo. The Forever Yes show had opened in March. It had a lot of publicity. There was a lot of interest in that. We did a very cool book for it. I was feverishly working on my own art.

It was in Chicago that I did some tattoos for a good friend of mine, Brian Wells, a terrific painter. I tattooed him a few times with very unusual stuff that he had me design, unusual not just in subject matter, but workmanship. He wanted dumb drawing that looked like a kid did it. That was challenging because my natural tendency is to make tattoos look as good as you can. Brian liked tattoos that may have looked awkward, but they held meaning to him and he had a highly developed sense of aesthetics. It really opened up my head to a more sophisticated approach to this as a medium that could be almost anything.

He had me do a tattoo in 1993 based on the famous Robert Rauschenberg piece, *Erased de Kooning Drawing*, where Rauschenberg took a drawing from Willem de Kooning to deliberately erase as an act of art. He erased it to almost nothing. Brian wanted an erased tattoo.

We decided we needed something iconic and we settled on the black panther. I worked it all out on paper. I insisted he erase it down, got the smudges, and then copied it on his arm. He loves going into tattoo shops and telling them he has an Ed Hardy tattoo. When they ask to see it, he pulls up his sleeve and deadpans, "I don't know what went wrong."

But Malone always wanted to go to Japan, so we went. Toward the end of this trip, I spent more than five hours on one guy's arm, another five hours plus on another guy, both arms and his chest. An hour and a half on another fellow who didn't sit well. Most of the guys took it like stones, but it is torture to inflict on someone who can't take it. "I hate this kind of grind." I wrote in my journal. "Never again?" With a question mark—like the old tattoo design for navy guys, "U.S.N. never again."

Malone was sick a lot of the time, but we went to an antique toy museum in Kyoto, as he had always been a fan of Japanese toys. I went to a *kabuki* with the famous actor, Ganjiro, part of a venerable acting family, who Francesca and I got to know when he appeared in Honolulu. I went backstage and brought him a small tribute painting. I was painting in hotel rooms in Chicago, Japan, L.A. I would carry sets of acrylics, drawing supplies, paper, and little canvases and work wherever I was. Any time I could grab to do my own artwork, I did. But I needed to hone in and focus. I resolved this would be my final work trip to Japan.

Photo: Dan Thome

ABOVE: Tattoo models in Trajan's Marketplace, Rome, 1985.

AT LEFT: Tales of the South Pacific: Ed tattoos the natives in Peleliu, Palau, 1983.

BELOW: Ed with Dr. Fukushi, holding "wet skins," Tokyo, 1983.

AT LEFT: Tokyo rockabilly girl, 1985.

COUNTER-CLOCKWISE FROM BOTTOM LEFT:
Three views of the "Max Ernst Jukebox/
Figure Leaping into Space/ Return to Sender
Goddess" wrap-around tattoo, 1981–82.

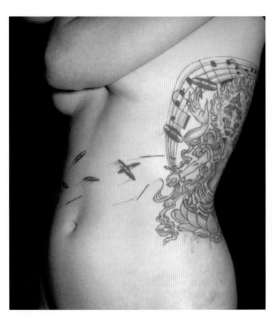

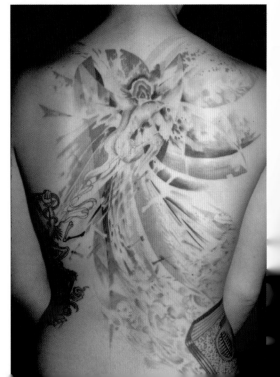

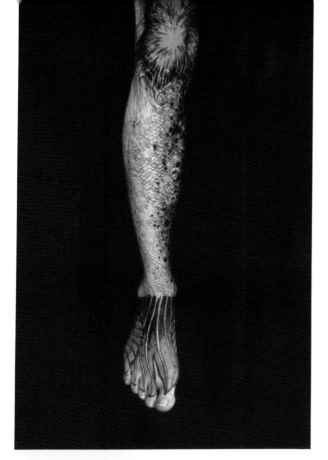

Photo: Patricia Steur

TOP LEFT: A visual pun on
Bill Salmon's leg. 1982–87.

ABOVE: Ed, Francesca, and
Rocky, Honolulu, 1989.

AT LEFT: Freeway Panther,
1991.

Photo: Cat Gwynne

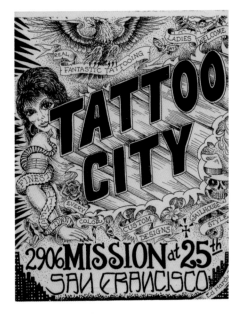

THIS SPREAD: Selection of Tattoo City and Realistic Tattoo flyers.

ABOVE: *Rose of No Man's Land,* watercolor, 1988. (Tom Patchett collection)

FAR LEFT: *The Rock*, watercolor, 1988. (Mary Lynn Price collection)

AT LEFT: Art for the poster to the exhibit, "Pierced Hearts and True Love" at the Yerba Buena Center, San Francisco, 1992.

BELOW: 2000 Dragons, on display, Track 16, Santa Monica, 2000.

Photo: Mary Lynn Price

TOP: The first Ed Hardy store, Melrose and Fairfax Avenues, Hollywood, 2005.

MIDDLE PHOTOS: Madonna and Steven Tyler of Aerosmith in *Love Kills Slowly*.

AT RIGHT: Adrien Brody and Christian Audigier, the marketing genius behind the brand.

AT RIGHT: Ed in San Francisco, around the corner from his studio, 2008.

BELOW: Two Generations of Tattoo: Ed and Doug Hardy, Tattoo City, San Francisco, 2012.

22.
2000 Dragons

I was spinning too many hats on too many sticks, trying to keep everything in the air. All the travel, my personal artwork, tattooing like a son of a bitch, going back and forth to Hawaii, other trips that weren't for tattooing, organizing shows and everything else, I wasn't paying close enough attention to Tattoo City.

I found out that Freddy Corbin, a terrific guy, great artist, and a charismatic character who had essentially become my manager at Tattoo City, was also a heroin addict. I was the last person in town to know. Somebody told me he saw him down standing in line for the needle exchange on Haight Street. I went ballistic. I realized it was impossible for me to run the shop and the crew and keep this Hawaiian fantasy of surfing and painting going. We had the little apartment which, of course, nobody else used.

Freddy was actually over in Amsterdam on vacation with a woman he'd just married who had fallen fatally ill from infections associated with her drug use. When I met him at the San Francisco airport, I was on the verge of choking him. A friend of mine who was a recovering addict came along for moral support and talked me down. At any rate, he was officially fired and I knew I had to move back to San Francisco.

We had sold the apartment at the Hamilton in 1996 and used the money to buy a Victorian flat on Francisco Street behind the Art Institute, where we stayed on our trips to the city. We had two dogs—Sonny and Ruby, Rocky's offspring, born right before he died—and a cat, Mr. Kitty, and a storage unit stuffed full. We moved twenty tons out of Hawaii, boxes and boxes of books, all my surfboards. We briefly put the house in Hawaii up for sale, but the market had dropped and we only received ridiculous, cheap offers and changed our minds. We got a property manager, put a tenant in the upstairs, and kept the downstairs, where there was a side entrance to my studio and Francesca's sewing room. We bought a microwave and made a place where we could stay on our brief forays there.

I rented a studio above a strip club off Broadway, a few blocks from Tattoo City, where I could do my artwork, and went back to work doing tattoos at the shop. We looked at real estate every weekend in San Francisco for a year, hoping to find a bigger space. Property values kept rocketing up. We eventually expanded our real estate search to Berkeley and Oakland, although we had never before lived in the East Bay. After several months we found a fantastic place in Oakland, a big lot covered with trees. In the back, there was a small garage built for a Model A that I turned into a cool studio. It was a huge adjustment in all ways, but we made a lot of friends and began learning about all the virtues of Oakland and Berkeley. Francesca had a great sewing room and our garden yielded amazing produce.

Once we settled in that house, and started taking the dogs for walks and enjoying the neighborhood, I began to realize how fucked up my leg was—I'd had back problems ever since returning from Gifu in 1973, and now had developed sciatica. I was pulling a shift at the shop starting at ten in the morning, working until early afternoon to beat rush hour on the Bay Bridge, and making lots of art in my studio, doing a number of large paintings. I started showing with Ruth Braunstein in San Francisco.

Then I met Manuel Ocampo, a painter originally from the Philippines who was living in L.A. He was a young guy who had caught on with collectors and had a great career going. I first saw his work at a groundbreaking L.A. show at the Museum of Contemporary Art called Helter Skelter. It showcased a huge range of very wild work by SoCal artists that demolished the cliché of that era as an immature, brainless, sun-soaked place devoid of "serious culture." Ocampo's work hit me as hard as any art I'd ever seen, really opened my head with its combination of transgressive black humor, masterful painting, and totally unexpected themes. We connected soon after he came to Honolulu to show some of his work.

It was Manuel who introduced me to Tom Patchett, a successful TV writer for Carol Burnett and Bob Newhart, among others, who had established a gallery called Track 16 at the new Bergamot Station arts complex in Santa Monica, where he also kept his own massive collection of art and Americana, a lot of which had been rummaged from the Pasadena flea market.

Tom had become a fan and collector of Ocampo. He came to San Francisco to visit me with a young curator from the gallery named Laurie Steelink, who came out of the fine art world. Both Laurie and her husband, Bill Becchio, earned their undergraduate degrees at the San Francisco Art Institute and their graduate degrees at Rutgers. She had done a lot of interesting stuff around the eastern seaboard, and had been deeply involved in the Fluxus movement, before taking this job at the gallery. Most important, both Laurie and Bill had done tattooing. She knew about me, and understood the tattoo thing and its relationship to so-called high art. It also turned out that I'd met her husband Bill when they both were undergraduates at the Art Institute. Sitting behind him at a lecture, I had spotted an outline of a bomb he had someone tattoo on the back of his head, visible through his short hair, unusual for the time.

Tom bought one of my key works, a framed watercolor triptych of the "Rose of No Man's Land," which I had hanging in Tattoo City, and came over to the apartment to look at my other art. He offered me a show on the spot. He wanted to do a joint show with me and Ocampo, which was a real coup for me because Manuel was a big deal in the international art scene. He and I had become tight. We were swapping pieces and doing collaborative painting together when I visited his studio in Los Angeles. It was an honor for me to get into this gallery with him.

Track 16 was a gigantic space. The front room was about three thousand square feet and there was a series of other rooms. They did things like a show on the history of punk rock in Los Angeles that displayed musicians' shirts, photographs, records, record covers, all these original Raymond Pettibon flyers for the punk shows at Madame Wong's (Pettibon's brother was in Black Flag). Exene of X played the opening. It was a totally connected, L.A.-centric, pop/movie star/record business kind of thing. Tom did it because it was cool.

The show I did was called Permanent Curios. Patchett wanted me to include some of my flash and, at first, I resisted. But we cooked up the idea to do an entire installation around tattoos. We built a small structure we called the Tattoo Hut. I made up fake business cards for "Doc Hardy" and "Mojo Manila," and we drew wacky, ironic flash. I filled out the walls with this, and flash from my earlier street shops and hung a shower curtain for an entrance. When you slid back the shower curtain, a motion sensor was triggered that set off an old tattoo machine, rigged to make an especially irritating racket. It was in a vise, like tattooing is a vice.

I painted a dummy rail and put together a mix tape from the forties and fifties of songs that evoked that era to me: "Cherry Pink and Apple Blossom White" by Perez Prado, "Harlem Nocturne" by Johnny Otis, "I'm a Man" by Bo Diddley, and Ernest Tubb's "My Filipino Baby" (a nod to my partner in the project), all coming out of a speaker behind one of Patchett's old Bakelite radios. The music was on repeat. I sprayed the walls with a mixture of Vaseline and green hospital soap and everybody who had ever been in a tattoo shop said it smelled exactly like a tattoo shop. Walking into classic shops, you were hit on all the senses. We put chicken wire from the top of the dummy rail to the ceiling, like Colonel Blake's Wild West Museum in Corona del Mar when I was growing up.

The morning the show was going to open, when I walked in there and the tattoo machine and the music went on, it gave me the chills. Instant time travel. It felt like I was ten years old and walking into Bert Grimm's. As I'd always been pretty much a flat art guy, this was a revelation. All the shops I'd built were done with every detail intentionally and minutely planned, but to build one as a replica of my compulsive "real life" pursuits opened my head up to a new dimension.

Another great show opportunity came up that same year, along with the opportunity to rub shoulders with one of the great art heroes of my youth. I'd met Houston artists Jack Massing and Michael Galbreth—The Art Guys—when Ruth Braunstein paired us up for a show at her Braunstein/Quay Gallery. I was proud to be showing with Ruth, who represented Pete Voulkos and John Altoon, two of my other art heroes from my formative years. The Art Guys offered to give me a solo show at their large studio, where they occasionally put on shows of work they liked. When they told me they were associated with Walter Hopps, the curator of the legendary Ferus Gallery in Los Angeles during the sixties that I had so faithfully attended, I made tracks for Houston in early 1998. The Art Guys installed a huge amount of my work and held a lively opening with many sales. And I did, indeed, meet Hopps, at that time the director of the prestigious Menil Collection in Houston. He bought some of my work and we stayed in close touch until his death in 2005.

When I told Tom Patchett my plans to publish a comprehensive retrospective of everything I had done, he wanted to partner with me. In 1999, we mounted an exhibit, Tattooing the Invisible Man, at Track 16 to go with the book's publication. In that front room alone, we had eight hundred things on the wall—everything from the pencil flash that I drew when I was ten years old to my most recent paintings, works in all kinds of media, and a "racing stripe" of hundreds of four-by-six photos of tattoos I'd done running along the walls. This show drew a lot of attention and I noticed people who were tattoo clients starting to buy my art. Oliver Leiber, for one, who I had tattooed extensively and was the son of songwriter Jerry Leiber, bought several pieces.

In September 1999, we set up a trip to Japan with three of the other Tattoo City tattooers, as tourists, not working. One of them, Colin Stevens, had been raised in Japan and served as the resident interpreter.

While I was in Japan, I was deep in the final stages of the Tattooing the Invisible Man exhibit, painting watercolors, walking around with these young guys, going to museums during the hot, humid days, and seeing *kabuki* and other cultural delights at night. My left leg was starting to give out and was in a lot of pain, but I was determined to visit one of my favorite ancient Japanese places.

While we were in Kyoto, the other guys went off to visit a young tattooer in Osaka. Colin and I took a short train ride to Fushimi Inari, a Shinto shrine in southern Kyoto that dates back more than 1,200 years. Thousands of closely-built vermilion *torii* gates straddle a network of trails leading up a sacred mountain. We started climbing.

We were standing in the light rain by a small lake. There was an old woman deeply intoning a sutra, surrounded by ceramic white foxes that are the symbol of good fortune and glad tidings. These Inari shrines have swarms of fox statues, different sizes. In the middle of the pond, standing straight up on his fins, was a giant, completely white koi. I went all chicken skin before he splashed back in the water. I am deep in fucking Japan now, I thought. It was hypnotic, the kind of complex convergence of ancient tradition, symbolism, and nature, beyond words. That country got into my blood.

Around that time, Malone called one day with a curious proposition. He had been contacted by somebody from Philadelphia named Larry McGearty, who founded Retroactive Menswear in 1989. He sold rockabilly gear to Japanese hipsters. He dealt in dead stock: new, unsold clothing sent to Japan, where it was marketed as vintage Americana. He wanted to use Sailor Jerry's designs to create a "new" retro clothing line with this growing market in Japan in mind.

Malone didn't want to have anything to do with anything outside of the shop. After Jerry died, Mike paid a considerable sum to his widow Louise for the tattoo business and that included everything, even the rights to the designs. He told me if I handled the business, we could split whatever we made fifty-fifty. I talked to Larry. He was a personable guy, sincere, who really dug what Jerry did. He had a couple of tattoos. Since even before the first *Tattootime*, I had been crusading to have Sailor Jerry recognized as the tattoo hero he was. We put his name out there as much as we could, included his flash in exhibitions and you could see awareness of his work on the rise. McGearty was partners with a big time ad agency in Philadelphia and they did have a good eye. They became interested in doing a whole line of hipster Sailor Jerry products, like bowling-ball bags and purses, accessories for the rockabilly lifestyle. We signed the deal and Malone and I started receiving quarterly royalty checks, a few thousand bucks each.

It seemed strange, but incidental to me. Stranger things still lurked around the bend, things I could have never imagined, as tattoo art—a phrase that practically didn't exist when I started— sunk ever more deeply into the mainstream culture.

The approaching millennium triggered my determination to make a memorable work involving dragons. I decided to paint two thousand dragons on a two-thousand-foot surface to mark the occasion. On New Year's Day 2000, I started, and Francesca snapped a picture of the first brush mark on the paper. I bought an old ledger to keep tedious, minute records of every aspect of the project: how many feet I painted that day, the number of dragons I did, what music I listened to. I photographed it all, Scotch-taping the photos together and putting them along the wall so I could see the sequence.

Bud Shark, with whom I had been doing prints in Boulder,

Colorado, turned me on to Tyvek, the material they use to make FedEx envelopes. It is both extraordinarily lightweight and strong. I ordered a four-foot-by-five-hundred-foot roll from DuPont. A friend built a roll-through easel for me. I was working in a small garage built in the twenties, barely big enough for me, my paints, and the easel. I could only see about five feet of the scroll at a time and I numbered each dragon in Chinese. I didn't paint constantly, still worked at Tattoo City four or five days a week. Life was still complicated, so I would get in the studio when I could. We made a couple of trips to L.A. and New York. In early February, we spent over a week in Belgium, to see a huge retrospective of the eccentric visionary painter James Ensor (1860–1949), who was one of my favorite artists since high school. We spent a lot of time in the museum show, traveled to Ensor's house and studio in Ostend, and saw a lot of other great art.

I finished the dragon scroll on July 28—2,000 square feet, in 125 hours work time, 52 days of painting scattered sporadically over the seven months.

I knew dragons. I had made an extensive study of the theme, not simply as shapes and designs, but the mythology and meaning behind the dragon. They are the most powerful symbol in Asia. Of course, it's a symbol throughout the world, but in Asia it stands for strong, essentially positive forces and ties in with the whole Taoist thing. I had drawn, painted, and tattooed so many dragons, I could do them in my sleep.

I started one like this, one like that. As I got into it, I thought, *There can be big ones.* I began throwing paint around more, working with my body and my whole arm, instead of only the ends of my fingers that you use to do a tattoo or an etching. I always wanted to work loose, like those New York–school action painters— Bill de Kooning, Franz Kline, and those cowboys.

The dragons got pretty big—the largest was about thirty feet. Some were tiny, maybe an inch long. I've been influenced enough by Japanese design to have enigmatic things coming in from the sides, but on this painting I took advantage of all the breathing room afforded me. I could have waves roll in and die out. I left one section with nothing happening. On another part of the scroll there are no dragons, only a couple of clouds, then a couple of little dragons, and next some big thing erupts.

I painted a part that looked like a peeling wall with dragon frescos showing through. In one section I took a rag of red paint, swished it across the top, and let it run down, then broke it off with a hard edge and a small dragon emerging from the red. Most of the dragons were Asian, although toward the end I put in a large Quetzalcoatl, a feathered serpent to represent Mayan and Aztec art, and segued into a whirlpool I copied from one of my favorite late-nineteenth-century Japanese artists. That was the only thing I really copied on the entire scroll, but it is a very cool whirlpool. The whole thing seemed symphonic to me.

Painting this changed me in a fundamental way, opened possibilities I didn't know I could explore. From then on, I was high on working larger, looser, expanding the spontaneity I'd begun exploring when we moved to Honolulu. Thirteen years being reconnected to my personal art had been great, running studio time in tandem with tattooing, but this was a new dimension.

Laurie at Track 16 devised an ingenious way to display the scroll using airplane wire and bulldog clips. She installed it like a maze, four feet high and five hundred feet long. The scroll turned to accent the composition as it developed. When Francesca saw the whole scroll installeded for the first time, its serpentine design crawling around the room, suspended by wires, she immediately saw an unexpected resemblance. "There is the 2,001st dragon," she said.

The millennium was a big year for me. In addition to the big scroll, my alma mater, the San Francisco Art Institute, awarded me an honorary doctorate. The components of my life were beginning to blend together more tightly.

After Track 16, the scroll, through Bud Shark's connections, went to the Museum of Contemporary Art in Denver in 2001. In 2002, 2000 Dragons showed at the Yerba Buena Center for the

Arts in San Francisco. Donald Richie wrote an essay for the catalog. We took the scroll to a biennial exhibit in Ecuador where I was the sole U.S. representative and showed it in an old deconsecrated cathedral in Cuenca, a world heritage city high in the Andes. From there it went to Guayaquil and Quito. Each time it is displayed, you get a different take on it. Most recently, it was exhibited in summer of 2012 at Diverse Works, a nonprofit Houston art space.

I was hobbling around the Yerba Buena opening. My left hip finally had to be replaced in 2002. I came home from the surgery with a dislocated hip, but had no idea until I went for my first postoperative checkup a month later. I knew something was wrong from the time I left the hospital, but, I deferred to the doctor. The pain was intense and I developed a jones for Vicodin. I had never been a pill head in my life and here I was, eating all these painkillers and sitting around in a fog watching old TV shows.

Another doctor handled the second surgery. When I was healed enough to walk, I had enough. I wanted to go where it was warm. I wanted to get back in the water. I wanted to go home to Hawaii. We put the Oakland place on the market and moved back to Honolulu.

In March 2003, Track 16 mounted a joint show with me and Bob Roberts. Originally we were going to make it a three-way with Malone, but Malone was too busy with other things. To advertise the show, we printed an old-fashioned, rainbow-colored boxing poster and posed bare-chested with our fists up: "Mad Dog Mutant vs. Don The Dog." It was, after all, an "Exhibition Match." Laurie and Mary Lynn Price, another close friend on whom I did an all-color, no-black abstract backpiece evocative of underwater life, produced a short documentary on Bob and me. Along with the film, an article about the exhibit, with eight pages of color photographs of our paintings appeared in the "Tattoo Art" issue of *Juxtapoz* magazine.

The editor of the hip, new art magazine was my old pal Robert

Williams, who advertised his "Zombie Mystery Paintings" at the *Queen Mary* tattoo convention. Williams, who started out working with Big Daddy Ed Roth and was an underground comics star with R. Crumb and the others at *Zap Comix,* understood street arts like tattoo. He led the issue with a piece about Tattoo City featuring me and the whole crew. But it was the paintings from the exhibit in the magazine that blew away Tatsuro Ishihara.

Tatsu and his partner Steven Hoel ran a small fashion operation called Ku USA. They had a line of casual Asian-influenced wear that Tatsu designed and a small store on Melrose Avenue in Hollywood and another couple of little shops in Tokyo. It was Steven who got me on the phone and told me they wanted to use my tattoo images on clothing. I wasn't interested. I had tattoo T-shirts in the shop for years and had no interest in putting them on production clothing.

I had been doing T-shirts since I saw Kid Jeff and Big Daddy Roth airbrushing shirts at the car shows in 1958. I had worked with Ed Nolte, who had a silkscreen business in the late seventies and we did a bunch of shirts with my some of my more Asian images. We did a set of silk-screened prints of the animals in the Asian zodiac. It was fun, but I didn't think there was any money in it.

I told Steven no, I didn't want to be bothered. But Steven was patient and persistent, and proposed a trip to San Francisco. I told him he could come up if he wanted. He drove up and brought a bunch of their products.

When he walked into the tattoo shop, I thought we were going to have to call a medic. He had never been in a tattoo shop. The thousands of bright, shiny, flashy colored designs staring down from the walls was sheer image overload and practically put him flat out on his back. He couldn't believe what he was seeing. "This could be phenomenal," he said.

Their clothing was all quality. Smart and cool, sort of reserved, casual-wear stuff with an Asian angle, the clothes featured themes lifted from classical Asian art or Buddhist calligraphy, designs guaranteed to strike a chord with me. Steven also impressed me as an enthusiastic, honest man. I started to think this might be cool, after all.

He and Tatsu were very aware of the Sailor Jerry gear and they sleuthed it out that I was partly responsible for that. Steve knew the Sailor Jerry line from attending trade shows. He wanted to know what was going on with the Sailor Jerry deal. When I told him, he suggested I might not be getting paid what I should. "I'll go to those shows and see what they're selling," he said.

I liked these guys and signed a deal for them to use my tattoo designs. I gave them access to my flash and they went through a lot of material. The first line had one shirt emblazoned with a ghost with cherry blossoms in her hair, screaming, with lightning coming out of her mouth. Another had the heart and skull with ribbons that say "Love Kills Slowly."

23.

Christian

Christian Audigier, fresh out of the hospital from a heart attack, wandered into the Ku store on Melrose, where they had some Ed Hardy shirts in the window. He was the fashion visionary who put the Von Dutch name on trucker's hats and made a fortune. The Von Dutch store was on the same block, although he and the Von Dutch company had recently come to an acrimonious parting of the ways. He bought a couple of the Ed Hardy shirts, intrigued by what he saw, and came back the next day.

Steven and Tatsu had been getting ecstatic responses to their Don Ed Hardy line at trade shows, but they were seriously small time compared to someone like Christian. They had been talking about finding somebody with deep pockets who could take this big time. They had been speaking with a Korean company that made jeans. Steven said to me, "This could be as big as O. P." I couldn't believe that tattoo T-shirts could ever be in the same league with surf wear like that.

Christian returned to the Ku store and wanted to know who this Ed Hardy was. He had been out with some friends, who flipped for the shirts. "Oh, Christian, is this your new line?" He was actively looking for his "next big thing" and I guess that he saw the Ed Hardy designs as something that could be marketed in the way that he knew how—get a product on celebrities and let it market itself. And he was right.

When Steven called and started to tell me about the guy, I didn't know him from Adam, but I knew about Von Dutch. He was one of my early pinstriping heroes. Dutch (Kenny Howard) was the first car painter to create elaborate, eccentric pinstriping and flames on the burgeoning kustom kar scene of the early fifties. He was offbeat, opinionated, and difficult to deal with, but a visionary in his field. Before long, cars with wild paint jobs were often referred to as having been "Von Dutched." The Von Dutch clothing line, mainly trucker caps and T-shirts, had been extremely successful and stirred up a lot of controversy among the hipster hot rod people, who felt that Von Dutch's name and legacy had been usurped. Dutch died years before and rights to his name and images, initially sold by his daughters, had changed hands many times. The look really was just his distinctive swooping signature and the flying eyeball he originated. Christian created a street-fashion sensation out of this slight material.

Christian was a charismatic Frenchman, raised in Avignon. He always claimed he arrived in the United States in 2000 with $500 in his pocket. He was star-struck with the idea of being a designer and was involved with a number of brands. He helped launch American Eagle and pioneered "celebrity wear," paying paparazzi to photograph Britney Spears, Justin Timberlake, Madonna and others coming out of his store, wearing his gear. No matter what else he is, the guy is a marketing genius.

Christian wanted to buy the master license to the art that was in the collection. Basically that meant he would find people to produce products with my imagery. Steven was excited about a deal with Christian. He said this could be exactly what we needed; Christian could be the guy to take the line where it could go. I Googled him and found an article about a lavish birthday party he threw for himself, where guests included Puff Daddy and all these other people. I called Steven back. "This guy is at ground zero of everything wrong with contemporary culture," I said.

On the other hand, I added, if he was really that kind of a powerhouse, it couldn't hurt to talk with him. I flew in from Hawaii later that week and went with Steven to Christian's glitzy, rented mansion in Beverly Hills. It was a world of which I knew nothing.

After some discussion, Steven, Tatsu, and I decided to go for it, and returned to "Bubbly Hills" to lock in the deal. We had hastily formed a limited partnership, which meant Francesca and me splitting profits with the twenty-odd people in Steven and Tatsu's Ku USA consortium. Christian offered us some good faith money up front and we signed the contract.

He had a giant, imposing, *L*-shaped sofa covered with the Von Dutch logo. "Christian, you've got to have that redone now with Ed Hardy," Steven said.

"I know," said Christian.

He pretended he still didn't know anything about me, but he had done his homework, and bought every book about me he could lay his hands on. "I will make you an enormous international star," he said. "I'll make this a global phenomenon. We'll fly you around the world. We'll bring you in in a Bentley. You'll sign autographs for thirty minutes and do press conferences."

I told Christian I had no interest in being the figurehead. I just wanted to get paid and to be left alone. I might have put it more diplomatically, but that was the basic idea. We didn't really do a good job with the legalese, which left a huge amount of money on the table that Christian was able to simply take for himself. We found this out later, of course, but when you see random objects like lighters with Ed Hardy imagery, it's because the licensee paid Christian "key money," typically $200,000 or more, to get the right to license a product category.

Within a couple of weeks, he found a location on the corner of Melrose and Fairfax, across the street from Fairfax High School, right on the dividing line between the hip boutiques and the high-end retail, a key intersection in Hollywood. Christian showed me the place when I went down to sign the contract. There was an antique store on the site and he simply paid off the owner and bought the lease, waving the money under her nose.

I went down a couple of weeks later and Christian drove me by the antique store. The antique dealer had already moved out. He had a hipster sign painter putting up giant Ed Hardy designs on the outside of the store. They had some obscenely expensive SUV covered in Ed Hardy. I pulled up in my budget rental car, wearing my usual button-down shirt and gray cardigan. The young guy working there acted like he had to be polite to this square, old man. He spied my watch. "Oh, wow," he said. "Is that vintage?"

"Timex," I said. "Bought it at Long's for ten dollars."

It dawned on me that all these people working in the store, Christian's cousins and who-all, were each wearing watches that cost upwards of five thousand dollars. These were not my people. There was a billboard above the store featuring a current porn starlet wearing Ed Hardy. I began to see where this was going. I did not attend the gala opening.

In February 2005, however, Christian asked me to paint something onstage as part of the show during an extravagant birthday party he was throwing for himself at a vacant lot at Hollywood and Vine. It was Ed Hardy Babylon—a full *L*-shaped stage with the Ed Hardy emblem signature emblazoned on everything, young models sporting the clothes, even little dogs wearing the new line of Ed Hardy pet couture. There was a van full of over-the-top Ed Hardy customized motorcycles, Ed Hardy energy drinks, you name it.

I dutifully packed some brushes and flew down to Hollywood, only to find a DJ with a giant, elaborate system set up where I was supposed to paint. The DJ knew nothing about it, and neither did anyone else. Christian could not be found. At the end of the event, with monitors running excerpts of me from the various documentaries, Christian triumphantly appeared with a gyrating line of the models, glitter raining down on them. At the after-party at a nearby trendy bar, I finally found Christian, and asked what happened to me painting. "I thought you didn't want to be presented in public," he said and wandered off with his yes men.

Tom Patchett watched the retinue depart. "Hardy, these guys all look like Russian Mafia," he said.

Christian pressed me for more designs. I had licensed him about twelve hundred images, mostly consisting of flash I'd painted in my Sailortown days. But he always wanted more. He could be highly dramatic, imperious—he would snap "cigarette" and hold out his fingers, while a minion stepped forward with a smoke and a light—and I started to hear stories about him. He was definitely a complete narcissist, a real piece of work. The Von Dutch guys were suing him.

A lot of people had warned me about the clothing business. They said it can be full of money, but also treachery and deceit. I was told to be very careful and not expect too much. I didn't. When Christian took over, I realized they were quickly ramping it up, but I didn't pay close attention.

In February 2005, the Ed Hardy designs were the big hit of the clothing trade show, MAGIC 2005, in Las Vegas. Christian poured so much money into promotion, it was depraved. The shirts were an almost instant phenomenon, a cultural meteor. Movie star Adrien Brody wore the screaming gorilla T-shirt to the premiere of the new blockbuster *King Kong* that May. Annual sales went from $50 million to $100 million. By 2009, annual sales would exceed $700 million.

Madonna loved Ed Hardy. Christian kept a wall of more than seventy paparazzi shots of Madonna wearing Ed Hardy gear. She dressed her daughter, Lourdes, in Ed Hardy as well as the little kids she adopted from Malawi. She gave her husband, British film director Guy Ritchie, the trucker's caps that Christian made of my *Skins & Skulls* series from the British club scene, cleverly popping the skull drawings on the caps.

As the brand grew, Christian's megalomaniacal side started to show up. He had a design team reworking my original artwork and he was adding his own name to everything. It became "Ed Hardy by Christian Audigier" and I wasn't happy about that. Steven bought some hundred-dollar T-shirt that had the name

"Christian Audigier" on it a dozen or more times, and the name "Ed Hardy" only once. After not advertising for the first few years, they began advertising. He began putting his face on billboards about Ed Hardy in Los Angeles.

The Ed Hardy thing kept getting bigger and bigger. They were opening stores everywhere. I would get around to the stores once in a while. I went into an Ed Hardy store in New York and found a shirt where my imagery was paired up with the iconic Che Guevera head. I got on the phone immediately. They couldn't alter my images like that. Tom Patchett put me together with a talented Los Angeles litigator named Art Cohen.

Our ownership group, Hardy Life, was still managed by Steven, and he and Christian didn't remotely get along. Each one thought the other was a scumbag and the relationship was hugely acrimonious.

With the rise in sales, Christian went to Steven and negotiated with him to pay for certain things annually in exchange for a reduced royalty rate. This was where it was clear how sophisticated Christian was and Steven wasn't. He ended up selling the royalty cow for a bowl of milk. That deal cost Hardy Life $50 million in royalties easily over the course of three years. These are numbers I can't even conceive in the first place, so I try not to let it bother me.

Not only did Steven realize that he had been duped, but the unauthorized editing of my artwork really made it clear how low Christian would go. And Steven was right to a point—this was a guy trading on my name and not paying enough for it—so we agreed to sue Christian and the parent company, Nervous Tattoo, for $100 million for breach of contract.

You want to talk about something that I know nothing about, it's the legal world. That is something I hope never to be involved with again. The lawsuit was the biggest waste of time and money Francesca and I have ever been through. It went on for a couple of years. Our company spent more than five million dollars on legal fees.

I was still tattooing. We continued to write and publish books on tattooing and other alternative arts. We were living in Hawaii and I was doing as much art as I could on my own. 2000 Dragons propelled me into new enthusiasm and passion for my personal art. We had kept the tiny, three-hundred-square-foot apartment in San Francisco, where we stayed when we were in town.

So, yeah, the brand thing was bringing in money, but it also was bringing in a lot of grief that I hadn't expected. I was reading legal briefs in Hawaii, sitting there wishing I could go to the beach. Miserable shit, the kind of thing I had always wanted to avoid. But it infuriated me that Christian would take credit for my designs. I kept telling the attorneys, "Colonel Tom Parker was not Elvis. Elvis was Elvis."

Ed Hardy was a mysterious figure, not a famous tattoo artist. We heard all kinds of things: "My cousin knows Ed Hardy," "Ed Hardy's dead," "Ed Hardy is a broken-down tattooer who maybe did a few of the designs." Or maybe he didn't exist, like Mrs. Butterworth or Aunt Jemima.

I could have stopped them with an injunction anytime from producing any more products with my art, something Christian feared. You could see him starting to brand his own products and create new lines that looked like mine. Meanwhile, the brand was rocketing to success and we had to strike a deal to let them use the artwork and continue to pay our royalties. The whole thing was totally nuts.

While this was going on, we were in the process of selling part of our company Hardy Life, a sale we completed in May 2009, and transitioning it into Hardy Way, which is a joint venture with a public company called Iconix. They are a brand management firm in the clothing field that handle Joe Boxers, Candee's, Jay Z's Rockawear, and another dozen brands.

When I went down to Los Angeles for the depositions, Hubert Guez, the new CEO of Nervous Tattoo, came to hear my statements. He could see that I was no scumbag, but only an artist trying to protect his work. To his credit, he reached out to me and a few weeks later in October 2009, we settled the whole thing.

We were at the National Tattoo Association convention in Seattle in April 2007 when word reached us that Mike "Rollo Banks" Malone had killed himself. A lot of people who knew Malone were aware of his decline and troubling circumstances. Some of his friends urged him to attend the convention, even suggesting they would rig an RV and drive him from Chicago, where he was living. I was going to be the subject of a roast and we wanted Malone to be one of the roasters. At first, he said he would consider the invitation, but he eventually turned it down.

Several months earlier, I had come down from an exhibit opening in Minneapolis to see him. We spent an afternoon celebrating somebody's birthday at a tattoo shop Malone co-owned, had a piece of cake, and sat around telling the youngsters a bunch of stories. We were supposed to get together the next morning, but he called and said he didn't feel well enough, so I went home without seeing him again. I knew he had Crohn's disease and was diabetic. He was not taking care of himself. He had put on a lot of weight. He lived in an apartment where nobody could go, a small, cluttered cave where he wheeled around in a chair.

Malone lived a checkered life. He fell hard for a woman who did cosmetic tattoos in the Midwest and began visiting there regularly. He'd introduced Doug to that scene and Doug made the move in early 1999, scoring a job at a busy shop. Much later, Dough told me that right before his Midwest move, he and his girlfriend had been living on Japanese instant noodles. Malone moved a few months later to open a shop in a suburban region of Minneapolis that proved to be a gold mine, although the romance with the cosmetic lady ended badly. He briefly kept the China Sea shop open, in the hands of a guy he knew from the mainland who worked for a percentage to keep the doors open. When this individual's life went haywire, Malone closed the historic location in January 2000.

It wasn't the first time Malone left the islands. In the eighties, burned out with Rock Fever—the claustrophobia of being in such a small place with limited options on many fronts—he moved to Austin, Texas, and that went well for a while. He opened a hip tattoo shop, tattooed a bunch of interesting people, tooled around town in an old Cadillac, wore cowboy boots and married a pop music critic for the *Austin Chronicle* named Margaret Moser. Those were good years for Malone, but they lost their house when real estate prices crashed and retreated to Honolulu. Margaret stayed with him for a while, but they split the blanket and she went back to Austin.

By the time he moved to Chicago, Malone was connected with a protégé, a young tattooer Malone met in Minneapolis. Malone taught him about tattooing, really brought him along. He lived in the apartment below and tried to clean up Malone's messes. Some time prior to this, Malone had been seeing a woman who lived in Los Angeles, a lady he had met on an airplane originally and reconnected with later. It seemed he had a new, positive outlook, but she broke off the relationship and he let himself go— serious weight problems, night feedings—but you couldn't talk to him about it. Malone was an extremely private person. He introduced me to Francesca and was my closest brother in tattoos, but you couldn't say, 'Hey, bud, want to talk about it?' That was never going to happen.

In a handwritten suicide note, Malone left me half of his estate, including his interest in the Sailor Jerry brand. He split the other half between Kandi Everett, his former girlfriend and tattoo partner, and the guy downstairs who had taken care of him. I never knew if Malone owned any property or what, but when Kandi went back to Chicago to check out the situation after a flood in the basement, she found a lot of Malone's collections and possessions missing, including all the sheets of original Sailor Jerry flash. These had become worth quite a bit of money on the burgeoning tattoo collectible market. We knew that, over the years, Malone was selling some bit-by-bit, but this was something different.

Malone knew his protégé had drug problems in the past, but he thought they were behind him.

Malone had not been dead long when we received a letter from the advertising agency in Philadelphia that produced the Sailor Jerry merchandise. They were selling the brand to a liquor manufacturer, one of the Sailor Jerry licensees, and we no longer would have any rights in the matter. A friend looked over the contract and said we had been properly excluded. The brand had grown to where we had been receiving substantial checks every quarter, maybe a hundred grand a year split between us. Not a lot by corporate standards, but I knew how much ink I would have to scrub into skin to make that much dough and all I had to do for this was endorse the check.

The Ed Hardy brand had grown quite big by then, and, of course, we looked into whether the Sailor Jerry licensees could do this, but I had entered into the original deal so stupidly, without any legal advice, there were very few avenues to pursue. Once again, we bore the consequences of entering worlds I was ill equipped to handle, and too careless to insure with informed advice beforehand.

Out of nowhere came a letter from the distillery that bought Sailor Jerry. I think they didn't know who I was, but they knew how big the brand had become and were afraid I might raise a stink if they didn't make some kind of gesture. We met in Los Angeles. The liquor company sent people from London. Kandi came over from Hawaii and Malone's little friend was there. They made us a generous offer, but wanted to make sure no Ed Hardy rum would appear to compete with their Sailor Jerry brand, which had become very successful. They withheld half my end of the deal for five years, after which, if there was no Ed Hardy rum, they would pay me.

Malone was a huge loss. It was not only that he had so much talent, but he also taught and inspired so many people in the tattoo world. He directly trained many, including my son. Those who connected with Mike in that capacity were fortunate. He was also important in the bigger picture of the tattoo world with his Mr. Flash business, which he started around 1980. He codified tattoo images in an organized, structured way, with his clear, eminently workable and distinctive variants of classic designs and reams of original creations. His flash could be found in shops around the world and made a lot of money for people. Some shops didn't have anything but his flash. Rollo was never comfortable with putting himself out in public, always too self-effacing. He also resented my willingness to step forward, a kernel of friction between us for decades.

The mind-boggling success of the Ed Hardy brand only encouraged Christian's worst tendencies. He pushed the limits on the lavish lifestyle. He lived like the Sun King. His staff was liveried, the women wore French maid's outfits. Everybody spoke French. He was ridiculous, but after more than a billion dollars in Ed Hardy sales in five years, he could afford to be whatever degree of ridiculous he wanted.

None of us had been to the Nervous Tattoo office until 2009, when my business affairs man Dave Rosenberg went to see the new product lines. He pulled his crappy rental econocar into a lot full of exotic automobiles—Bentley, Porsche, Ferrari—and they put him in an Ed Hardy Humvee golf cart to drive to Christian's studio. Inside a massive warehouse with the walls covered floor to ceiling with pictures of Michael Jackson, Christian held court before a bevy of models laying around on couches and motorcycles.

We bought out Steven and Tatsu and their other partners, more than a dozen, including some I never met, and put the brand in the hands of Iconix. They brought in a new design team, who actually consulted with me. Negotiations continued with Christian to buy back the master license, but none of this required my attention.

Christian handed out more than seventy sub-licenses. We owned the brand, but Christian would control the sub-licenses, receiving money for granting the license that contractually he didn't have to share with us. He made a vast amount of money selling sub-licenses; people wanted in so bad.

I listened on a rare conference call with Christian as he explained his populist marketing vision of a brand so broad and diffuse, anybody can participate, a mixture of democratic principles and avarice. Christian didn't see any need to balance the number of products on the market against diluting the brand. They were discussing a two-dollar disposable Ed Hardy cigarette lighter and Christian kept hitting on the idea that the brand should be for everyone. Of course, the unspoken subtext was that he's getting a big piece of change out front. What I used to tell people was that I was winding up with the little toenail of the elephant.

At one point, I think there were seventy Ed Hardy stores in the world. A lot of those have subsequently closed, but that was a lot of stores. There were several stores in Manhattan, several around Los Angeles. There were stores in London, stores in Tokyo. Germany was the second-biggest market after the United States. People told me the stores in Australia were huge and lavish. Currently, the big growing markets are Brazil, India, and China, where more than twenty stores will be open by the end of 2012.

Friends would send me photos from tiny villages in obscure parts of Eastern Europe of Ed Hardy goods in store windows. It was beyond belief. From air freshener for your car to sun-tan lotion for indoor tanning beds, there was an Ed Hardy product to suit your lifestyle. Francesca came back from Costco one day with a cardboard dashboard protector with a leaping koi, some flowers, and the Ed Hardy bubble script signature about a foot high across the whole dashboard. We were on a walk on our hill one day and saw a car with Ed Hardy car-seat covers. It was everywhere.

Funny what happened. After draping celebrities head to toe in Ed Hardy gear from Paris Hilton to Hulk Hogan—one of my favorites was the shot of Elizabeth Taylor in her wheelchair and jaunty Ed Hardy hat—Christian shot himself in the foot. His brief romance with reality TV star Jon Gosselin practically single-handedly killed the brand. After Gosselin left his wife and their eight kids (featured on a top-rated cable TV show) in August 2009, Christian flew him and his new girlfriend to St. Tropez and covered him in Ed Hardy gear (which he already had been wearing on the show). In an instant, the most-hated-man-in-reality-TV, the deadbeat dad of all-time, poisoned the brand. The buyer for Macy's cited Gosselin when he dropped the line that fall.

There was a lot of chatter when the brand started turning up on *Jersey Shore*, but nobody gave those folks the clothes. They bought them. The Hardy brand was already a legitimate part of *Jersey Shore* culture and this prompted some discussion about whether the exposure was a good thing for Ed Hardy. Abercrombie and Fitch had paid the producers to keep their line *off* the show—product displacement?—but those were the same guys who had to withdraw the racially inflammatory "Two Wongs . . ." T-shirt, so what do they know? Such a concern smacks of snobby elitism to me, but I've never watched *Jersey Shore*. Or Jon Gosselin's show, either, whatever it was called, but Homer Simpson showed up on his TV show in Ed Hardy wear, too.

We bought back the master license from Christian in 2011. He could have gotten twice as much if he had sold the year before, instead of stringing everybody along for his own purposes. It may never be 2009 again for the Ed Hardy brand, but it did become an authentic cultural phenomenon. To me, they harnessed the psychic power of the tattoo and that is what took everybody for the ride.

24.

The Last Tattoo

I did my last tattoo at Tattoo City in 2008. I finished up a dragon I started the year before on Mary Joy, one of the tattooers in the shop, and then hung up my machines. I had slowly backed away from the epic work, especially after having my second hip replacement in Hawaii a couple of years before. It went easier the second time, but it was still difficult and definitely cooled down my surfing. I don't do that much anymore.

I was still putting on quite a few large pieces. Toward the last couple of years, I told people that I would no longer do big body work. I might do an arm. I'd do a sleeve. It wasn't only souvenir tattoos the size of a quarter with a signature. But I had slowed down enough to where I thought, actually, I don't have to tattoo at all. It's too hard on my body and I decided to save my energy for my personal art.

How many artists have seen their work spread so far during their lifetime? Not many. And they're more in the Picasso realm. That part of it is unreal to me. Of course, I have finally lost the chip on the shoulder about tattoos, my obsession with the way tattooing was looked upon. Even before the brand, I had been backing off my attitude. Francesca was asking, what did I have to prove? I was regularly exhibiting my own personal art, as well as curating shows based around tattoo themes. There were museum shows, international exhibits. I had written and published almost thirty books under our Hardy Marks imprint. The press constantly wrote about the work and interviewed me.

In 2009, a surprise benefit of the brand was San Francisco gallerist Rena Bransten becoming aware of my work. Rena is one of the longest-established and respected art dealers in the Bay Area. My old friends Ron Nagle and Hung Liu had been showing with her for years. Ron called and said, "Hey, Rena wants you to call her." She was a fan of the Ed Hardy clothing—coincidentally, the Ed Hardy store had opened on the ground floor of her building—and discovered I made art, as well. In the fall of 2009, Ron and I had a two-person show there and she continues to represent me.

In 2010, our longtime friend, award-winning filmmaker Emiko Omori, released *Ed Hardy—Tattoo the World*. She started shooting footage for this feature-length documentary shortly after Realistic opened in 1974. She first released a thirty-minute film, *Tattoo City,* in 1980, built around her experience getting a full-back dragon tattoo. In filming me painting the 2000 Dragons scroll, she decided to use that event to anchor a feature-length treatment of my life in tattoos, utilizing film she had shot over thirty years.

Our life is good. Doug moved back to San Francisco in 2009 and helps manage Tattoo City and Hardy Marks Publications. He's been tattooing twenty years now, hard to believe. After lots of ups and downs with our moves, Francesca continues her work and interest in textiles and fashion and is connected with a global network of like-minded people. We are focusing on what really counts and I'm trying to ease off from my manic *modus operandi.*

When the brand thing hit, it went crazy. It's not Coca-Cola, but it was some kind of unparalleled phenomenon. That's why our partners, the Iconix Brand Group in New York, bought the master license from Christian in 2011 for a substantial amount. This, however, does not provide Francesca and me with any increased income. You have to give Christian Audigier credit—he saw the power in the images and knew how to market them. The

Ed Hardy brand ushered in tattoo designs as a look in the culture. Big-shot fashion guys like Marc Jacobs, who has a few tattoos, started making hipster handbags and women's shoes with obviously tattoo-inspired designs. Tattoo subject matter, design treatment, and lettering are now ubiquitous.

I think I understand what Christian saw in the designs. They were meant to be emblematic, like heraldry. They're bold—the whole point of classic Western tattoo designs is that they read clearly on the skin. Heavy shading, dark and light values, an instantly recognizable silhouette of the shape. It's a dagger and a heart. It's a crawling panther. It's an eagle. This was the crucial common element to classic tattoo designs.

These things are distillations of human interests and hopes. And they represent. *This stands for me.* This is not just a flag, a cross, a pinup—this is who I am in some small but important way.

I knew that about tattoos. I was surprised that it had that much appeal in the outside world. I did not foresee a role in mainstream culture for tattoos, but when I would start running into people wearing the designs and introduce myself, an enormous number of people did not know they had been tattoo designs. They liked them for what they were. This iconic imagery, richly freighted with powerful symbolism, stands out in an age when everything had become more soft focus, more diffuse.

To me, integrating art into life is a way to help get through the whole thing. Wake up to how positive it is to have something that lights up your life. Whether it's a painting in a frame, a sculpture on a pedestal, or a tattoo on somebody's skin, it connects you with something indefinable, a celebration of what people might accomplish. We all know how this is going to end, but art is my life.

At age ten when I looked at Len's dad's tattoos, it was a goshdarn bolt from the blue. I knew that I wanted to do this. And I went for it. My early drawings were pretty accurate tattoo designs. Everything I ever did was another step on that path. I immediately saw through the prevailing attitudes about tattoos. They were part of all the nonindigenous culture, thought patterns, and ways of behavior that were rammed down people's throats by the over-arching control system.

That's what I learned from Billy Burroughs. Lay low, stay anonymous, keep your eyes open, and watch out. It's all about control. That's the lesson of the sixties. The same lesson we learned from hot-rod culture, surfing, LSD, rock music, everything: I'm not buying into your game.

Tattoos, it turns out, are also about freedom, a kind of ultimate expression of personal domain. Tattoos bloom in the most suppressed corners of society—prisons, the military—in the face of almost universal social condemnation. Tattoos have even finally come to China in a big way; hundreds of artists are now working there. During the Maoist era, there was nobody tattooing in China. Those people have an incredibly rich tradition of deep art and ornate culture to draw from. Tattoos have returned to all the Pacific island cultures, where the Christian missionaries closed down the native tattoo traditions more than a century ago, and invaded Europe, where the tattoo tradition had largely been relegated to navy ports. Tattoo is one of the few true examples of global culture, easily permeating otherwise strict boundaries of geography, language, or ethnic identity. One world—one tattoo.

I started in tattooing in 1967 and I watched the form crawl out of a tawdry underground. I remember the first time the first academic came around to interview me in my shop in San Diego. When we published *Tattootime* in 1982, it was the first tattoo magazine. Now there are dozens of magazines and hundreds of books about tattoos.

Like Lyle Tuttle always says, "tattoo" is the magic word. It hits people in a way that no other visual medium does. And it is not simply visual, but visceral. Everybody has an opinion about it and everybody has a gut reaction. And because they are permanent, tattoos raise all these issues about life and death.

I used to be highly critical about tattoos. I was such a smart-ass. I knew how tattoos were supposed to look. Some sailor came into the shop in San Diego once and I looked at the tattoo on his arm. "Who did that fucked-up eagle on you?" I said. Immediately I could tell that this was his favorite tattoo and who was I to be critical? One person's tattoo is nobody else's business. If they like it, if they feel good about themselves because of it, that's a successful tattoo. You can criticize it on formal levels. It could have been shaded different. It doesn't accurately look like what it's supposed to be. But a tattoo is an art of collaboration. Somebody put the tattoo on the person who is wearing it. It is probably the most personal form of art.

I've done God knows how many tattoos. I see my designs on people everywhere. Why do people like tattoos? Why do people like art? Why does a certain song get you? This is the realm in which tattoos operate. It's completely illogical, except if you dig it and it makes you feel good, then, it's fine and you understand it.

Nobody can say why they do what they do. There are no formal schools of thought. There are no Ten Ways to a Better Tattoo. A tattoo is something somebody wants. It evades all that intellectualization. It evades rational thought. And that's what I'm after with art of any kind.

I've always said I don't know why people get tattoos, but I do think people get tattoos for themselves, first. Showing the tattoos may or may not matter. And some people definitely do intend their tattoos to be seen, to make a statement: I'm the meanest cat on the block, or the best lover, or what have you. But you get them, first and foremost, for yourself. Of course, with the back tattoo, there is that drawback. It may be the biggest open canvas on your body, but you don't get to see it, unless you're in in the changing room at Macy's with the double mirror. You can forget you have it. You go to the beach and sometimes wonder, "What are they looking at?"

If you're going to have a goofy tattoo, it helps to have a good sense of humor. I hope some of these people who get tattoos when they're young do, because they may look funny when they get older. Halloween for life.

Tattoos can be markers of your journey, like those old stickers on your car, decals you put on your wind wing that tell the world, I'VE BEEN TO IDAHO.

People get them as psychic armor. In pretechnological societies, tattoos could be apotropaic, make you look like a badass, ward off the weird creatures in the night, or scare your enemies when you come out of the bush screaming. The Woads, whoever they were all those years ago in Ireland and Scotland, were marked up like animals.

I love tattoos with writing. These bold statements, written in the skin—*Death Before Dishonor; Born to Lose*—for better or worse, are assertions of what the person stands for. Scripted tattoos, carefully lettered pieces of writing, poetry, quotations, whatever, have recently come to make up a large part of requested work. Definitely more literate people are getting tattooed and the sophistication of their choices is amazing. Reinforcement reminders of values and how to aim their lives, like a permanent shopping list. Skin poetry.

My tattoos tell the story of my life. I can trace the times and people of my life through the tattoos on my body. Each one means something to me. On my fiftieth birthday, my son Doug put a tattoo on me and I'm glad I had good space left on my arm. He did a World War II vintage cartoon, the *Who me?* duck, a classic bit of old flash.

Although I do have a few small joke tattoos from early in my career, I'm not much into that now. A tattoo does not have to be serious, and a lot of people could use more of a sense of humor about the whole thing, and life in general. Anyway, I still have plenty of room in case I see something I truly do like. You never know. As Bob Roberts always says, having those areas of clean skin is like money in the bank.

ACKNOWLEDGMENTS

First, I am very grateful to Joel Selvin, who proposed the idea of this book and whose humor, insight, and patience made it happen. Also to Lisa Louis, whose efforts and interviews from the early 1990s were a great help. Overall, the unusual journey documented here would not have been possible without the support of my wife Francesca and son Doug.

Kudos to all those whose stories appear in the text, and for anecdotes they have shared with me. My current favorite is from Dennis Cockell. As a staff member at Buckingham Palace in recent years, he unofficially tattooed, on site, scores of people, including some running the place. Special recognition also goes to the great "talking chief," Lyle Tuttle, our prime living repository of tattoo history, who deserves a book of his own.

My gratitude goes to the countless people who chose to be tattooed by me, as well as collectors who have bought my work in other mediums. The gallerists, curators, and museum directors who have supported my work deserve a big tip of the hat, particularly Tom Patchett and Rena Bransten. I am especially grateful to Bud Shark, David Salgado, and Paul Mullowney for our ongoing inspiring collaborations in creating multiple originals. I am also profoundly indebted to the close friends who have documented, preserved, and championed my journey: Alan Govenar; Emiko Omori; Mary Lynn Price; Mike McCabe; Chuck Eldridge; Wendy Slick; V. Vale; Thomas Woodruff; and many others. For continuing my tradition, our Tattoo City crew: Doug, Trevor Ewald, Mary Joy, Aleph Kali, Jen Lee, and Kahlil Rintye. As *consigliere* for our business endeavors, Dave Rosenberg's ongoing expertise and advice are invaluable.

Thanks to all of my fellow obsessed sidekicks—many of them named above, but especially Comrade Hung Liu and The Baron of Sculptural Intelligence, Ron Nagle—for our ongoing, crucial, and inspiring art conversations. Last but not least, I am indebted to Laurie Steelink, whose talents bridge a variety of the above roles.

Joel Selvin would like to thank . . .

Ron Nagle introduced me to Ed and Francesca, who treated me like an old friend from the night we met. Rena Bransten invited me to the party. Frank Weimann, Elyse Tanzillo, and the entire staff of The Literary Group took care of business. Rob Kirkpatrick, Nicole Sohl, and everybody else at Thomas Dunne Books who made it happen. Carol Mastick typed the flawless transcriptions. Dave Rosenberg of Hardy Marks went above and beyond. Doug Hardy offered inspiration and encouragement. Carla Selvin, my darling daughter, provided care and devotion. Thanks also to Francesca Passalacqua, who is as embedded in this book as she is in Ed's life, and my most special, humble thanks to the master himself, Don Ed Hardy. He is a man whose single-minded artistic vision and dedication of purpose reminds me of the greatest musicians—Hank Williams, Muddy Waters, Bob Dylan—and I am honored to have played a part in helping Ed tell his important and inspiring story.

INDEX